AFGHANISTAN – THE BEAR TRAP

ABOUT THE AUTHORS

Brigadier Mohammad Yousaf was born in 1937 and was commissioned as an infantry officer into the Frontier Defence Force Regiment of the Pakistan Army in 1961. Subsequently his career took him through the usual sequence of command and staff appointments, including active service against India. He also attended the Command and Staff College at Quetta and the National Defence College at Rawalpindi.

While commanding an infantry brigade he was selected by the Director of the Inter-Service Intelligence (ISI) to head its Afghan Bureau, a post he held from 1983 to 1987, until he resigned as a matter of principle and left the Army. During these four years he was responsible for training, and operational planning of the Mujahideen inside Afghanistan and later inside the Soviet Union.

Since retiring he has kept in close touch with events and Mujahideen leaders in Afghanistan. He now lives in Karachi with his family. He has written a short book on General Akhtar, his superior at ISI, who was killed in an aircraft crash in 1988, along with President Zia.

Major Mark Adkin was commissioned into The Bedfordshire and Hertfordshire Regiment in 1956 and served with it and The Royal Anglian Regiment in Germany, Malaya, Mauritius and Aden. On leaving the British Army he joined the Overseas Civil Service and was posted to the Solomon Islands. Transferred to the Gilbert and Ellice Islands, he was one of the last British District Officers anywhere in the world.

His final overseas post was as a contract officer for five years with the Barbados Defence Force, and it was as the Caribbean operations staff officer that he participated in the US invasion of Grenada in 1983. He now lives in Bedford and has written books on military subjects, including *Urgent Fury*, *The Last Eleven?*, *Goose Green* and *The Charge*, all published by Pen and Sword Books.

AFGHANISTAN-
THE BEAR TRAP

The Defeat of a Superpower

by
Brigadier Mohammad Yousaf
and
Mark Adkin

CASEMATE
Havertown, PA

Published by

CASEMATE

2114 Darby Road, Havertown, PA 19083

ISBN: 0-9711709-2-4

Cataloging-in-publication data is available from the Library of Congress

To General Akhtar Abdul Rehman Khan,
Pakistan Army,
Director-General Inter-Services Intelligence, 1980-1987

CONTENTS

MILITARY SYMBOLS USED ON MAPS

UNIT SIZES

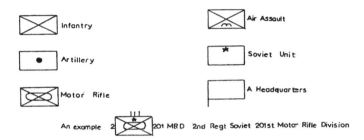

An Army Group

An Army

A Division

A Brigade

A Regiment

A Battalion

UNIT TYPES

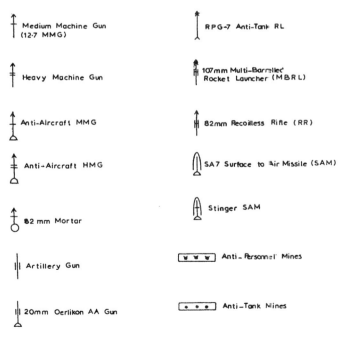

Infantry

Artillery

Motor Rifle

Air Assault

Soviet Unit

A Headquarters

An example 2 201 MRD 2nd Regt Soviet 201st Motor Rifle Division

MUJAHIDEEN WEAPONS

Medium Machine Gun
(12·7 MMG)

Heavy Machine Gun

Anti-Aircraft MMG

Anti-Aircraft HMG

82 mm Mortar

Artillery Gun

20mm Oerlikon AA Gun

RPG-7 Anti-Tank RL

107mm Multi-Barrelled
Rocket Launcher (MBRL)

82mm Recoilless Rifle (RR)

SA7 Surface to Air Missile (SAM)

Stinger SAM

Anti-Personnel Mines

Anti-Tank Mines

MAPS

A NOTE ON SOURCES

The information for this book came almost entirely from personal experience and observations during my time at ISI, and more recently when I returned to Peshawar. I know the Mujahideen, some of their Commanders and all their Leaders well. We worked and planned together for four years and I have discussed the situation today with many of them. This book, therefore, has not been written with extensive use of works of reference, or from the stories of journalists. I disagree with much that has been written about the war in Afghanistan. Sometimes the facts are wrong, more often the interpretation is wrong. This does not mean that all books on the war are valueless, far from it, but merely that I found very few to be reliable aids when compiling my manuscript. Those that were included Mark Urban's *War in Afghanistan*, Macmillan Press, 1988; David C. Isby's *War in a Distant Country*, Arms and Armour Press, 1986; and Robert D. Kaplan's *Soldiers of God*, Houghton Mifflin Company, Boston, 1990. Of these I found the first-mentioned to be particularly authentic and accurate.

PUBLISHER'S NOTE

AFGHANISTAN – THE BEAR TRAP

Twenty years ago, as today, the military balance could not have been more uneven. Intent on conquering Afghanistan, the Soviet Union poured in vast resources of men, modern equipment, air power and sophisticated command and control facilities. Their enemy, the Afghan Mujahideen, were outgunned and outnumbered and yet it was they who were to prevail thanks to their superior local knowledge, resilience and limited external support, on this occasion from the CIA, secretly channelled through the Pakistani Government.

The lessons in *Afghanistan – The Bear Trap* have never been more relevant than they are today in what has been so recently declared by the US President as The War Against World Terrorism.

For a clear understanding of what the pitfalls are of a major military intervention into one of the World's most primitive and hostile environments, reading *Afghanistan – The Bear Trap* can arguably not be bettered. Written by their puppet-master, Brigadier Mohammed Yousaf, then Director of the Afghan Bureau of Pakistan's ISI over the crucial years 1983-1987, no-one was closer to the heart of the Mujahideen's operations.

In this remarkably frank book, he describes with commendable clarity the extraordinary death by a thousand cuts that was to be the shocking fate of the Soviet army. As well as being mandatory reading for military planners, it is guaranteed to fascinate all with a close interest and concern for the outcome of the current crisis.

INTRODUCTION

DEATH by a thousand cuts — this is the time-honoured tactic of the guerrilla army against a large conventional force. In Afghanistan it was the only way to bring the Soviet bear to its knees; the only way to defeat a superpower on the battlefield with ill-trained, ill-disciplined and ill-equipped tribesmen, whose only asset was an unconquerable fighting spirit welded to a warrior tradition. Ambushes, assassinations, attacks on supply convoys, bridges, pipelines, and airfields, with the avoidance of set piece battles; these are history's proven techniques for the guerrilla. For four years, from 1983-1987, it was my task to plan and coordinate these activities.

I was an infantry brigadier in the Pakistan Army when I was suddenly summoned to take over the Afghan Bureau of the Inter-Services Intelligence (ISI). I went reluctantly, and with foreboding. The ISI has, like most covert intelligent organizations an intimidating reputation both inside and outside the Services. It is considered to be the most effective intelligence agency in the third world. It is also vast, with hundreds of officers, both military and civil, and thousands of staff. Its head — the Director General — who was the then Lieutenant-General Akhtar Abdul Rehman Khan, was the most powerful man in the armed forces, with daily direct access to President Zia.

When I received the news of my posting over the telephone I was a brigade commander on a divisional exercise at Quetta. I could not believe it, and asked the staff officer to recheck as I had never had intelligence training, never held an intelligence appointment, and so felt sure there had been an error. To my dismay there had not. I was to report to Islamabad within 72 hours. It was unbelievable. For a while I thought it was the end of my professional career. Such a posting is generally not welcomed by senior officers as, invariably, you make more enemies than friends. Overnight you become a different person in the eyes of your peers. Even superiors outside the ISI regard you with deep suspicion, as part of the ISI's function is to keep careful watch on the generals to ensure reliability to the régime.

Certainly in those days of martial law under Zia, apprehension, even fear, of what the ISI could do was very real.

The next day General Akhtar telephoned me and I took the opportunity to protest that I had neither the experience nor the aptitude for a job within the ISI. His curt response was that neither had he when he first took over as Director-General. He did, however, assure me that the job he had in mind would be to my liking. And so it was.

As it turned out I was not directly involved in intelligence gathering. My duties, month after month, year after year, involved operations; operations against the second most powerful superpower in the world – the USSR. It was the most momentous challenge of my life. The responsibility was frightening. As Director of the Afghan Bureau of the ISI I was tasked not only with training and arming the Mujahideen (Soldiers of God), but planning their operations inside Afghanistan. When I looked at the enemy order of battle on the map in my operations room I counted no fewer than one 4 star, five 3 star, and some fifteen 2 star Soviet generals, not to mention at least twenty-five Afghans, all of whom outranked me.

Throughout my time in the ISI I was concerned with formulating and implementing a military strategy to defeat the Soviets. My aim was to make Afghanistan their Vietnam. Operations were of course also directed against the communist Afghan Army, but I emphasize that my main enemy was the USSR. It was the invader. Without its massive presence the conflict would have been over long before I took up my post in October, 1983. My duties were military. Although I was keenly aware of the effect of politics on the outcome of the fighting I was seldom, if ever, directly involved in political decision-making. Nevertheless, as time went on, the whims and prejudices of politicians, including those within the Mujahideen, often made the actual fighting of the war a nightmare of frustrations and disappointments. Had it not been for General Akhtar, my only superior during most of my time in the ISI, shielding me from the political intrigues I would surely have resigned within months.

Despite this the reader will need to understand that there are seven recognized Mujahideen political parties, headquartered in exile, in Pakistan, each with a leader. Of these, four can be broadly classified as Islamic Fundamentalists, while three are Islamic Moderates. They are referred to in the text as the 'Parties' or the 'Party Leaders'. These Leaders are not to be confused with the Mujahideen commanders in the field. They all belong to one of the Parties, but are termed Commanders.

My time, until late in 1987 when I retired from the Army, was spent in trying to organize and administer rival Mujahideen groups so that they might present some sort of unity on the battlefield. I had to attempt to coordinate one of the largest guerrilla campaigns in modern times, with a staff of sixty officers and 300 senior NCOs and men from the Pakistan Army. To the

Mujahideen I could issue no orders – an advantage taken for granted by my Soviet and Afghan opponents. I had to achieve operational results by cajoling and convincing, not commanding. Somehow I must continue to improve and develop on what had been achieved by my predecessor so that eventually the tactics of a thousand cuts would produce such a haemorrhaging of men and money that the burden would be unbearable.

I was compelled to operate under an elaborate smokescreen of secrecy. Most senior generals of the Pakistan Army had no idea of my duties. Even my family was unaware of the real nature of my task. This need for absolute anonymity stemmed from the official denial of the government that Pakistan was aiding the Mujahideen. No one in authority would admit that weapons, ammunition and equipment were being channelled through Pakistan, by Pakistanis, to the guerrillas. Even more taboo was the fact that the ISI was training the Mujahideen, planning their combat operations, and often accompanying them inside Afghanistan as advisers. Of course the arms supply was an open secret; everybody knew it was happening, but although the involvement of Pakistan in the field was guessed at, it was never, ever, publicly admitted. Throughout the war the diplomats kept playing their game of pretence with Pakistani ambassadors in Moscow and Kabul, and a Soviet one in Islamabad.

Because the role of Pakistan was so sensitive, because I had no wish to embarrass my country, or jeopardize its security, and would do nothing that might prejudice operations against the Soviets, the writing of this book was delayed. When I retired in August, 1987, the Geneva Accord had yet to be signed, no Soviet withdrawal had started, but the Mujahideen were gaining the upper hand. There was little doubt that the USSR had had enough. Mujahideen military victory was in sight. Although I spent the early months of my retirement recording the highlights of my time with the ISI, it was not my intention to write a book. Indeed, I was most strongly advised against such a course. Now, in late 1991, there is no danger of compromising either state secrets or the prosecution of the Jehad. The once covert activities of the Mujahideen, ISI, or Pakistan, are no longer secret, but common knowledge in my country, if not outside. With the retreat of the Soviets what I have exposed of the struggle against them is no longer of operational importance. Today all training activities by Pakistan have ceased, the training camps have been abandoned, ISI personnel do not venture inside Afghanistan, and Mujahideen no longer raid across the Amu River into the Soviet Union.

Even the system of distribution of arms has changed, while the quantity has been substantially reduced. The Military Committee of Afghan leaders with which I worked on planning operations, has been disbanded, and a new system of control by the Afghan Interim Government (AIG) substituted. So I am persuaded that this book may serve a useful purpose for posterity and for historians, if only to highlight lessons for political and military leaders.

There is much to be learned, or rather re-learned, about the conduct of guerrilla warfare from the Afghanistan experience. If some of these can be assimilated and applied in the future then writing this book will have been worthwhile.

After three years, things have changed for the worse with the Mujahideen in Afghanistan. In February, 1989, when the last Soviet soldier crossed back into the USSR everybody expected a Mujahideen victory within weeks. In Kabul resistance was on the point of collapse, its citizens faced starvation, the Afghan Army was supposedly about to surrender, and foreign diplomats were packing their bags. A second Saigon was about to happen. All Afghan watchers predicted a Mujahideen triumph, they only differed as to whether it would come in weeks or months. It never came at all. To a soldier, who had been so intimately involved, it was a devastating disappointment. Somehow a Mujahideen defeat had been snatched from the jaws of victory. This book is an attempt to explain why.

Nevertheless, I have not written a history of the Afghan war. My objective has been to set the record straight with regard to how things happened, and why they happened. I seek to explain the workings of a guerrilla army, how it operated, its failings as well as its merits, to record the reasons, as I see them, why a triumph for the Mujahideen was denied them in the months following the Soviet withdrawal.

Some, perhaps most, of the things I describe have never been made public before — hence the sub-title of the book — although I have been careful that nothing I say can damage current or future operations inside Afghanistan. For the first time the true extent of the assistance given by Pakistan to the Mujahideen in training, logistics and on operations is made known. During my four years some 80,000 Mujahideen were trained; hundreds of thousands of tons of arms and ammunition were distributed, several billion dollars were spent on this immense logistic exercise and ISI teams regularly entered Afghanistan alongside the Mujahideen. Certainly some of the motives and actions of the US to which I allude as being distinct possibilities will be denied — perhaps correctly. Where I feel that all is not as it seems, where doubt exists as to the cause of events, such as the air crash that killed President Zia, I attempt to set out the known evidence honestly, and then draw conclusions. These conclusions are entirely personal, but ones which I cannot wipe from my mind. Probably, I shall for ever remain uncertain.

Many books have been written on the war, some describe the cut and thrust of battle on both sides, year by year, while others, more numerous, are merely accounts of journalist's journeys with the Mujahideen. Invariably these books flatter a particular Mujahideen Party or Commander, depending on who was the author's host. It is extremely difficult for the media to know what is happening in Afghanistan. First, it is so remote. There are no comfortable hotels, the fighting is taking place hundreds of miles away from

Peshawar, in Pakistan, where most journalists congregate. There is no way of dashing out after breakfast, watching or filming a shootout in the streets, then getting a story to New York or London that evening. Secondly, and arising from the first, there is the physical stamina required to go inside Afghanistan. The gruelling effort of marching for several weeks in those unforgiving mountains without proper food or shelter deters all but the most hardy. Add to this the sickness and the danger and it is not surprising that Mujahideen Commanders assess prospective companions with caution. Only a few get taken in. Then, at the end of it all, they may see no action. Their supreme efforts in keeping up for day after day are often poorly rewarded in terms of a readable story.

For a few all this was quite unacceptable, so they would persuade a Commander to set up a mock battle, sometimes with Mujahideen in Afghan uniforms, buildings wired for demolition in advance, all in true Hollywood style. The Mujahideen enthusiastically rushed around firing all types of weapons, there was much smoke, much noise, much enjoyment and much filming. Of course the journalists had to pay, give the Commander publicity and prestige, but the films sold well in the US or elsewhere. It was an altogether more civilized way to wage war, and for both parties to make money. Even when writing a genuine article, it usually became a channel to promote the views and aspirations of the Commander who took them in. He is their hero, his views are expounded, while the reader gets an overly extravagant picture of a personality, his performance and his importance.

To avoid falling into this trap I have seldom mentioned Mujahideen Commanders by name when describing a particular operation. I have chosen examples that I believe to be typical of the fighting, some of which were failures, but I have not praised one Commander while disparaging another on the basis of the old Army dictum, 'No names, no pack drill'. Similarly, I have not named people who are still serving, or who operated under the veil of secrecy, where this could damage their reputation or endanger their lives. Apart from this the names used are the real ones.

Despite the above safeguards there will be some who oppose this book's publication, if only for the sake of perversity. My immediate superior at the time of my retirement, while showing an interest in the idea, insisted that I should get any draft approved by the Army. This would have been the kiss of death to my efforts. The Pakistan military would have chopped it to pieces in their efforts to eliminate criticisms. So when, after two years, I decided to put my handwritten notes into a more presentable form I could seek no official help.

My first problem was that nobody in the family could type. I bought a typewriter and persuaded my eldest daughter that she should learn on my manuscript. I give her credit for eighty pages of laborious two-finger effort before she gave up in disgust. Next, I had to resort to letter-writers in

Karachi, pretending that it was some sort of official paper rather than a book. I could not just hand it over and await its completion. This would have been to court disaster, as what I was doing would be public gossip within days. To use just one writer was out of the question, so I visited five or six. To each I would give 15-20 pages to work on, while I stood around the shop, sometimes peering over his shoulder, sometimes shooing away other curious customers, and generally becoming thoroughly bored and frustrated. At the end of the day I would collect up all the pages and take them to the next man the following day. To type and correct over 400 pages at this rate takes time, especially when I often had to wait up to a week before I could find a writer available. After a while I ran out of letter-writers, and had to start again with the first one. A dreadful experience.

Still I was far from finished. If publication in Pakistan was going to involve endless bickering and bureaucratic delays, with no guarantee of a book at the end of it all, then the answer seemed to lie in the USA, my ally in the war. As a former ISI officer, whose inclination to write about his experiences was known to some, I resorted to sending the manuscript to a friend in New York, who introduced me to Mark Adkin. This book is the outcome of the ensuing partnership.

I have endeavoured to convey the 'flavour' of this guerrilla war by describing my experiences, or those of others known to me, during my tenure with the ISI. It was, while the Soviets occupied the country, a campaign in which a late twentieth century army fought against an early nineteenth century one. The Afghans who annihilated the British during their winter retreat from Kabul in 1842 were virtually identical to those indestructible fighters who killed over 13,000 Soviet soldiers and wounded some 35,000, and sent its army scurrying home after nine years of bitter fighting. The people have not changed much over the centuries; even Alexander's Macedonian pikemen who marched up the Panjsher valley 2300 years ago would easily recognize the jagged, barren, rocky skyline today. Time does not change much in Afghanistan.

To my knowledge the mystery of why the Mujahideen never marched into Kabul within weeks of the Soviet withdrawal has never been fully explained. It has usually been put down to internal feuding. I believe this is only part of the answer. To me the evidence, albeit circumstantial, points to a covert decision by their main backer — the US — that the Mujahideen should not be allowed an outright military victory. I believe they could have had their triumph despite their quarrels if it had been in the US interests. Unfortunately it was not. Both superpowers are much more comfortable with the present stalemate.

Nothing in this book is official history, but I have made every effort to get my facts correct. Any errors are mine, as are the opinions and comments. I wish to concede, without any reservations, that I could have achieved nothing during my time with ISI without the devoted, unstinting and unending labours of my officers and staff. They worked day and night, without any public recognition, for the success of the Jehad. I owe them a lot. I hope that this book will, in a small way, be seen by them as an acknowledgement of their contribution.

Finally, I salute the Mujahideen who, for all their faults, have once again proved an unbeatable opponent. No matter how many political reasons may have been espoused for the Soviet's retreat from Afghanistan, they would never have gone without the efforts of these Soldiers of God.

Crash, Culprits, and Cover up

'Zia's death must have been an act of God.'
Benazir Bhutto, *Daughter of Destiny*, 1988.

The Crash

When the camouflage-painted Pakistan Air Force C-130 transport aircraft hit the ground it did so at an angle of 65 degrees. It was nose-diving, flaps up, wings level, landing gear up and locked, with all four engines functioning normally. It impacted at 190 knots. After a brief moment a monstrous ball of orange flame consumed it as the fuel tanks exploded. Both clocks in the flight deck later showed 3.51 pm exactly on a clear, bright day, a few miles north of the small garrison town of Bahawalpur. Precisely five minutes earlier it had lifted off at the start of its 70-minute flight to Islamabad. After some two minutes of terror all on board had the merciful relief of instantaneous oblivion.

It was 17 August, 1988. Moments before Hafiz Taj Mohammad, who was walking towards his field near the village of Dhok Kamal, near the Sutlej River eight miles north of Bahawalpur, heard the roar of engines and looked up. He watched incredulously as the lumbering plane, which was still rising steadily through 5000 feet, suddenly dropped its nose to fly almost straight at the ground, before, with some superhuman effort, it climbed again. Then, as though its strength had finally gone, it plunged down to extinction. To the man below there was no outward reason, no missile, no mid-air explosion, no fire, no engine trailing smoke, nothing to forewarn of such a disaster.

Dead were the President of Pakistan, General Zia-ul-Haq, and the man who might have succeeded him had he survived, General Akhtar Abdul Rahman Khan, Chairman of the Joint Chiefs of Staff Committee. Gone were the two most powerful men in Pakistan, the head of state and the man who, for eight years until 1987, had headed the ISI. At a stroke the Afghan resistance fighters, the Mujahideen, had lost their two most influential champions. Dead were the US Ambassador, Mr Arnold Raphel, who had known the President for twelve years, and Brigadier-General Herbert

Wassom, the US Defense Attaché in Islamabad. Dead also were eight Pakistani generals with their staff, and the crew — thirty-one persons in all.

Disquietingly, neither President Zia nor General Akhtar should have been aboard the plane. Both had been persuaded against their wishes to attend a demonstration of a solitary American M-1 battle tank, which the US was keen to sell to the Pakistan Army. It was not a function that required their presence. Such a comparatively low-level event would normally have been handled by the Vice Chief of Army Staff, General Mirza Aslam Beg. It was the first time Zia had left the heavy security of his official residence since he had dismissed the government of Prime Minister Junejo three months before.

It was only on 14 August that Zia had finally given in to the pressure from his former military secretary and Defence Attaché in Washington, Major-General Mehmood Durrani, now commanding the armoured division. He insisted that the President's presence was diplomatically desirable, and would give added weight to the Pakistani delegation. After all Zia had retained the post of Chief of Army Staff. Against his better judgement he agreed to go.

Similarly, General Akhtar had no intention of going to Bahawalpur until a mere twelve hours beforehand. His change of mind was brought about by the persistent phone calls of a former director in ISI, to the effect that Zia was about to make some controversial changes in the military hierarchy about which Akhtar should know. Akhtar consulted with the President, asking for an urgent meeting. Zia, who was then committed to the tank demonstration trip, suggested Akhtar accompany him as they could discuss things on the aircraft. The fate of both was sealed.

The callsign of the President's plane was PAK 1, but the actual aircraft he would use was not selected until shortly before the flight. Usually two of the C-130s based at the Air Force base at Chaklala, a few miles from Islamabad, were earmarked. Then, once the decision was taken, the VIP passenger capsule could be rolled into the aircraft and secured shortly before take off. This was a 21-foot-long by 8-foot-wide plywood and metal structure weighing 5000 pounds, which was fitted out to give some comfort, including an independent air conditioning and lighting system, to an otherwise notoriously uncomfortable aircraft interior. The second aircraft, PAK 2, would follow PAK 1 as a backup. There was a routine security search of both planes prior to departure. For this flight there was a problem. The airstrip at Bahawalpur was small and could only accommodate one C-130, so PAK 2 would land 150 kilometres away at Sargodha. Once the President left Chaklala there was no possibility of his changing aircraft.

There would, however, be two other smaller planes on the airfield. The first was the Cessna whose task was to circle the vicinity of the airport as a precaution against missile-armed terrorists. This had been routine practice since an unsuccessful missile attack six years earlier. Then there was the eight-seater plane of General Beg who, as the official host, had to get to Bahawalpur in advance of the demonstration. The US military attaché's small jet that would take him and the ambassador south would be parked at Multan. If the crash was sabotage the two Americans were not part of the target.

The actual demonstration, in front of so much Army brass, was a big embarrassment to the Americans. The much-vaunted Abrams tank failed to score many hits and the billion dollar deal evaporated in the enervating heat.

While the President and the senior officers ate lunch at the officer's mess PAK 1 sat on the tarmac, baking in the sun. An armed military guard was on duty around the aircraft, but there had been a minor fault with a cargo door so the seven crew technicians worked on it. The pilot, Wing Commander Mash'hood Hassan, who had been personally selected by Zia, together with his co-pilot, navigator and engineer, arrived back at the plane for pre-flight checks in advance of the passengers. These four men would be seated on the elevated flight deck, which was separated from the VIP capsule by a narrow door at the top of three steps, on the left side of the aircraft.

Zia, with his party, arrived at around 3.30 pm, and knelt towards Mecca before saying his farewells. He had persuaded both the senior US officials to join him for the return flight. They did so with no apparent concern. General Beg made excuses when the President tried to prevail upon him to board PAK 1. He would use his own plane as he had business to attend to at Lahore. It was a known practice of Zia's to fly with the maximum number of top generals or officials to minimize the risks of a sabotage plot. Shortly before departure two crates of mangoes arrived for the VIPs, which were loaded in the rear without any check, together with a case of model tanks.

Strapped into the sofa and easy chairs inside the VIP capsule were Zia, Akhtar, Afzaal (Chief of the General Staff), Raphel, Wassom, and the President's military secretary, Brigadier General Najib Ahmed. Zia, Raphel and Akhtar sat close together so they could chat during the flight, although conversation is difficult as the C-130 is an excessively noisy aircraft. At 3.46 pm PAK 1 lifted off after the Cessna security plane reported nothing untoward. On the flight deck the take off routine had been uneventful, with clear communications to the control tower. The fact that the aircraft lacked either a black box flight recorder or a cockpit voice recorder would later be the subject of censure, but at lift off none of the crew or passengers had the slightest hint of the catastrophe that was little more than two minutes away. Mash'hood gave his arrival time at Islamabad over the radio as the plane pulled up into the sky and began to turn on to its correct course.

On the ground General Beg's pilot was preparing to take off; at Sargodha PAK 2 was airborne, as was the Cessna. All were on the same radio frequency as PAK 1, so all heard the ground controller request PAK 1's estimated position, and the response, 'Stand by'. Then nothing, no mayday call, total silence, despite the increasingly frantic calls from the control tower as it was realized that something was radically wrong.

To the passengers the horror of the sickening plunge, with bodies hanging by their safety belts, unable to move, screams drowned by the uninterrupted roar of the engines, was indescribable. Then, the sudden, few fleeting moments of relief as the plane seemingly came under control and started to climb again, with the occupants lolling in the opposite direction or jammed hard back into their seats. But, finally, yet another terrifying dive as PAK 1 gave up the struggle to survive.

The Culprits

In judicial terms it was either misadventure or murder. When the news broke, the chances of finding any Pakistani who believed it was an accident were a million to one against. Zia was a man with umpteen enemies. There had been at least six previous attempts at assassination, including a near miss by a missile fired at his plane. Probably his most uncompromising opponents within Pakistan were the Bhutto family. Zia had, despite the international outcry to commute it, confirmed the death sentence on the present Prime Minister Benazir Bhutto's father — this, to the man who, as prime minister, had personally picked Zia, then the most junior lieutenant-general, for promotion to Chief of Army Staff over the heads of his seniors. Zulfikar Ali Bhutto had made a decision that, three years later, he would pay for with his head. On 4 April, 1979, he was hanged in Rawalpindi jail. Thereafter the family feud was unrelenting. Zia imprisoned Benazir Bhutto and her mother, banned Bhutto's political party, and had his sons Shah Nawaz and Mir Murtaza convicted of serious crimes in absentia. In exile Mir Murtaza established an anti-Zia terrorist group named Al-Zulfikar (The Sword) in Kabul, where it shared offices with the PLO. From there, and Damascus, it carried out a campaign of killing and sabotage which, in 1981, included the hijacking of a Pakistan International Airlines passenger jet. Then, in 1985, Shah Nawaz died a painful death in sinister circumstances in Paris, it being rumoured that he had been poisoned by Zia's agents. There was, and still is, an implacable hatred between these two families. Benazir Bhutto claimed the crash was 'An act of God', before going on to win the general election three months later, to become Pakistan's first woman prime minister.

Zia was a military man who, along with Akhtar, was the last officer to have been commissioned from the Indian Military Academies just before the partition of India in 1947. Once in politics he would often boast that 'The Armed Forces are my constituency', and he never vacated the post of Chief of Army Staff that Bhutto had given him. But even within the military he had few friends. He quickly developed an uncanny knack of spotting potential rivals for power. These were removed from the scene by sacking, or posting to positions well away from the political centre at Islamabad. His only role as Chief of Army Staff had been to vet the promotions and postings of all officers to the rank of major-general or above. Numerous disgruntled Service chiefs were secretly delighted that Zia was dead.

Potential assassins were not restricted to Pakistanis. Ever since Zia had backed the Mujahideen in their struggle against the Soviets and their Afghan allies, Pakistan had been swamped with KHAD agents bent on undermining his government by a terror campaign of bombing civilians. KHAD is the Afghan secret police organization, trained and advised by the KGB. At the top of its hit list was President Zia, closely followed by General Akhtar. The Soviets were withdrawing from Afghanistan solely because Zia had given sanctuary to the Mujahideen and had, for nine years, been arming, training and advising them in a bloody guerrilla war that had cost the Soviet military 13,000 lives. The USSR blamed Pakistan for continuing to encourage and supply the Mujahideen in their attacks during the withdrawal, which was half-completed at the time of the crash. It had gone so far as to warn Pakistan, through the US Ambassador in Moscow, that it intended to teach Zia a lesson.

Then there was India. Pakistanis and Indians had slaughtered each other on three separate occasions, in 1947, 1965 and 1971. India's Prime Minister Rajiv Gandhi was convinced that Zia was supplying weapons to Sikh terrorists. They had murdered his mother, and now several thousand armed Sikh insurgents were active in India. Zia was accused of meeting their leaders, and giving shelter and training to the guerrillas inside Pakistan. To counter this, Delhi had established a special branch of its Intelligence Service, with the unpretentious title of the Research and Analysis Wing (RAW), specifically targeted on Pakistan.

Even the US government shed few genuine tears at Zia's death. It was the State Department's belief that Zia had outlived his usefulness. With the Soviets leaving Afghanistan, the last thing the US wanted was for communist rule in Kabul to be replaced by an Islamic fundamentalist one. American officials were convinced that this was Zia's aim. According to them his dream was an Islamic power block stretching from Iran through Afghanistan to Pakistan with, eventually, the Uzbek, Turkoman and Tajik provinces of the USSR included. To the State Department such a huge area shaded green on the map would be worse than Afghanistan painted red.

On the very day of the disaster the Pakistan Chief of Air Staff ordered a Board of Inquiry set up to inquire into the circumstances of the crash, assess damage and costs, apportion blame (if any) and make recommendations to avoid similar occurrences in the future. Air Commodore Abbas Mirza presided, with three other senior Pakistan Air Force (PAF) officers sitting as members. To provide technical advice and expertise six USAF officers were hurriedly flown from Europe to join the inquiry. They were led by Colonel Daniel Sowada.

For two months the Board deliberated and sifted evidence. Witnesses were interviewed, while exhaustive laboratory tests were carried out regarding the aircraft structure, instruments, engines, propellers, and flight controls, both in Pakistan and the USA, with the full cooperation of Lockheed, the aircraft's manufacturers. One after another possible causes of the crash were eliminated with meticulous care. Crew fitness, fatigue and stress were ruled out. There had been no pilot error. Adverse weather was not a factor, nor was fuel contamination. No inflight fire had occurred prior to impact; the aircraft was structurally intact when it hit the ground; there was no metal fatigue; engines and propellers were functioning normally, as were hydraulic fluid, electrical power and control cables. No evidence of a high-intensity internal explosion was found. Finally, no missile or rocket had been used to down the plane. The inevitable conclusion – a criminal act of sabotage had killed thirty-one people.

The Board was of the opinion that the crew in the cockpit had been instantaneously and simultaneously incapacitated by the use of a chemical agent such as a fast-working nerve gas. The presence of an odourless and colourless gas would not alarm the crew, so they would not don helmets and masks to breathe oxygen. It was established that none of the flight crew was wearing helmets at the time of the crash. The Board commented that such a chemical agent could have been packed in a small innocuous container such as a drink can, thermos flask or gift parcel, and smuggled onboard without arousing suspicion.

It was not possible to substantiate the type of gas used as 'no proper autopsies on the flight deck crew were carried out'. Only the body of Brigadier Wassom was examined before the authorities at the military hospital at Bahawalpur were ordered not to perform autopsies. He had been in the VIP capsule, not on the flight deck, and all that could be deduced was that he had not suffered injuries from any explosion prior to impact. Neither had he breathed in any toxic fumes, as would have been the case with a fire before the plane hit the ground. The instructions not to perform autopsies came as a shock, as it was a routine procedure. Later, it was stated that all the bodies had been completely destroyed in the fire, rendering autopsies impossible. When General Akhtar's family wanted to see his body before burial, they were refused, on the grounds that it was totally disintegrated, with nothing of any substance left.

This reason was not believed. Witnesses at the crash site said that, while the passengers at the rear of the aircraft were virtually totally destroyed, this was not the case with the senior officers in the capsule or the crew in the cockpit. The condition of Wassom's body did not prevent thorough examination. Zia's Holy Koran survived, charred but easily recognisable, as did Akhtar's uniform cap, together with his personal file cover with its crest, and the words 'CHAIRMAN JCSC' still clearly readable. A US official was to announce that the bodies were not available for autopsy as Muslim custom requires burial within 24 hours. While this is true in normal circumstances, it never applies within the Services, as shown by the Army medical staff at Bahawalpur when they automatically made preparations to proceed.

The Board had no members qualified to undertake criminal investigations, but they did record that, 'although 31 death certificates have been received no physical body count was carried out at the wreckage site or in the hospital. The possibility of someone not boarding the aircraft at Bahawalpur cannot be ruled out'.

Although the ISI was initially tasked with investigations, its efforts appeared less than enthusiastic. Service personnel at Bahawalpur were surprised that they were not subjected to rigorous interrogation. The discovery of a murdered policeman nearby was not successfully investigated, while the efforts of interrogators to extract a confession from the pilot of PAK 2 were bizarre, as well as unrewarding. A recent killing of a Shiite leader had been blamed by his followers on Zia. Both the pilot of PAK 2 and co-pilot of PAK 1, Flight Lieutenant Sajid, were Shiites, so it was suggested that the PAK 2 pilot had persuaded Sajid deliberately to crash the plane in a suicide mission. Only when the Board of Inquiry showed that such actions would have been physically impossible was the unfortunate man released.

So it was an act of mass murder. The likely method was pinpointed by the Board, although the culprits remained unidentified. As explained above, many people, organizations, even nations, had powerful personal or political motives for wanting Zia removed. What has gone before are the facts as far as I have been able to ascertain them; what follows are my own comments on how it might have been done.

First, I will deal with the point sometimes made that the violent roller-coaster movements of the aircraft indicated a last despairing attempt by somebody to fly the plane. If it had been a crew member he would certainly have shouted some warning over the radio, but there was absolute silence. Assuredly the crew were incapacitated. Afterwards it was suggested that the voice of Brigadier Najib Ahmed had been heard calling out to the captain, and that he had managed to get into the cockpit where his cries had been picked up on the radio as the pilot's hand was still locked to the switch. One version of this theory has Najib actually trying to control the aircraft. I believe this is nonsensical. Once PAK 1 got out of control there was no way anybody could physically leave his seat and struggle forward, climb the steps, open the door and get onto the flight deck. Finally, there is no mention of anyone hearing Ahmed's voice in the Board of Inquiry's report. Had such a thing happened it would have been there. The erratic climbing and plunging has another explanation. According to a Lockheed C-130 expert, if this type of aircraft flies unattended its nose rises steeply, a mechanism in the tail reverses this and the plane dives. The plane over-corrects, again with the same results. This might occur several times before a crash. The technical term for this pattern is 'phugoid'.

I believe the primary aim was to assassinate Zia. The original plan may have been to murder Akhtar as well, and at the same time, but I doubt it. It was really asking a lot to kill them simultaneously. Akhtar was detested by many senior officers, he was near the top of KHAD's hit list, and he was assumed by many to be ready to step into Zia's position if he died. Perhaps it was part of the plot to get him on board PAK 1 that afternoon, but if so it was a very last-minute arrangement. On balance I feel his death was probably regarded as an unexpected bonus by the killers.

Certainly the use of a plane crash was selected as the means because the chances of evidence to incriminate the plotters surviving would be minimal, even if it was later established as sabotage. The use of ultra-sophisticated poison gas, capable of killing four crew members simultaneously, points to the involvement of at least one intelligence agency. The problem would be the source of the gas. Pakistan would be unlikely to have it, but the KGB and CIA would surely have access. Both KHAD and RAW could have obtained it through their Soviet contacts. If the conspirators were among the Pakistan military then it is conceivable that the CIA could have supplied it, albeit for another purpose.

Also highly probable is the involvement of the Pakistan military, certainly at comparatively junior level, probably at senior as well. Neither the KGB nor KHAD or RAW could have halted the autopsies at a military hospital. With military involvement, the obtaining of the President's flight schedule becomes comparatively simple, as does getting around security at airports, and the actual planting of the device inside an aircraft.

The planners must have been getting desperate as week after week passed without Zia showing any inclination to use his plane. The tank demonstration was not likely to interest him without considerable persuasion, and was probably used as a last resort. The problem was to convince him to go without making him suspicious. Quite possibly somebody convinced General Durrani, the tank division commander, that Zia's attendance would add to the importance of the event, and was in Durrani's own interests. His subsequent success in inducing the President to go could have been entirely innocent.

We must assume that the lethal gas device had already been obtained while awaiting an opportunity, and the person destined to plant it given his instructions. He was undoubtedly in the military, probably a technician within the Air Force, possibly, if my theory is correct, from No. 6 Squadron PAF. This is the unit that operates the C-130 transports out of Chaklala a few miles south of Islamabad. A decision had to be taken as to when to plant the gas. Once it was confirmed that Zia would fly to Bahawalpur the choice lay between doing it there or at Chaklala, when it was clear exactly which aircraft would be PAK 1.

Most theories suggest the planting of the device was done at Bahawalpur, but I believe it much more likely to have been Chaklala. At Bahawalpur there would be no Air Force personnel except the crew, so none of them would do it — unless they were willing to go down with the plane. How could the plotters be sure an Army man could get on the guarded aircraft? The device had to be put in the cockpit which involved climbing up the steps, through the door, on to the flight deck. This was virtually impossible for a soldier, and certainly did not happen with the mango delivery. The crew working on the cargo door perhaps? But they were to fly back to Islamabad. Neither they nor the security guard would allow a soldier or civilian into the aircraft, let alone go climbing up into the cockpit. I cannot say with absolute certainty it was not done at Bahawalpur, but if it was it was a highly risky operation with the odds against success.

At Chaklala an intelligence agency would have an easier task in infiltrating the permanent Air Force staff. Access to the C-130s was part of the everyday duties of the technical or maintenance personnel. A perfect opportunity occurred when the VIP capsule was rolled up inside PAK 1. It identified the aircraft and, with the bustle of activity in strapping it to the floor and pre-flight checks, nobody would have questioned anybody going into the cockpit, perhaps changing a fire-extinguisher or inserting the device in an airvent. If the sabotage was carried out at Chaklala then it would have needed two devices to set it off — a timer and an altitude device. The timer would be set to activate the altitude switch. With the former a four-hour time lapse would be safe, allowing for one hour before the plane took off, just over an hour's flight, and then as PAK 1 sat on the strip at Bahawalpur the altitude device would be armed. All that was needed would be the climb to the required height, then inside the cockpit the deadly gas would escape. If Chaklala was the scene of the sabotage then it was a double-arming device that was used, otherwise PAK 1 would have crashed shortly after take-off and suspicion would have been focused on the Air Force base personnel.

The plot worked flawlessly, except for one major calamity: both the US Ambassador and the military attaché died. Certainly, whoever carried out this multiple murder had not intended these two senior Americans to be among the victims. There was no way of knowing that Zia would invite them to join him for the journey at the last minute. The conspirators were appalled. They anticipated the most thorough, penetrating and wide-ranging investigation which would undoubtedly uncover their identities. It never happened. The final phase of this merciless terrorist act was the US cover-up.

The Cover-up

The State Department would have much preferred an accident, some sort of technical failure, pilot error, anything rather than sabotage. If it was a murder of two high-ranking US officials then the American public would expect, indeed demand, to know the culprits. For such an outrageous act of terrorism the outcry against the perpetrators would be loud and long. The government would probably find it impossible to silence the clamour to exact retribution. Depending on who had done it, exposure could mean the ruin of US policy objectives in the area, and elsewhere in the world.

Supposing the KGB, or their surrogates in KHAD, were responsible, how would revealing the USSR as the organizer of mass murder, of the assassination of a head of state, affect the build-up of goodwill between East and West? How could the US avoid a major outbreak of hostility between themselves and the USSR? Almost certainly the Soviet withdrawal from Afghanistan would be reversed. The implications of Moscow being to blame were unnerving.

Similarly, the dilemma was almost as serious if the plotters were within the Pakistan military. If investigation uncovered a clique of anti-Zia generals the American people would be outraged that, after all these years of massive support to the Pakistan Armed Forces and the Mujahideen, they had killed a US ambassador and a brigadier-general. It would be futile to say they hadn't intended to! US-Pakistan relations would be in ruins. Aid would have to be curtailed, the military might be forced into prolonged presidential rule, the democratic elections scheduled for November would be abandoned, and with them the prospect of the more acceptably moderate Benazir Bhutto becoming prime minister. As I have said earlier, the US was not sorry to see Zia go. The State Department was happy to see the Soviets out of Afghanistan, but decidedly unhappy with the likelihood of, as the US perceived it, Zia-backed fundamentalists taking over in Kabul. Nor did it like his determination to have nuclear weapons. By mid-1988 Zia was becoming a liability rather than an asset to the US.

Though unlikely, it was conceivable that some minor political faction or terrorist group, like Al-Zulfikar, had somehow achieved the impossible. The problem was, once serious investigations started there was no knowing what unwelcome worms might emerge from the can as the lid was lifted. Testifying before the House of Representatives Judiciary Sub-Committee on Crime in June, 1989, Assistant Secretary of Defense Richard Armitage justified the lack of any serious investigations into the sabotage by claiming, '[we were] hopefully moving Pakistan in a more democratic manner... . The military in Pakistan as well as their presidency just being decapitated, we were very alarmed there might be some backsliding'. In other words they were quite prepared to write off Ambassador Raphel's and Brigadier Wassom's murders if that meant not rocking the boat.

None of this soul-searching would have been necessary if no Americans had died — particularly such senior ones. The whole business was complicated by the fact that as recently as 1986 Congress had passed a law that gave the FBI the legal right, indeed the duty, to inquire into terrorist acts overseas that involved attacks on US citizens. It is often referred to as the 'Long Arm' law.

The State Department did four things immediately after the crash which, taken together, point unerringly at a cover-up. First, within hours, it sent a team of purely technical airforce advisers to assist the PAF Board of Inquiry. Secondly, it did not insist, through its embassy, on autopsies on the bodies of the victims, particularly the crew, but rather allowed them to be buried knowing that essential evidence as to how the crash was caused was being buried with them. Thirdly, it sent a Deputy National Security Adviser, Robert Oakley, to take over Raphel's post. He could be relied upon to sit on the lid of the can. Later, in June, 1989, he told a highly sceptical sub-committee that when he attended the National Security Council meeting to decide on the US response to the crash, he simply forgot all about the 'Long Arm' law. This, despite the fact that he had personally lobbied hard to get it passed. Fourthly, and most importantly, it vetoed the FBI's request to go to Pakistan. Oliver Revell, FBI's Assistant Director, had requested clearance and on 21 August had been given it verbally, but, within hours, it had been withdrawn — probably on the instructions of Oakley, who was by then in Islamabad.

General Beg, who had just avoided dying with his President, had circled the burning wreckage in his own aircraft before flying straight to Islamabad. There troops were alerted, key points protected, and a crisis cabinet meeting called. But there was no military takeover. Beg accepted immediate promotion to Zia's old post of Army Chief of Staff, while the civilian chairman of the Senate, the 73-year-old Ghulam Ishaq Khan, took over as head of the interim government. The November election would go ahead.

Almost certainly the military authority that halted the autopsies will never be named, nor will the details of the collusion that must have taken place so swiftly between the Pakistani authorities and the US Embassy in Islamabad. It was not until ten months later that congressional pressure finally forced the State Department to allow three FBI investigators to go to Pakistan. As Congressman Bill McCollum (R. Fla.) said, 'At this late date, can the FBI find out what actually happened in Pakistan? I don't know. But we intend to find out what happened at the State Department'. The FBI team seemingly lacked enthusiasm for the task. It was reported that 'awkward' questions were not asked; the agents appeared disinclined to investigate evidence that conflicted with the statement that the bodies were too badly burned to permit autopsies and, with their schedule arranged by the Bhutto government, were apparently more interested in sightseeing than cross-questioning witnesses. According to a *Washington Times* source they only left Islamabad for tourist trips. Their attitude made it quite clear that they were following instructions not to stir the pot.

There was much hypocrisy in high places at the funeral on 20 August, 1988. India had sent its President and declared national mourning at home, the Russian Ambassador laid a wreath with solemn ceremonial, while US Secretary of State George Schultz called Zia a 'martyr' and assured the Mujahideen fundamentalist Leader, Gulbuddin Hekmatyar, that the US would do all it could to ensure their success in freeing Afghanistan. The funeral had both a military and an Islamic flavour. Hundreds of thousands of Pakistanis gathered near the gold-plated Faisal Mosque to watch the coffin, covered in the national flag and flowers, and carried on the shoulders of soldiers, arrive for the final rites. Prayers were followed by the measured boom of a 21-gun salute.

There was genuine sorrow and foreboding among the three million Afghan refugees encamped just inside the Pakistan border. There was a great sense of loss among the Mujahideen, for Zia and Akhtar had been the architects of their successes in the field. Now, with the Soviets withdrawing, with victory in sight, continued, uninterrupted support would be indispensable for the final push to Kabul. As the reader will discover the Mujahideen were to be bitterly disappointed.

The Beginnings

'The water in Afghanistan must boil at the right temperature.'
President Zia-ul-Haq of Pakistan to Lieutenant-General Akhtar Abdul Rehman
Khan, December, 1979.

QUETTA is the capital of Baluchistan Province in Pakistan. My life as a soldier was completely changed because of Quetta, which has been a garrison town since the last quarter of the 19th century. Its name is a variation of the word 'kwat-kot', signifying a fortress, as it is the southernmost point in a line of frontier posts that date back to the days long before the partition of the Indian sub-continent into Pakistan and India in 1947. It grew from a dilapidated group of mud buildings into a thriving market community, and one of the most popular stations of the old British Indian Army. The military Staff College of Pakistan, which I had attended as a young major, was originally established at Quetta in 1907, and is today a college of international repute, with potential senior officers from many foreign countries competing for places. Students from Britain, Canada, Australia, the US, Egypt, Jordan, Thailand, Singapore, Saudi Arabia and elsewhere had all rubbed shoulders with me on the same course. The Quetta earthquake of 1935 flattened the town, killing some 40,000 people and making it the most destructive quake of modern times, until the June, 1990, one in northern Iran. Today it is an important Pakistan Army garrison town with a large military cantonment area housing numerous units and a corps headquarters. It is the centre of a base area for possible operations in Baluchistan, or along the border. A hundred kilometres to the NW, over the Khojak Pass, is the southern gateway into Afghanistan (see Map 1).

I was in Quetta when I received the telephone call that was to send me to my new posting with the ISI. It was September, 1983, and I was taking part in divisional war games as a brigade commander. Later, I learned that it was the so-called 'Quetta incident' that had resulted in that call being made. Some months before there had been a corruption scandal within the ISI, involving three Pakistani officers who had been arrested for accepting bribes from Mujahideen Commanders in exchange for the issue of extra weapons,

Map 1

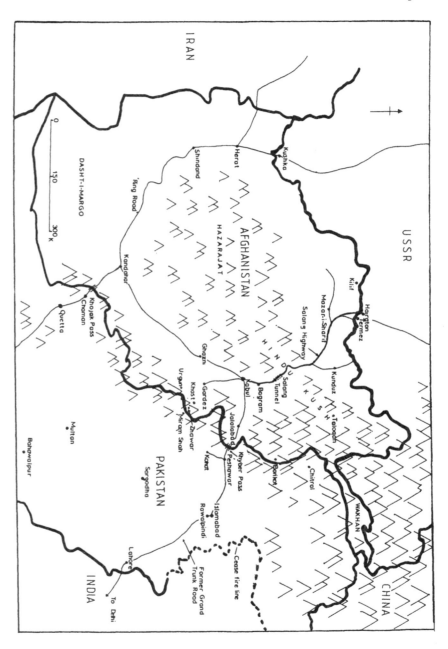

well above their allocation. These arms would fetch high prices in the frontier areas of Pakistan. The officers were court-martialled and imprisoned, while the brigadier, whose job I was to take, was moved sideways. As I was soon to discover, Quetta housed a forward detachment of my new organization, the Afghan Bureau of the ISI.

I was told to fly to Islamabad immediately and report to the Director-General of ISI, Lieutenant-General Akhtar. To say I was apprehensive would be an understatement. I was filled with misgivings. I knew nothing of intelligence matters, my career had followed the clear-cut pattern of a regimental infantry officer, with tours of duty with my battalion alternating with operational staff jobs, then as a commanding officer. As a full colonel I was on the operations staff of a corps; at no stage had I had any intelligence experience. So why was I being summoned to the ISI? Of all the thirty or so brigadiers whose postings were announced at that time I was the only one destined for an organization most officers regarded with intense suspicion, if not fear. The ISI was considered all-powerful, and the Director General second only in authority to President Zia, although he was outranked by numerous other generals.

The ISI had responsibility for all intelligence matters at national level. These covered political and military, internal and external security, and counter-intelligence. I knew of its role in outline and its reputation in some detail. The ordinary career officer felt, with justification, that the ISI was watching him personally, that it had its informants reporting on his attitudes and reliability. If an officer was on the ISI staff his peers, and indeed his seniors, tended to shun him socially. I had even noticed this myself in the few hours I spent at Quetta after my posting became known to my comrades on the exercise. I was no longer one of them.

Another reason for my anxiety was having General Akhtar as my immediate superior, not only because of his appointment but because of his daunting reputation. An artillery officer by training, he had fought against India three times, and as a very young officer had witnessed the horrors of mass murder at partition. I believe his hatred of India stemmed from those atrocities at the time of Pakistan's independence. He had a cold, reserved personality, almost inscrutable, always secretive, with no intimates except his family. Many had found him a hard man to serve due to his brusque manner and his reputation as a disciplinarian. He had many enemies. His success in reaching such high rank had been due to his energy, his boldness and his readiness to drive his command to its limit. I had served under him once before as a battalion commander in his division, so I knew at first hand what a difficult taskmaster he could be. He was totally loyal, totally dedicated to his profession, and, as I was to quickly realize, totally determined to defeat the Soviets. He was later to confide to me that it was his cherished wish to visit Kabul after the war had been won, to offer his prayers of thanks for victory. Although he lived to see the Soviets in retreat, he never got his wish.

Within 72 hours of receiving the phone call, I was being ushered into General Akhtar's house in Islamabad. As a soldier he looked impressive, with an immaculate uniform, three rows of medal ribbons and a strong physique. He had a pale skin and was intensely proud of the Afghan blood he had inherited. He carried his years well and I recall thinking he looked far younger than 59. He knew that I did not want the job, so he started by asking me how much I knew of the ISI's role in the Afghan war. Apart from general rumours and the recent Quetta incident, I knew nothing, so he took considerable time to brief me, stressing that he had personally selected me for the job, and that his decision had the backing of the President. All very flattering, but I now knew the enormous responsibilities that I was about to shoulder. Like many of my contemporaries at that time, I was not convinced of the wisdom of our government's policy on Afghanistan. I doubted whether the Soviets could be defeated militarily, and, with the presence of enormous numbers of refugees inside Pakistan, I felt that, sooner or later, we would face the same problems that some Arab countries were having from Palestinians on their soil. Within a few weeks I knew I was wrong.

In late 1983 Pakistan was a Muslim country under martial law. The Chief Martial Law Administrator was the President, Zia. There had been little exceptional about Zia the general, but Zia the politician was a shrewd and ruthless man, whose appearance belied his toughness. Benazir Bhutto once described him as 'a short, nervous, ineffectual-looking man whose pomaded hair was parted in the middle and lacquered to his head'. I certainly recall that for the man who ruled Pakistan he seemed, on first acquaintance, somewhat inoffensive, always rising from his seat and coming forward to greet guests most effusively, never waiting for them to approach him. But those that underestimated him did so at their peril, the prime example being Benazir's father.

The Armed Forces governed the country and Zia controlled the Armed Forces, the senior ranks of whom he watched and manipulated cunningly to ensure his own survival. Each province in Pakistan was then under a military governor, a senior general who owed his appointment to the President. Of these the North West Frontier Province (NWFP) and Baluchistan bordered Afghanistan. They were the front-line provinces, with a large proportion of the Pakistan Army deployed within their boundaries, watching the frontier, and able to move forward to previously reconnoitred battle positions should the Afghan war threaten to spill over the border. Pakistan felt insecure. India was on her eastern flank, an enormous nation of 800 million hostile Hindus, with whom Pakistan had fought three times. To the west lay Afghanistan

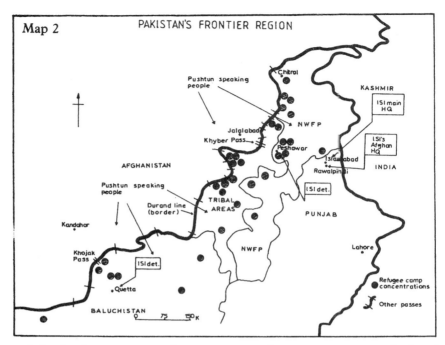

Map 2 — PAKISTAN'S FRONTIER REGION

and the Soviets, a communist superpower whose army was now deployed within easy reach of the mountain passes into Pakistan. Potentially, it was a highly dangerous strategic situation. India and the Soviet Union were allies; should they combine, Pakistan faced the prospect of being squeezed out of existence. I was fully aware of these threats. Like all officers, I knew that our military contingency plans were drawn up on the basis of fighting the Indians or, since 1979, the Soviets. Our nervousness was heightened by the fact that the USSR was a nuclear giant, and India had developed a nuclear capability, which we were seeking to emulate for obvious reasons of self-defence.

Pakistan's position was further complicated by the long-standing dispute with India over Kashmir in the NE, the simmering troubles in Baluchistan where there was a breakaway independence movement, and the centuries-old instability of the NWFP (see Map 2). The NWFP had always been a tribal area which defied control by a central government. In 1893 a British bureaucrat called Sir Mortimer Durand demarcated a new border, thereafter called the Durand Line, between what is now Pakistan and Afghanistan. While this line gave every strategic advantage in terms of dominating heights to Pakistan (then part of India), which suited imperial defense, it ignored tribal, ethnic or cultural realities. It cut through the Pushtun people's homelands. Britain had never seriously sought to subdue these warring tribes and clans. Even those areas east of the Durand Line were left to their own devices in the mountains. The whole of the NWFP had been an armed camp for the British, every regiment in India had its tour on the frontier, where the Pushtun tribesmen provided excellent training for the military, with an endless stream of incidents, and sometimes full-scale punitive expeditions. It was much the same for Pakistan. The Pushtuns were never ruled by the British, and at independence Pakistan took over the timeless situation whereby local tribes in this area continued to control their own affairs, and to move to and fro across the border much as they pleased. By and large we left them to get on with their trading and feuding without government intervention. The British had found this the easy option and so did Pakistan.

Into these frontier areas had poured a vast flood of refugees from Afghanistan. At that time over 2 million people had encamped along a 1500-kilometre stretch of border, from Chitral in the North to beyond Quetta in the south. Hundreds of tented and mud-hut camps teemed with people, mostly old men, women and children, all of whom were destitute. As will become clear later, the existence of these refugee camps played a key role in the struggle for Afghanistan.

When the Soviets invaded Afghanistan in December, 1979, Zia had immediately sent for his Director-General of the ISI, General Akhtar. He wanted an assessment of the situation facing Pakistan. He wanted answers to several questions, but most of all he wanted to know how he, Zia, should react. As a military man, he had turned, not to diplomats or politicians, but to a fellow soldier, a former military college classmate, for advice. He had told Akhtar to produce what soldiers call, 'an appreciation of the situation', but on a national, grand-strategy level. An appreciation is a meticulous, logical, step by step examination of a given situation, where all relevant factors are considered, along with likely enemy objectives, to produce a recommended course of action and an outline plan to achieve it.

Akhtar had made his presentation to Zia, forcefully recommending that Pakistan should back the Afghan resistance. He argued that not only would it be defending Islam but also Pakistan. The resistance must become a part of Pakistan's forward defence against the Soviets. If they were allowed to occupy Afghanistan too easily, it would then be but a short step to Pakistan, probably through Baluchistan Province. Akhtar made out a strong case for setting out to defeat the Soviets in a large-scale guerrilla war. He believed Afghanistan could be made into another Vietnam, with the Soviets in the shoes of the Americans. He urged Zia to take the military option. It would mean Pakistan covertly supporting the guerrillas with arms, ammunition, money, intelligence, training and operational advice. Above all it would entail offering the border areas of the NWFP and Baluchistan as a sanctuary for both the refugees and guerrillas, as without a secure, cross-border base no such campaign could succeed. Zia agreed.

The President told his Director-General to give him two years in which to consolidate his position in Pakistan and internationally. In 1979 Zia had just provoked worldwide consternation and condemnation by executing his former prime minister; his image both inside and outside Pakistan was badly tarnished, and he felt isolated. By supporting a Jehad, albeit unofficially, against a communist superpower he sought to regain sympathy in the West. The US would surely rally to his assistance. As a devout Muslim he was eager to offer help to his Islamic neighbours. That religious, strategic and political factors all seemed to point in the same direction was indeed a happy coincidence. For Zia, the final factor that decided him was Akhtar's argument that it was a sound military proposition, provided the Soviets were not goaded into a direct confrontation, meaning the water must not get too hot. Zia stood to gain enormous prestige with the Arab world as a champion of Islam, and with the West as a champion against communist aggression.

Initially, for the first few months, the Americans disappointed Zia. They adopted a wait-and-see attitude. President Carter was locked into the intractable Tehran hostage crisis, which soured American opinion against Islamic radicals, while advice from the Pentagon and CIA was that, with or without Pakistan's backing, Afghanistan was a lost cause. They believed that the Soviet Army would control the country within weeks. Why, therefore, get involved? Why throw good money after bad, and needlessly antagonize the Soviets by aiding the Afghan resistance? It was a country within the Soviet sphere of influence, and the US policy-makers had seen it slipping into the communist camp for over twenty years. They had been unwilling or unable to stop it then, so what chance was there now with the Soviet military in situ?

I had always been incredulous at the Americans' Afghanistan policy over the previous two decades. Their response to Soviet encroachment had seemed to be based on ignorance, apathy and appeasement, so their initial slowness in reacting positively had come as no surprise to me. The communist coup in Kabul in 1978, the climax of years of political and economic infiltration and subversion, produced no expressions of disapproval, no break in relations, in fact quite the reverse – the new regime was given automatic recognition. A top expert in Soviet affairs, Adolph Dubs, was sent out as the US Ambassador on the basis of business as usual. Within months Dubs died in a hail of gunfire from Afghan troops, under Soviet advisers, as they sought to 'rescue' him from four kidnappers in a Kabul hotel room. His death merited a weak protest, and the start of the phasing out of the already stagnant US aid programme. Nine years later another ambassador was to die violently in suspicious circumstances, again with possible Soviet involvement. This time the reaction was a cover-up.

It was 18 October, 1983, when I reported to the most carefully guarded office of the ISI, from which the war in Afghanistan was directed. Like all the other staff in this Afghan Bureau, I wore civilian clothes, little realizing I would never wear uniform on duty again. My headquarters was established in a large camp of some 70-80 acres on the northern outskirts of Rawalpindi, 12 kilometres from Islamabad, where General Akhtar had his office in the main ISI buildings. Inside the high brick walls were offices, a transit warehouse through which 70 per cent of all arms and ammunition for the Mujahideen came, at least 300 civilian vehicles with garage facilities, several acres of training area, a psychological warfare unit, barracks, messhalls for 500 men and, later, the Stinger training school, complete with simulator. It was called Ojhri Camp. Outside was the main road between Rawalpindi and Islamabad. Across the road was a Pakistan Army camp, and on the other sides the sprawl of houses that make up the fringes of Rawalpindi. International jet airliners flew directly overhead as they made their approach to Islamabad airport. Its very location within the confines of a major town made it inconspicuous. Of the countless thousands of passers-by none suspected it for what it was – the command post for the war in Afghanistan.

From being a straightforward infantryman I had become, overnight, a secret soldier. I referred to my staff by cover-names, never discussed work with my family, never answered the telephone directly, changed my car and number plates frequently, and never announced my travel arrangements in advance. Despite all these precautions I lived quite openly in a rented house in Islamabad. I normally carried a pistol but, as a mere brigadier, I did not rate an escort, or guard at my home. It was only towards the end of my stint with the ISI that I was told that I was near the top of the KHAD hit list, with a price of 10 million afghanis ($50,000) on my head. During those four years I was never aware of any personal danger to myself or my family. I put that down to professional incompetence on the part of the communist agents, as I was far from well hidden, although my social life was virtually non-existent. I never visited the US Embassy; I never attended diplomatic functions or formal military occasions. The only exception was with the Chinese. Every year General Akhtar and I would go to the Chinese embassy for dinner after the official signing of the arms protocol, whereby China agreed to supply us with specified types of quantities of weapons and ammunition for the Mujahideen. This was typical Chinese. They always insisted on absolute accuracy in all their dealings. I remember the colossal fuss that was made, involving high-ranking embassy officials, when just one small box of ammunition among thousands went astray. We later recovered it, but very politely they had insisted we move heaven and earth to do so. What a contrast to everybody else.

I was answerable only to General Akhtar; he reported to the President – it was as simple as that. Our chain of command completely bypassed the usual military hierarchy. Later, when we moved back to a more democratic government with a prime minister, Akhtar was supposed to report to him as the chief executive of government. I can only say that it was nearly a year before we at ISI were allowed to brief him on our role in Afghanistan. Zia did not want to let anybody know what we were doing, even the prime minister, if there was any possibility of his not staying in the post. The role of my bureau was top secret. Although it was well known that Pakistan sheltered the refugees and the Mujahideen, and that supplies were channelled to them across Pakistan territory, officially it was always emphatically denied.

In theory the top post in Pakistan's military establishment was that of Chairman of the Joint Chiefs of Staff Committee (CJCSC). He presided over meetings of the three Service Chiefs of Staff (COS). The position was a sinecure, a post without authority or influence. For one thing the CJCSC commanded no troops, and for another with Zia still Chief of Army Staff (COAS) it made the holder senior to the President within the Services – an obvious non-starter. Eight years after Akhtar was made Director-General of ISI he was promoted to four-star rank and appointed CJCSC by Zia. This was less than 18 months before these two men died together in the plane crash.

On my first day I was taken round the offices, and to see the main warehouse, where I received my first shock. Lying in the open, in piles, under an arched roof were all types of small arms, mortars, rocket launchers and recoilless rifles, together with their ammunition. Just about every safety rule I had ever been taught for arms storage was being broken, and this within a densely populated area. The logistics officer's response to my concern was, 'Sir, we are fighting a secret war; you will soon get used to it'. He was proved correct.

Meeting the various officers of my staff quickly gave me a better understanding of how we ran the war, although I was not impressed with the atmosphere of distrust, and apparent lack of cooperation within the Bureau. Several officers warned me to watch my back as they felt some of the staff had been imposed on us as spies from the Director-General's office. Our main headquarters and warehouse were located at Rawalpindi, but there were two forward detachments, one at Peshawar and another at Quetta. Each had operational, intelligence, logistics and liaison duties. They were located close to the offices and warehouses of the various Mujahideen Parties and Leaders to facilitate cooperation between ourselves as the supplier, and them as the receiver of the weapons and ammunition. The Quetta detachment had its own small warehouse because of the great distance from Rawalpindi. This enabled supplies arriving at Karachi by ship to be moved directly there instead of via our main warehouse – a substantial saving in time and cost.

During my time with the ISI the momentum of running a large-scale guerrilla war increased tenfold. The workload quickly threatened to overwhelm our original establishment, so I was authorized to expand. From

1984, through to 1987, over 80,000 Mujahideen went through our training camps, hundreds of thousands of tons of weapons and ammunition were distributed, while active operations were being planned and carried out in all of the 29 provinces in Afghanistan. I eventually had an establishment of some 60 officers, 100 Junior Commissioned Officers (JCOs), who approximate to US or British warrant officers, and 300 NCOs.

My headquarters had three branches. Under a full colonel was the Operations Branch, which also included training and intelligence. This branch was responsible for controlling the day-to-day planning of operations, the selection of targets in accordance with the overall strategy, and the allocation of tasks to the Mujahideen. It also coordinated operational intelligence from various sources and supervised training courses for the Mujahideen, which at that time were few and ill-coordinated. The next branch, also commanded by a full colonel, was in charge of logistics. Its primary task was the collection, allocation and despatch of weapons and ammunition. The third section was a lieutenant-colonel's slot. It dealt with psychological warfare – the operation of three border radio stations, distribution of leaflets and conducting interviews.

The Afghan Bureau which I controlled could not cope with all aspects of supporting the war. General Akhtar had set up another department, also under a brigadier, responsible for what I would term the 'software' of war – the provision of clothing and rations (in this case rice, pulses and flour) for the Mujahideen. These were purchased in huge quantities throughout Pakistan, with CIA money, for distribution to the guerrillas. I cooperated closely with this department. Over two years after my appointment yet another branch was created on the express orders of the President. Because of the rampant corruption within the Pakistani-staffed Commissionerate [sic] for Afghan Refugees (CAR), which was handling the supply of food and clothing for all refugees in Pakistan, the ISI was required to take over these duties for Afghan villagers remaining in Afghanistan. This policy of trying to alleviate the suffering of these people was an attempt to get the population to remain in areas of Mujahideen operations so that they would continue to provide information and succour. It was another brigadier's appointment, but although it was funded largely by the US Congress these funds were separate from the arms money.

During my first few weeks I resolved to listen and learn. I decided that 1984 would be the year for making changes and increasing the tempo of our activities. It would be foolish to try before I had fully grasped what was possible, what was not, and I had met some of the Mujahideen Leaders and Commanders. One thing that pleased me was that my new job was operations orientated. I was not directly involved in intelligence gathering, but rather in controlling active operations in a war against the Soviet Union. It was a daunting, but immensely challenging undertaking. As a professional soldier it was to be the ultimate test of my abilities. By coincidence, not long before my posting to ISI, I had had to organize a divisional study period on the Soviet Army, its tactics, organization, capabilities, and the threat it posed to Pakistan. My research had led me to rate the Soviet soldier highly for his performance in World War 2, but that was 41 years ago, when the Germans had marched on Moscow. Then the Soviets had been defending their homes; now they were themselves the invaders with entirely different motives for fighting. It was time I studied the Soviets' more recent performance. Before I attempted to plan anything for 1984 I needed to know what had been happening inside Afghanistan over the last four years. I needed to know about my enemies, their strengths and weaknesses, their locations and objectives, and I needed to learn a lot more about the Mujahideen if I was to drive the Soviets from Afghanistan.

CHAPTER 2

The Mujahideen

'Oh Gods, from the venom of the cobra, the teeth of the tiger, and
the vengeance of the Afghan — deliver us.'
An old Hindu saying

THERE were some 15 million people in Afghanistan in 1979 when the Soviets invaded. Today that figure has shrunk to around eight million, with up to two million dead, and over five million refugees in Pakistan and Iran. Its people are a mixture of tribes, with a mixture of languages and cultures, but a common religion — Islam. Islam provides a way of life and moral code to all groups. The great majority of Afghans are Sunni Muslims, though about a tenth are Shi'as. Although an over-simplification, it is possible to divide Afghans into two broad groups. To the south and east of the Hindu Kush mountains are the Pushtun, while to the north are the Tajiks, Turkomans and Uzbeks, speaking, or at least understanding, Dari (Persian). These latter people share their origins and culture with their neighbours north of the Amu River in the Soviet Union. I confess that my knowledge of these people was sadly deficient when I was appointed to oversee their armed struggle against communism. My foremost task, on assuming my duties, was to get to know my men.

Understanding the Afghan guerrilla fighter was to be a continuing process. Only after I had met many, seen them under training, watched them in action, discussed their problems with them and visited their bases inside Afghanistan did they gain enough confidence in me for them to listen when I tried to influence them in their conduct of battle. Even then, I was still sometimes politely ignored. To start with I expected too much. It took a while to adjust to the fact that I was no longer 'commanding' regular soldiers, but rather 'guiding' guerrillas. It was a fascinating process of learning. I have an immense admiration for the Afghan warrior. He has stood the test of time, he has never yet been conquered, and in 1980 he took on the Soviets, and in eight years forced them out of his country, an achievement second to none. Nevertheless he is no superman. He has, like most of us, his faults, mostly associated with inflexibility. Because I feel it is important for the reader to 'know' the Afghan, even if only slightly, at the outset, I have assembled together in the first part of this chapter some clues as to his character.

A small group of Afghans clustered around a wood fire, arguing. Two of them were disputing as to who was the bravest. To prove his point, one of them leaned forward and thrust his hand into the fire. He held it there, with the flames eating at his flesh. Despite the excruciating agony he made no sound, only the locked jaw, the screwing up of the eyes, and the slight shaking of his arm, indicated the supreme effort of will necessary to conquer the pain. For a few moments he kept it roasting in front of his audience. When he pulled back his hand it was bright red, dripping fluid. The man had established his courage.

Courage, physical courage, is central to the Afghan character. The incident described above actually happened, although it is an extreme example. This man was certainly overcoming fear, which is what courage is all about, but he was demonstrating a special facet of Afghan bravery — the ability to suffer pain stoically, without fuss, and silently. It is deemed unmanly for an Afghan to cry out, or scream, if gravely injured. This is inculcated into his character as a child, as a part of his upbringing. Cuff a five year old Afghan boy and tears will flow as other children, but hit the same child at seven and he will hardly flinch. To be without courage is abhorrent; such a person is despised.

Mujahideen wounded in the war faced the most daunting journeys on makeshift stretchers, or strapped to the back of horses, for days, sometimes weeks on end, over the mountains to Pakistan in search of medical treatment. Not for them the swift flight in a helicopter to a hospital miles from the fighting, as is normal with modern conventional armies. For guerrillas the time between being hit and receiving qualified medical attention is more often measured in days, rather than minutes. Amputations without anaesthetics were commonplace, using a knife, or even an axe, to chop off a mangled foot or leg. Many died of shock. I remember one Commander requesting, as a priority item, a surgeon's saw so that operations could be slightly less brutal and bloody. It was pure coincidence that this appeal came from a Commander nicknamed 'The Butcher', for his propensity for executing captured KHAD agents by personally slitting their throats. Those wounded who lived endured the torment of every movement, every slight twist or turn, during their nightmare journey to a doctor. Seldom did they utter more than the occasional moan. This willpower, this refusal to give in, or show what they considered to be weakness, is a great virtue in any soldier.

I do not mean to imply that a Mujahid is never frightened. He knew fear, but not the fear of death. I found that most were afraid of mines, and were hesistant to attack posts closely protected by minefields. Their concern was living the life of a cripple, in a society where physical stamina and hardiness are indispensable. Mines tended to blow off feet, or legs, or hands, not kill.

How could a man raise his family, tend his sheep, build his house and climb the hills without his legs? The prospect of such a life was infinitely more frightening than death on the battlefield.

The combination of courage, and their fervent religious belief in the cause for which they fought, made the Mujahideen formidable warriors to defeat. They were fighting a Jehad — a Holy War — a crusade against unbelievers, Kafirs, as they were called. As devout Muslims they knew and followed the teachings of the Holy Koran literally. Once a Jehad was declared by their religious leaders it was the duty of all men to fight, to save their faith, to defend their honour, to protect their independence, and to guard their land and families. Age was of no importance in joining a Jehad. Boys of 13 or 14 and men in their sixties or seventies, with snow-white beards, frequently fought side by side.

The call to arms against the communists, against invading infidels, was the major unifying factor that held together the different tribes. While the Soviets, and their Afghan allies, remained in the country the Mujahideen could sink some of their internal differences to combine against a common enemy. Not that feuding was ended, far from it, but rather that the divisive effects of their tribal quarrels, jealousies and hatreds could sometimes be temporarily contained by an appeal to Islam — to the overriding demands of the Jehad.

Mujahideen means Soldiers of God — those who fight for Allah in his war against unbelievers. It is an honour, a duty that is welcomed by the true Muslim. Unless you fight in a Jehad you cannot be a Mujahid. The Holy Koran states that a man killed in a Jehad becomes a Shaheed, a martyr. Commanders would never report that they had had so many killed in an operation, but rather that, 'God be praised, we had five Shaheed'. The Mujahideen's willingness to die in battle stems from the promise by Allah that Shaheeds go immediately to Paradise. No matter how many sins they have committed in this life, to die as a Soldier of God ensures complete forgiveness. A special place in Paradise is assured. Shaheeds are buried as they fall, in the clothes that they died in, bodies bloodied and unwashed, and without coffins. They go to Allah exactly as they died for their faith. There is no greater glory for the Muslim warrior.

It is not only the man who dies in a Jehad that is venerated. There is reward also for those who fight and live. Such a person is called a Ghazi, and Islam promises him rich rewards in Paradise. According to the prophet (peace be upon him) the Mujahid who spends one night on guard duty has performed equally with the ordinary man who prays for a thousand nights.

The battle cry of the Mujahideen is 'Allah o Akbar'— God is Great. They will shout this as they rush forward, as they fire their weapons, when they see a target hit, even on training when no enemy is in sight. It is a cry that has been heard down the centuries. Still today it can inspire the modern Mujahid, as it did his great-great-grandfather amongst the same crags and rocks when he confronted the British invader.

Not every male is fighting as a Mujahid at the same time. Within every family there is a system of dividing up the military and civil responsibilities of the menfolk. Mujahideen are volunteers who receive no pay, but a man may spend only three or four months in the field, and the remainder of the year as a shopkeeper, a farmer, on contract work in Iran, or perhaps in a refugee camp caring for the womenfolk of several families. When a man feels he has had enough he goes home and is replaced, eventually, by another relative. Thus, a Commander might boast 10,000 men under his control, but in practice it is unlikely, unless there is a major offensive under way, that he could muster more than 2000.

Most Afghans try to live up to their code of honour — Pushtunwali. Aside from courage there are two aspects of this code — vengeance and hospitality. 'Badal' is the Pushtu word for vengeance. The need to secure revenge for any slight, any insult, has been a part of the Afghan's life throughout his history. Blood feuds between individuals, between families, and between clans or tribes, are endemic. The Afghan will never turn the other cheek, a killing must be avenged by a killing, and so it goes on from generation to generation. A family will never forget a debt of honour. Revenge may not be swift, the injured party may bide his time for years if need be, until at the right moment he strikes. A son must kill his father's murderer. In many instances his mother will insist he does so, otherwise she will disown him and he will be disgraced. If the murderer himself is dead, then his son, or his brother, or his uncle, must die. Thus is the feud perpetuated. Even a Jehad does not stop badal.

Sometimes hospitality clashes with vengeance. To refuse a person shelter, or sanctuary, is unthinkable to an Afghan. Even if the person seeking hospitality is a bitter enemy he cannot be refused. While in that man's house he is absolutely safe; his host would fight to protect him, give him the choicest food, and treat him as a member of his close family. In an Afghan's home, even the poorest one, a guest will receive the best. If this entails killing an only sheep, so be it; no effort, no sacrifice is spared. A stranger, particularly a foreigner, sitting down to eat with a group of Afghans from the large communal pot will get the meatiest portions handed to him without hesitation.

Add to the above the Afghan's hardy physique, his ability to endure privations, his great resilience, and you have the makings of a first-class guerrilla soldier. Peacetime life is tough, the mountains and deserts of Afghanistan are an exacting, severe environment. A summer temperature of 130 degrees fahrenheit is commonplace, while in winter, in the high mountains, 20-30 degrees of frost is normal. Many peaks of the Hindu Kush top 20,000 feet, and are forever capped with snow and ice. Their very name means 'Hindu killer', from the time when the people of Afghanistan raided the plains of India for slaves, many whom perished on the terrible march through these unyielding mountains. The endless stretch of sand and rock in the SW is aptly called Dasht-i-Margo — the Desert of Death. A hard country has bred a hard, proud and fierce people.

From the military point of view the Mujahid starts with substantial advantages. Physically he is better able to withstand the extremes of the terrain and climate than his much softer Soviet opponent. He is fighting for his faith, his freedom, and for his family, which gives him an enormous moral ascendancy.

In practical terms the Mujahid can live off the land, or rather from the villages, until the Soviet scorched earth policy became widespread. Even when he takes rations on the march all he needs is nan (flat bread) and tea to sustain him for days on end. The fatty bread is carried wrapped in a blanket, or cloth, and becomes rotten with age, making it the most revolting of meals. Nevertheless, it is eaten. The Mujahideen can walk for days, even weeks, on the minimum of food; then, when the opportunity comes, they will stuff themselves with huge quantities, stocking themselves up like camels for the next journey.

An Afghan man rarely goes unarmed, even in peacetime. To him his rifle is a part of his body, a piece of clothing without which he feels uncomfortable. A weapon to a man is like jewellery to a Western woman — he is rarely seen without it. It is a symbol of manhood. A favourite before the war was the old British .303 rifle, some dating back to World War 1, others copies made in Pakistan. Afghans buy and sell weapons as Americans do cars. This closeness to arms means that the Mujahideen take readily to training on new weapons, and usually obtain startlingly good results. On many occasions I came across trainees in Pakistan who had not got high enough shooting results who refused all food until, with extra practice, they improved. To be able to shoot straight is of far greater practical value than to be able to write. In their life the gun is mightier than the pen.

After their weapon, the next most valued possession is their blanket. It is usually a greyish-brown colour, and is used day and night for a wide number of purposes. The Mujahideen uses it as a coat, or cloak, for warmth in winter, or against the wind; they crouch under it to conceal themselves from enemy gunships, as it blends perfectly with the mud or rocks; they sleep on it; they use it as a sack; they spread it on the ground as a table cloth, or upon which to display their wares; often it becomes a makeshift stretcher and sometimes it is a rope; several times a day it becomes their prayer mat.

While I was with the ISI serious efforts were made to clothe the Mujahideen adequately to face the winter. The months from December to March were hardly conducive to living in the field, or even in caves, without proper winter clothing. Even then, fighting died down in the winter and few operations were possible. An interesting sidelight on the question of clothing concerned boots. Normally the Afghan wore open sandals, which were totally unacceptable in the snow, but we found that the issue of boots was not initially popular. The reason was that the army boot has numerous lace holes, which meant that putting them on, and taking them off, was a time-consuming business. For the Mujahid, who was expected to remove his boots and wash his feet five times a day before prayer. this was a not inconsiderable chore. We had to look for boots with only two lace holes.

It should not be thought that the Mujahideen were completely devoid of weaknesses as guerrilla soldiers. As I discovered, their rigidity, their resistance to change and proud inflexibility caused serious problems in the tactical field, apart from the endless bickering over imagined slights, and refusal to cooperate with other Parties or Commanders.

An example occurred in 1984 with the Soviet's oil pipeline. This pipeline, that followed the Salang Highway to Bagram Air Base, was exposed above ground all the way, and as such was an obvious target for guerrilla attacks. But when I came to instruct Mujahideen Commanders on how to destroy it with the minimum of effort I came up against objections. I explained that this was a simple operation for a handful of men, or even one man on his own. The best way would be to approach silently at night, between the two guard posts which were always at least 500 metres apart, place the charge, set the time pencil and get out. Perhaps a few anti-personnel mines on the likely route of the repair party would improve things, and if necessary a group with a heavy machine gun (HMG) could cover the nearest post in case of trouble. My trainees refused to accept this. The posts were too close, they said.

To prove my point I organized a night exercise whereby two groups of trainees manned posts 500 metres apart, with the task of trying to hear another small party of four men who would, at some time during the night, crawl up and place charges. Needless to say the explosive was positioned without either post being aware. Still it was unacceptable it could not be done in their area; there would be mines along the pipe; or the terrain was unsuitable.

In fact what was wrong with my method was that it lacked noise and excitement. It was not their way to fight, with no firing, no chance of inflicting casualties, no opportunity for personal glory and no booty. Their method was to bombard the posts with heavy weapons by night at long range, move closer to fire mortars, get 30-40 men to surround them, and at short range open up with machine guns, RPGs and RLs (rocket launchers). If the garrison withdrew, the posts were captured and the Mujahideen secured their loot in the form of rations, arms and ammunition, all of which could be used or sold. Then, only then, was the charge laid on the fuel pipeline. If the garrison stuck it out the pipeline remained untouched.

It often took a serious setback, with quite severe casualties, to force a Commander to review his methods. Like most soldiers the Mujahid hated digging. He was decidedly unhappy in a static defensive role; it was alien to his temperament; it restricted his freedom to move, and he could seldom be convinced of the need to construct overhead cover. Similarly his fieldcraft was often poor as he was disinclined to crawl, even when close to an enemy position. The hard stony ground, or the possibility of mines, may have had something to do with it, but I had the impression that it was a bit beneath his dignity. Walk, or crouch perhaps, but crawling was seldom acceptable.

In summary the Mujahideen have all the basic attributes of successful guerrilla fighters. They believe passionately in their cause; they are physically and mentally tough; they know their area of operations intimately; they are extremely courageous with an inbred affinity for weapons, and they operate from mountain areas which give them both sanctuary and succour. These virtues are tempered with the vices of obstinacy, and an apparently insatiable appetite for feuding amongst themselves. To defeat a superpower they needed four things: to sink their differences for the sake of the Jehad; an unassailable base area, which President Zia provided in Pakistan; adequate supplies of effective arms to wage the war; and proper training and advice on how to conduct operations. It was my responsibility to provide and coordinate the latter two.

Within a few days of taking over I was taken on tour to visit Peshawar to see for myself how this forward detachment of my Bureau worked, to be introduced to my staff, and, most important of all, to meet Party Leaders, their officials and any Commanders that might be there. They needed to see their new brigadier, and I had to make a start at getting to understand them.

Peshawar is the provincial capital of the NWFP. Like Quetta, it has always been a frontier town, always a centre of trade, always in a military area. Like its sister town in the south it sits close to a main route into Afghanistan — the Khyber Pass is only 40 kilometers away to the west. These days its people, its sights, its smells, and its stories, are from Afghanistan. The markets sell Afghan carpets, sheepskin clothing, brassware, and momentoes of the war. Souvenirs taken from dead Soviet soldiers were commonplace, with cap badges, belt buckles, uniform caps and fur hats displayed by the score, although the source of supply for these items has now dried up. From Peshawar all traffic westwards goes through the tribal areas, the homeland of the Pushtuns. They live on both sides of the Durand Line, they own land in both Pakistan and Afghanistan, and they move between both countries about as casually as an American might travel between North and South Carolina. Peshawar lies at the western end of the Grand Trunk Road which, in the days of British India, stretched back through Rawalpindi and Lahore to Delhi. Now Peshawar is surrounded by Afghan refugee camps, with Afghans outnumbering all other inhabitants.

Peshawar contains the heart of the Afghan resistance movement in exile. Here are the offices of its political Parties, here is its bureaucracy, here its Leaders live and work, here are its arms warehouses, from here the majority of its supplies are carried forward to border dumps and thence into Afghanistan. It is to here that Commanders and Mujahideen come for replenishment and news. It is Peshawar that attracts the journalists and the spies as a magnet attracts metal. For the latest gossip, rumour, report or whisper, you must start in Peshawar. Quetta also has branch offices of the Parties, warehouses, plus an ISI detachment, but they are on a smaller scale than in Peshawar.

For the sake of clarity I should explain again that reference to a Party means one of the seven Afghan resistance political parties, that were shortly to be formed into an alliance. The political heads of each Party are termed Leaders to distinguish them from the Mujahideen Commanders who actually commanded in the field. With one or two exceptions Leaders did not fight battles, although most went into Afghanistan from time to time to visit their senior Commanders at their bases. Like the majority of military forces the Mujahideen had their political bosses, from whom their Commanders were supposed to get their instructions, and who supplied them with the means to fight − money and arms. As I was to discover, the gap between those who fight and those who do not was difficult to bridge. Some of the Leaders were the subject of much criticism, if not contempt, for their soft living, smart cars and well-furnished villas. It was the age-old disdain of the soldier who risks his life and lives hard for the politician who does not. Enemy agents made the most of this suspicion. Behind this primitive command structure was the ISI, my Bureau in particular. Our task was to keep the Parties stocked with supplies, and somehow get all the different Parties and hundreds of Commanders, scattered all over Afghanistan, to fight effectively.

When I arrived in Peshawar on that first visit in late October, 1983, the Seven-Party Alliance had yet to be put together. Until the Quetta incident Commanders had usually received supplies direct from ISI, but the opportunities for corruption were so great, and with Commanders being so numerous, together with a multiplicity of small Parties, the system had become a nightmare. General Akhtar had managed to halt supplies to Commanders and channel them through the Parties, but there were still too many clamouring for recognition. It was plain to me that without some semblance of unity at the political level we could not begin to make improvements in the military field. My meetings in Peshawar were polite, but somewhat formal. I could only meet the Leaders separately. This was because they would not sit in the same room with each other. I had to be careful what I said, so as not to appear to be promising something to one

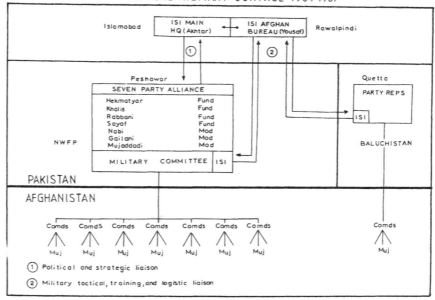

Party or another. I was speaking to men who, although devout Muslims, although committed to the Jehad, were fuelled by personal rivalries, prejudices and hatreds, which often clouded their views and dictated their actions. I had to remember that first and foremost they were Afghans, then they were politicians with political ambitions, then they were fighting a war.

As the head of ISI General Akhtar could only devote some 50 per cent of his time to Afghanistan. Of that, I believe 75 per cent was spent in trying to achieve some sort of harmony between fractious Leaders. I was to be grateful to him in the coming years that, after approving a strategy in principle, he left me free to make the military decisions and solve the military problems, while he tackled the political ones.

By early 1984 General Akhtar was determined that some sort of formal alliance be formed by the Parties. Some recognized high-level body was vital to act as a filter for the supply of arms and money to the users, and through whom we could attempt to coordinate action inside Afghanistan. For weeks he fought his uphill struggle to get the Leaders to agree. Prince Turkie, the head of the Saudi Arabian intelligence services, who was also responsible for overseeing his government's financial aid for the Jehad, was brought to Pakistan to address them. All to no avail. The Islamic Fundamentalists would not work with the more moderate Parties. It was then that President Zia intervened. Further meetings were convened and, after protracted talks had failed to reach agreement, Zia's patience snapped, and he issued a directive at 2.00 am – the Parties were to form a Seven-Party Alliance and issue a joint announcement to that effect within 72 hours. He did not say what he would do if they declined. The Leaders were well aware that without Pakistan's, and that meant Zia's, backing, everything was finished. Although the new Alliance was established, even at the last moment one Leader held out for a concession – and got it. It was accepted that important decisions be made unanimously rather than by a majority vote. Typical Afghan bargaining.

It was then a firm principle that every Commander must belong to one of the seven Parties, otherwise he got nothing from us at ISI – no arms, no ammunition and no training. Without these he could not exist, so he joined a Party, provided he could find one to accept him.

I was to have many meetings with Party Leaders during my time with ISI, discussing logistics and training, and coordinating operations, but I did most of my 'nuts and bolts' business with members of their Military Committee. This consisted of the military adviser or senior staff officer from each Party. I had arranged meetings with these men on a less formal basis before the Alliance came into being, but from then on I went to Peshawar at least monthly to see them. They were men who had either had military experience or had shown promise in this field. In time, no less than three former Afghan Army officers served on this committee. General Yahya Nauroz had once been Chief of the General Staff, Colonel Wardak had been a senior commander, and Captain Musa had come to the Mujahideen straight from the Indian Military Academy at Dehra Dun. The 'high command' set-up of the Mujahideen is shown in outline diagrammatic form on page 39.

Although the Alliance was a significant breakthrough, our problems were not all solved, but they gradually become slightly less intractable. One underlying difficulty never went away – the split between the four Fundamentalist Parties and the Moderate Parties, of which there were three. Fundamentalist adherents differ from the Moderates in their attitude to Western influence on Islamic teachings. Both are Muslims, but the Fundamentalist is more rigid, more conservative and is opposed to accepting any aspect of the Western way of life. It is a question of degree. A Moderate can accept a woman in trousers, but not in a mini-skirt, a Fundamentalist cannot.

The best-known and most controversial Fundamentalist Leader is Gul Badin Hekmatyar. He was born in 1946, which makes him the youngest of the seven, and was educated at the Kabul Military School, and University, where he qualified as an engineer. He was jailed in 1972 for two years for anti-government (anti-communist) activities. I found him to be not only the youngest but also the toughest and most vigorous of all the Alliance Leaders. He is a staunch believer in an Islamic government for Afghanistan, an excellent administrator and, as far as I could discover, scrupulously honest. Despite his comparative wealth, he lives a frugal life. He is also ruthless, arrogant, inflexible, a stern disciplinarian, and he does not get on with Americans.

Hekmatyar has never been forgiven by the US for his public refusal to meet President Reagan during a 1985 visit to New York to address the UN. It was seen as a major slap in the face for America who was supplying so much money to keep the fight going, yet here was a Mujahideen leader spurning the hand that fed him. Hekmatyar came under great pressure to relent, including telephone calls from other Leaders in Pakistan, who told him bluntly that he was doing enormous damage to the cause of Jehad in the West. He was unmoved. His argument was that to be seen having talks with Reagan would be playing into the hands of the KGB and Soviet propaganda, which claimed the war was not a Jehad, but rather an extension of US foreign policy. KGB and KHAD agents forever emphasized that the Americans were paying for Afghan to fight Afghan, making the Mujahideen not Soldiers of God but American stooges. Hekmatyar could not, or more likely would not, understand why US aid had to be so public. He knew he had to accept it, but wanted it covert, deniable, not obvious for the whole world to see. For him, like many Afghans, it was humiliating to acknowledge publicly his indebtedness to a non-Muslim. America's apparent craving for gratitude was incomprehensible. It does appear to indicate a general lack of understanding on the part of the US in its dealings with the East. Aid donations are publicized so much that the receiver loses face and becomes resentful rather than grateful.

Personally, I felt Hekmatyar made a grave error of judgement and that his action damaged the cause of Jehad, confirming the US in its view that such men in power in Kabul would be as dangerous as the communists. I am convinced this incident coloured their thinking when the Soviets eventually withdrew and decisions had to be made as to American policy in the latter stages of the war. But it was not in Hekmatyar's character to bend.

The other Fundamentalist Leaders are Molvi Khalis, Professor Rabbani and Professor Sayaf. Khalis, although nearly seventy, still used to venture deep into Afghanistan. Rabbani is a Tajik, a scholar and great linguist, being able to speak six languages. Sayaf is a highly respected intellectual, with strong support from Saudi Arabia, whose government awarded him the King Faisal Intellectual Prize in 1985.

I did not realize it at the time but part of the problem was lack of communication between the US and Fundamentalist Leaders, who seldom travelled to the US, unlike the Moderates, such as Gailani and Mujaddadi, who went every six months or so – all expenses paid. The Americans, understandably, wanted to see how their money was being spent, they wanted to control things, to interfere; indeed, they felt they had a right to do so. This argument cut no ice with the Fundamentalists. They remained convinced that US help was entirely politically motivated, it was convenient for them to pay for somebody else to take a crack at the Soviets, and thus get even for their humbling in Vietnam. As somebody who got to know senior officials on both sides of what became a serious controversy, I feel the Fundamentalists were correct in their assessment of American motives, but foolish to make their opinions so obvious, as without full US support the Jehad did not, and still cannot, succeed.

The Moderates are led by Molvi Nabi, Pir Gailani and Hazrat Mujaddadi. The first-named is a weak Leader, who leaves the running of Party affairs to his two sons, both of whom have been accused of retaining funds due to Commanders. The eldest son was involved in the Quetta incident mentioned earlier. Gailani is a soft-spoken, liberal democrat, fond of an easy life, who spends a considerable time abroad. He is not a forceful leader and seems to have little control over his Party bureaucracy. Mujaddadi is another linguist. He is also a prominent Islamic philosopher, whose main claim to fame was to serve four years in prison, three in solitary confinement, on charges of attempting to assassinate Nikita Khruschev during a visit to Kabul. He appears to be let down by his deputies and Party officials, over whom he seems to have little influence. Their dubious activities have now brought the Party into disrepute.

Another thing I learned during my first few months was that cooperation between Commanders in the field was not going to be achieved easily, even after the formation of the Alliance. Rivalries and petty jealousies between Commanders did not just go away because of the Alliance. In some ways it exacerbated the problem, as different Commanders from the same area would join different Parties, thus widening existing gaps between them. A Commander considered himself king in his area; he felt entitled to the support of the villages and to local taxes. He wanted the loot from attacking any nearby government post, and he wanted the heavy weapons to do it with, as they increased his chances of success and prestige, which in turn facilitated his recruiting a larger force. Such men often reacted violently to other commanders entering, passing through or 'poaching' on their territory. I could foresee serious difficulties in coordinating joint operations. No Party had a monopoly of power within specific areas or provinces in Afghanistan, although some might predominate. For example, in Paktia Province Hekmatyar, Khalis, Sayaf and Gailani all had Commanders operating, but only if they combined could any large-scale operation be effective.

Each Commander had his own base, usually in the remoter mountain valleys, within or near small village communities, from which he received reinforcements, food, shelter and sometimes money. As each of the 325 districts had at least one local base, the total in the whole jumbled network could have been up to 4000. But bases, vital though they were, are static, and the Mujahideen were reluctant to move away to operate against a more important target. For months at a time the Mujahideen in remote areas were not involved in any fighting, then perhaps came a sudden flare-up of violence. There seemed to be little planning, no discernible pattern to their activities; they fought when they saw an opportunity or they needed loot, and when the time suited them. I have summarized the political-military system of control and liaison for the period of my time with ISI on page 39. It looks neat and tidy as a diagram, but in practice it could get horribly confused.

I saw an example of this haphazard type of offensive around the small Afghan garrison towns of Urgun and Khost in the latter part of 1983. From August to November large numbers of Mujahideen attacked both towns, although Khost was not actually captured. When the government forces counter-attacked, just before the onset of winter, they opened up the road against little opposition. The Mujahideen around Khost preferred to move across to nearby Urgun in case it fell without their help, which would render them ineligible for any share of the loot. It was typical tribal fighting for immediate tangible gains, localized in area, and with no higher strategic objective.

Another critical factor that struck me about the war was that it would be a slow one. I could see that everything took time to decide, to discuss, to get moving. The Afghan is infinitely patient, there is seldom a rush, time is of little consequence to him. Things might get done, but slowly; normal military timetables were not going to work. I had no illusions that I could hurry them up. I was about to control a guerrilla army whose speed on the ground was measured in terms of how fast a man, or a horse, could walk across difficult terrain. The point was, however, that this gave them greater mobility than road-bound convoys or heavily armoured vehicles.

By the winter of 1984 (winter is from December until March) I had acquired, though personal contact, visits and briefings, some understanding of the military capabilities, weaknesses and potential of the Mujahideen. I knew their command system through which I would have to work and I was confident that I could have meaningful discussions with General Akhtar, and my staff, on how we might enhance their effectiveness as guerrillas.

Next, I turned to look at the enemy.

CHAPTER THREE

The Infidels

'It is right to be taught, even by an enemy.'
Ovid, *Metamorphoses*, IV

COURTESY of the CIA and their spy satellites over Afghanistan, my operations room walls were covered with excellent large-scale maps. They showed a rash of red symbols and pins. These portrayed the known locations of dozens of different formations and units, both ground and air, Soviet and Afghan. My first step in devising any plans to attack my enemy was to know where he was. Map 3 indicates, in outline, what I saw in terms of Soviet formations down to independent regimental, and Afghan to divisional, level. It was quite an imposing display. In all some 85,000 Soviet soldiers were inside Afghanistan, with another 30,000 or more deployed just north of the Amu River in the Soviet Union. Battalion-sized units from these latter formations frequently came over the river for operational duties, although the bulk had administrative or training responsibilities.

The Soviet chain of command went back to Moscow. There political decisions affecting the war were decided in the Kremlin. The Soviet General Staff (Operations Main Directorate) had initially appointed Marshal Sergei Sokolov to supervise the invasion. He had established his staff at the headquarters of the Southern Theatre of Operations. Further forward, at Tashkent, was the headquarters of the Turkestan Military District (TMD) with Colonel-General Yuri Maksimov in command. I was interested to learn that his performance as the overall Soviet commander of the Afghan War was highly regarded. In 1982 he had received promotion to colonel-general and was made a Hero of the Soviet Union at 58 − two years earlier than usual. Under him was the 40th Army rear headquarters at Termez on the Afghanistan border. Its forward command elements were under Lieutenant-General V.M. Mikhailov at Tapa-Tajbeg camp, Kabul. His command had the rather cumbersome and misleading title of Limited Contingent of Soviet Forces in Afghanistan (LCSFA). Working alongside him, but with no troops under command, was the senior Soviet military adviser to the Afghan regime, Lieutenant-General Alexander Mayorov.

Map 3

SOVIET-AFGHAN DEPLOYMENT 1983-84

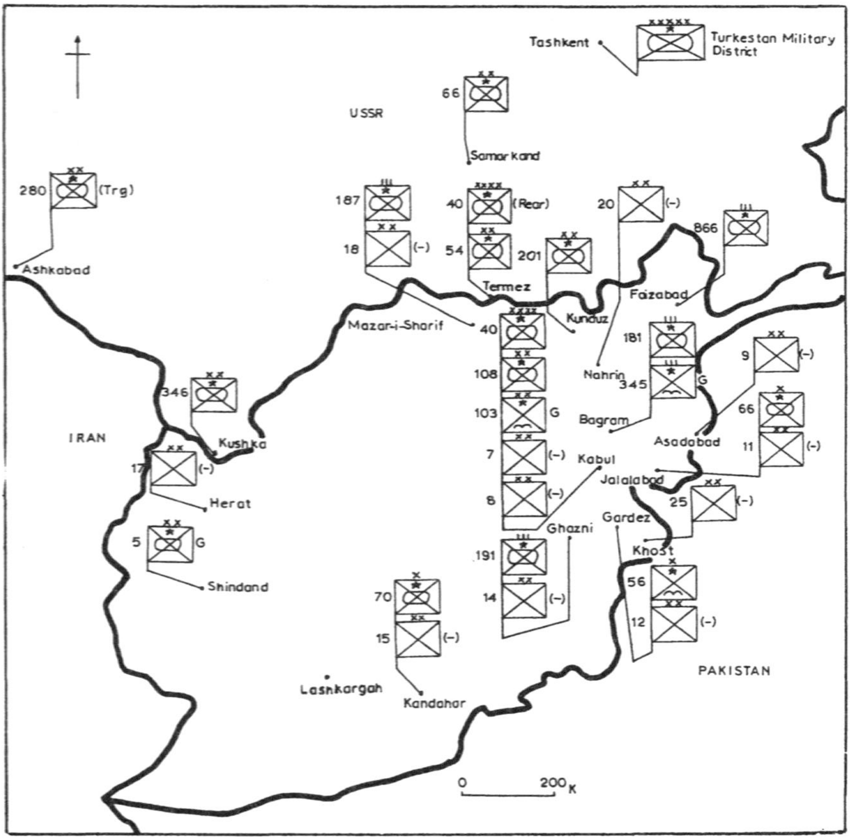

Tashkent — Turkestan Military District

USSR

66 — Samarkand

280 (Trg) — Ashkabad

187

40 (Rear)   20 (-)   866

18 (-)   54   201   Termez   Faizabad

Mazar-i-Sharif   40   Kunduz

346   108   181   9 (-)

IRAN   Kushka   103   G   Nahrin 345   G   66

7 (-)   Kabul   Bagram   Asadabad   11 (-)

17 (-)   8 (-)   Jalalabad

Herat   Ghazni   Gardez   25 (-)

5 G   191   Khost

Shindand   70   14 (-)   56

15 (-)   12 (-)

Lashkargah   Kandahar   PAKISTAN

0   200 K

45

At the time I thought it a little strange that in terms of numbers the Soviet pressure had not increased much since 1979. There was no evidence of their pouring more and more men into a bottomless bucket as the US had in Vietnam. It seemed they were not prepared to commit substantial additional formations to the war. If this deduction was true, it could be a critical factor for the success of future Mujahideen operations.

When the Soviets invaded they did not expect to have to mount a full-scale counter-insurgency campaign themselves. They had gone in with only four motor rifle divisions (MRDs), and one and a half air assault divisions (AADs) of paratroopers. These MRDs had been understrength cadre formations, fleshed out with hastily recalled reservists. They were composed of troops ill-trained for any war, let alone an anti-guerrilla one, and they arrived with obsolescent weapons and equipment, some dating back to WW2. This had been in marked contrast to their occupation of Czechoslovakia in 1968, which had required 250,000 troops in 20 divisions. We deduced from this that their original intention had been merely to stiffen the Kabul government under their newly installed puppet, Karmal. Their presence would hopefully give the Afghan Army sufficient confidence to get out into the countryside and flush out the resistance. In this they had been disappointed, but not sufficiently so to flood the country with overwhelming numbers.

As the map showed, in terms of combat troops not much had changed since 1979. There were now only three MRDs, one each at Kabul (108th), Kunduz (201st) and Shindand (5th Guards), with an AAD (103rd Guards) also based in Kabul. In addition there was a generous sprinkling of independent brigades and regiments at strategic points or important towns. There was a motor rifle brigade (MRB) at Jalalabad (66th), another at Kandahar (70th), plus an air assault brigade (AAB) at Gardez (56th). Independent motor rifle regiments (MRR) were at Ghazni (191st), Faizabad (866th), Bagram (181st) and Mazar-i-Sharif (187th). Finally, an independent guards air assault regiment (GAAR) was also at Bagram (345th) as a mobile reserve. The 346th MRD at Kushka and the 54th MRD at Termez were partially training formations, while the 280th MRD in the west near the Iranian border at Ashkabad was entirely for that purpose. The 66th MRD at Samarkand sometimes provided units for operations south of the Amu.

I knew from my Soviet studies that MRDs would probably have 11,000 men, the AAD about 7,000, while the strength of brigades and regiments were around 2,600 and 2,000 respectively. This would give just under 60,000 infantrymen, either motorized or paratroops. The remainder of the 85,000 were made up of artillery, engineer, signals, construction, border or security units, together with Air Force personnel.

My staff and I discussed the implications of the Soviet deployment. The first notable fact was that some 50 per cent of all their troops appeared to be tied up in or around Kabul. No less than two divisions were based there, with the majority of their artillery, transport, signals and engineer units, together with large numbers of other support and headquarters staff. The Soviets attached great importance to Kabul, with its airfield, which was the centre of government, and from which the war was controlled on a day to day basis. Only 50 kilometres north of Kabul was another huge concentration of Soviet personnel at Bagram. This air base had an independent regiment, a brigade from the 108th Kabul-based MRD and the independent GAAR, as well as the highest concentration of aircraft and Air Force personnel. Bagram was obviously regarded as the most critical air base in the country.

Another division was at Kunduz in the NE, and the two more independent brigades at Gardez and Jalalabad, each positioned opposite a main route to Pakistan. Clearly the Soviets regarded the capital and the eastern part of the country as the critical area. In the centre of Afghanistan the vast inaccessible jumble of mountains of Hazarajat, which made up almost half of the country, was almost devoid of Soviet units. Six hundred kilometres away in the west, a solitary division (5th GMRD) protected the second most important airbase, Shindand. To the south a single independent MRB was garrisoning Kandahar, opposite the route over the pass to Quetta. The Soviets appreciated that the centre of gravity was in the east, facing Pakistan, which was providing sanctuary for the refugees and Mujahideen. They had opted to hold the area Kabul-Bagram as the vital sector, with most of their other major units deployed to protect routes converging on this region, or to guard the Salang Highway that was its lifeline from the Soviet Union.

I also believed that the Soviets were sensitive in the north. Not only was their base area for the entire war effort just north of the Amu, but northern Afghanistan had had great commercial value to the Soviet Union for many years. In 1960 Soviet exploration had discovered several substantial natural gas fields near Shibarghan (see Map 6) in the northern province of Jozjan. It had an estimated reserve in excess of 500 billion cubic metres. In 1968 a 15-kilometre pipeline was opened, carrying the gas into the Soviet Union. Later, oil was discovered at Sar-i-Pul and Ali Gul 200 kilometres further west. Copper, iron, gold and precious stones are among the other profitable minerals that have been located in the northern and eastern parts of Afghanistan centred on or near the cities of Kabul, Kunduz and Mazar-i-Sharif. Precisely the areas that coincided with the Soviets military dispositions.

A further reason for my belief in the importance of the northern provinces was that they bordered on Soviet Central Asia. The people on both sides were Uzbeks, Tajiks and Turkomans. They shared a common ethnic identity and, despite the communist clamp-down on religious activities, they also shared the same faith − Islam.

My map also showed that the Afghan Army was deployed primarily in the east and north, mirroring the Soviets, with only a single division 'out of area' at Kandahar, and another at Herat in the far west.

From the Soviet and Afghan dispositions I was able to deduce several tentative conclusions upon which to base my own strategic thinking for the prosecution of the war. First, the Soviets were by and large content to hold a series of major military bases or strategic towns, and the routes between them, which indicated a mainly static, defensive posture. They did not seem to want to occupy large tracts of countryside. Second, they attached great importance to the Kabul-Bagram complex, and all approaches to it. Third, the provinces north of the Hindu Kush were critical to the Soviets for strategic (the Salang Highway ran through them), economic (gas, oil and mineral-producing regions) and political (the same people lived on either side of the border) reasons. Fourth, west and SW Afghanistan were not critical to the Soviets. Apart from the protection of Shindand, which, as a major air base, directly threatened the Persian Gulf, this part of the country was probably only considered as a buffer zone between themselves and Iran. Provided their road link north to Kushka via Herat, upon which the Afghan 17th Division was based, was kept open they would be happy.

The Soviet Forces had been in Afghanistan for four years, yet there was no evidence that they wished to escalate the war in terms of numbers. Despite the fact that they had underestimated the Mujahideen, and overestimated the capacity of the Afghan Army, they seemed content with improving their tactics, rationalizing their forces, developing the use of air power, bolstering their Afghan allies, and introducing more suitable weapons, in fact trying desperately to improve the quality of their troops rather than the quantity. I felt that they must realize that if they wanted to overrun the entire country quickly then they would need to triple the size of their forces inside Afghanistan. In 1964 the US had 16,000 men in Vietnam, yet within five years this figure had sky-rocketed to over 500,000 in an attempt to smother the opposition. The Soviets were not following the American example in this respect. I suspected that the reasons for this were more political and economic than military.

Internationally the Soviets had been vehemently condemned for their invasion. It had soured steadily improving relations with both the West and China, so to triple the size of their army in Afghanistan would certainly heighten the political outcry against the Soviet Union and boost the resolve of the US and others to sustain the Mujahideen. Economically the war was an enormous drain. Gorbachev was later to call it a 'bleeding wound'. Not only were the Soviets funding their own forces, but with the local economy in ruins they had to fund the Afghan government and army as well. Then, as their scorched-earth strategy took effect and refugees swarmed into Kabul and other large cities, they had to provide food for thousands of civilians.

Billions of roubles were needed from an already flawed Soviet economy. It was estimated that $12 million a day were required to keep the country and its war ticking over. Drastically to enlarge the strength of the occupying troops would be asking too much. In practical terms such an increase would have needed a much improved supply line from the north to Kabul, and one that was not subject to frequent attacks. The Salang Highway could not meet these requirements. All this was of some encouragement to me. If the enemy was fully committed militarily, then I knew exactly what we were up against; if there was unlikely to be massive reinforcement, I surmised the Soviets might have no trumps in their hand.

I already knew there was a political as well as military side to the Soviet strategy. The Kremlin, and indeed the Soviet General Staff, understood the fundamental truth that without Pakistan the Jehad was doomed. When President Zia, acting on the urging of General Akhtar, offered Pakistan as a secure base area, he condemned the Soviets to a prolonged counter-insurgency campaign that they were ill-prepared to fight. Like all armies, guerrilla forces cannot survive indefinitely without adequate bases to which they can withdraw from time to time to rest and refit. They need the means with which to fight, they need resupplying, they need to train and they need intelligence. Pakistan provided all these things to the Mujahideen.

For the Soviets this was extremely frustrating. By 1983 they had launched a well-coordinated campaign to make the cost to Pakistan of supporting the Afghan resistance progressively higher. Their aim was to undermine President Zia and his policies by a massive subversion and sabotage effort, based on the use of thousands of KHAD agents and informers. Every KHAD bomb in a Pakistan bazaar, every shell that landed inside Pakistan, every Soviet or Afghan aircraft that infringed Pakistan's airspace, and there were hundreds of them; every weapon that was distributed illegally to the border tribes, and every fresh influx of refugees, was aimed at getting Pakistan to back off. The Soviets sought with increasing vigour to foment trouble inside Pakistan. Their agents strove to alienate the Pakistanis from the refugees, whose camps stretched from Chitral in the north all the way to beyond Quetta, almost 2000 kilometres to the south.

The border areas of Pakistan had grown into a vast, sprawling administrative base for the Jehad. The Mujahideen came there for arms, they came to rest, they came to settle their families into the camps, they came for training and they came for medical attention. At the time we in ISI did not appreciate how fine a line President Zia was treading. As a soldier, I find it hard to believe that the Soviet High Command was not putting powerful pressure on their political leaders to allow them to strike at Pakistan. After all, the Americans had expanded the Vietnam war into Laos and Cambodia, which had been used as secure bases by the Viet Cong. The Soviet Union, however, held back from any serious escalation. I had to ensure that we did not provoke them sufficiently to do so. A war with the Soviets would have been the end of Pakistan and could have unleashed a world war. It was a great responsibility, and one which I had to keep constantly in mind during those years.

An interesting example of the sort of incident that could quickly get out of hand, or lead to international confrontation, involved Soviet prisoners of war, and occurred about a year after I arrived at ISI. At that time a few Soviet prisoners were kept by the Parties in their unofficial jails on the outskirts of Peshawar. On this occasion Rabbani had thirty-five such captives, together with several suspect KHAD agents, locked up near his warehouse. Three of these Soviets had been taken prisoner two years earlier, and outwardly at least appeared to have accepted Islam – possibly as a way of saving their lives. Because of this they were not secured or watched vigilantly. One evening, when everyone was at prayers, they overpowered a solitary sentry, took his weapon, and then smashed the armoury door to get more. After clambering on to the roof they demanded to be handed over to the Soviet embassy. Their captors did not agree. A long night was spent with the Soviets on the roof surrounded by well-armed Mujahideen. In the morning Rabbani's military representative tried to reason with them, but as he was doing so the Soviets spotted some men trying to get closer by a covered approach. The escapees opened up with a 60mm mortar, killing one Mujahid and wounding others. The battle was joined. Then, without thinking, one Mujahid fired an RPG-7 into the building, straight into the ammunition store. The explosion shook Peshawar, sending missiles and rockets flying in all directions and shredding the Soviets and KHAD agents. Fortunately, although the firework display closed the Peshawar-Kohat road, no civilians were injured. The Soviet press got wind of what had happened and later described the incident as an heroic last stand against impossible odds, with the prisoners killing scores of the enemy before being overwhelmed. Our government was highly embarrassed, as they always emphatically denied holding Soviet prisoners in Pakistan. We received explicit orders that all such prisoners must be held in Afghanistan. We had learnt a lesson, at the cost of a valuable arms dump, and allowing the water to come perilously near the boil.

1983 had been a comparatively quiet year in the field as far as the Soviets were concerned. There were no Soviet divisional offensive sweeps similar to those launched the previous year around Herat and in the Panjsher Valley. Nevertheless, I was able to study a regimental-sized operation which gave me some inkling as to how the Soviets had adapted themselves tactically to a guerrilla war. It occurred six weeks after I joined ISI.

On 26 November long columns of armoured personnel carriers, tanks, trucks and guns drove north up the Salang Highway from Khair Khana camp

Map 4

THE SOVIET'S FINAL OPERATION OF 1983

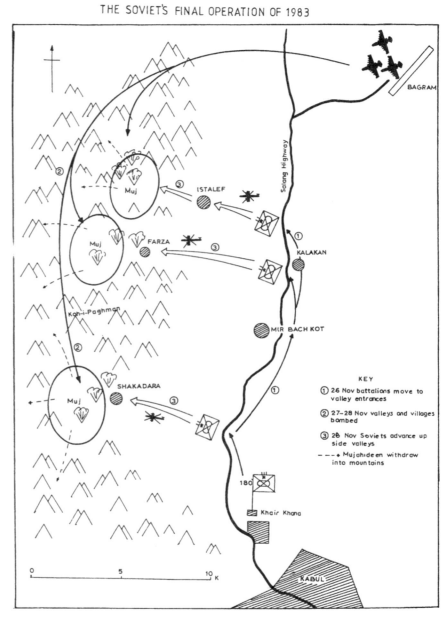

BAGRAM

Salang Highway

ISTALEF

Muj

③

FARZA

Muj

KALAKAN

③

①

MIR BACH KOT

Koh-i-Paghman

②

SHAKADARA

Muj

③

①

KEY

① 26 Nov battalions move to
valley entrances

② 27-28 Nov valleys and villages
bombed

③ 28 Nov Soviets advance up
side valleys

- - - ◆ Mujahideen withdraw
into mountains

180

Khair Khana

0   5   10 K

KABUL

51

on the outskirts of Kabul (see Map 4). They belonged to the 180th MRR of the Soviet 108th MRD. With them went Afghan Army units and helicopter gunships. The Soviet high command had been stung by the endless attacks on convoys using this critical life-line from the north. To the west of this road the massif, called the Koh-i-Paghman, rose up in places to over 12,000 feet. It was cut by several narrow east-west valleys that provided the Mujahideen with perfect covered approaches to and from the highway, from their bases in the mountains. Each valley had its tiny villages, with a larger one at the entrance, from which movement up and down the main road could be readily observed. The Soviets resolved to have a final attempt to clear three of these valleys before winter set in. From the equipment and weapons carried they appeared to have learned some expensive lessons.

Always edgy, always sensitive to sniper fire and ambushes at close range in the defiles, many troops now wore bulky metal-plate flak jackets. Special anti-sniper squads had been created to pinpoint marksmen. The firepower of the platoon had been boosted by the issue of the new AK-74 rifle, some with a single-shot 40mm grenade-launcher attached under the barrel, 30mm automatic grenade launchers with a range out to 800 metres and a high proportion of RPGs. Some platoons were being equipped with a highly demoralizing incendiary weapon. It resembled a bazooka and fired a shell up to 200 metres which exploded into a fireball on hitting the target. The standard APC of the MRD was the BTR-60 which mounted a 14.5mm heavy machine gun, a fine weapon provided the gunner could bring it to bear on his target. Often he could not, as his enemy had the disconcerting habit of overlooking him from high up steep slopes. Try as he might, the gunner could not elevate his gun sufficiently to engage. A 30° maximum elevation was perfect for the flat plains or undulating hills of Europe, but useless in the defiles of Afghanistan. By 1983 a workable solution had been improvised. Twin 23mm AA guns were fixed to the rear of a heavy-duty truck to give the required high rate of accurate fire at any angle up to the almost vertical.

The Soviet Air Force had learned from their low-level bombing runs. There had been a worryingly high proportion of bombs failing to detonate (the Mujahideen had sometimes used them as a source of explosive), so retard bombs which had a small parachute attached were now being employed. They descended more slowly and thus, even at minimal heights, gave enough time for the bombs to become armed before hitting the ground. Anti-personnel cluster bombs were another deadly innovation. They contained sixty bomblets each equivalent to an 81mm mortar bomb. The firepower was awesome, but without sound tactics it could not of itself bring victory, certainly not against a guerrilla force.

The column was split into three separate battalion battle groups each covered by gunships. Within a short distance the leading battalion swung left off the highway and headed towards the village of Shakadara. Ten kilometres further on the next battalion turned towards the Farza valley, and finally the last battalion moved into the Istalef valley, the northernmost of the three. The maximum distance travelled by any unit was 25 kilometres, but by nightfall on the 26th the battalions had merely positioned themselves astride the highway exits to each valley. The Mujahideen in the area were well aware of what was happening. On the following day the bombing started. Fighter bombers from nearby Bagram screamed up the valleys. Their targets were the people and houses below them. The air attacks, with the crash of 500lb bombs and palls of black smoke, were intended to kill indiscriminately, to terrify, to destroy houses and, supposedly, entrap any Mujahideen who might be in the valleys. On the 28th more bombers pounded the mountainsides and valley floor as the ground forces began pushing up towards Shakadara, Farza and Istalef, each of which was shelled and rocketed by gunships to supplement the air strikes. Not surprisingly, little was left when the Soviet troops arrived − some dead and injured civilians, piles of rubble, a few old men, women and children who had survived by cowering under rocks. Of the Mujahideen − nothing. The pretence of attacking and securing ground continued for another week before the entire force pulled back to Kabul.

There was nothing out of the ordinary in this comparatively small-scale operation. For this very reason it was illuminating for me. It was typical of Soviet tactics at this stage of the war. Road-bound units, bristling with guns, moved tortuously along the roads and tracks in broad daylight. There was no discernible attempt at surprise; the entire effort was slow-moving and ponderous, enabling the Mujahideen either to fight or disappear at their will. No serious attempt had been made to block the heads of the valleys, other than by bombs, and there was not much evidence of coordinating the air strikes with a swift approach by the ground forces. There was bombing, there was shelling, then there was a ground advance to find out what was left, a search and destroy mission with not much searching but a lot of destruction of buildings. No effort was made to position a proper cordon by using helicopters. The Soviets seemed content to stay in their vehicles for the most part, and when they did dismount it was usually only to sift through the debris wrought by high explosive on mud and brick. After a few days of this everybody had gone back, chalking up another victory for official reports. It reminded me of the boxer with his punchbag. Just so long as the boxer keeps his fist on the bag after making his punch an impression is maintained. When he removes his fist to strike again elsewhere the bag resumes its original shape.

It was not enough to know where the enemy was, or even to know his strength, weapons and tactics. I needed knowledge of his morale, his motivations and his will to fight. My recent studies of the Soviet soldier had left me with a high opinion of his fighting qualities, which was one of the

53

reasons I had been somewhat sceptical of the ability of the Mujahideen to defeat him in the field.

The German, Major-General von Mellenthin, who fought the Russians in 1943, rated their toughness, determination and willpower second to none. He wrote: 'Natural obstacles simply do not exist for him [the Soviet soldier]; he is at home in the desert, forest, in swamps and marshes, as much as the roadless steppes. He crosses broad rivers by the most primitive means; he can make roads anywhere ... in winter, columns ten men abreast and a hundred deep will be sent into forests deeply covered in snow; in half an hour these thousand men will stamp out a path, and another thousand will take their place; within a few hours a road will exist across ground deemed inaccessible by any Western standard.' Fortunately, as I was to discover, things had changed a lot in forty years, and the general had made no mention of mountains.

The Soviet soldier in Afghanistan proved to be a different man from his father in the 'Great Patriotic War', as they called World War 2. Then, the Soviets were defending their motherland, the Germans had killed or captured millions, overrun vast stretches of Russia and driven to the gates of Moscow. The Soviet troops fought with the ferocity and determination of cornered animals. They had no other option, theirs was a battle for personal and national survival; there is no greater cause. In Afghanistan things were completely different.

The modern Soviet soldier is a conscript; even his sergeants are the same. He is compelled to enlist at eighteen for two years. As a conscript recruit his life is normally miserable, often degrading. Prisoners or deserters described the intensive bullying to which they had to submit from private soldiers only six months their senior, as well as from many of their officers. The average Soviet had no motivation to fight in Afghanistan other than to survive and go home. He was not defending his homeland, he was the invader, detested by most Afghans, allies or enemy, and badly trained, fed and accommodated. As the American Vietnam veteran David Parks wrote in *GI Diary* in 1968: 'I never felt I was fighting for any particular cause. I fought to stay alive, and I killed to keep from getting killed.' I was quite sure many Soviet conscripts in Afghanistan would have expressed the same sentiments.

What puzzled me as a professional soldier was the almost total lack of even basic training given to men who were posted to operational units in the early days of the war. It was quite normal for a recruit to go on operations with only three weeks training behind him. Even worse was the prisoner who described how, during his first six weeks in the Army, he was merely given food and a uniform, no weapon and no training at all. Then he was posted to Afghanistan, to Mazar-i-Sharif, where he was immediately sent on village clearing and house-to-house searches, looking for Chinese, American or Pakistani mercenaries. Initially, as this man explained, he had to rely on his lessons on the AK-47 that he had received as a twelve-year-old school boy.

When it was realized that Soviet units would be needed to spearhead major operations and that the Afghan Army was totally unreliable, efforts were made to improve training standards, although this did not seemingly improve morale. Reinforcements were held back in the training divisions around Termez, but even this did not obviate the need for continuation training in operational units. The Soviet system did not work well. A conscript was in the Army for two years, with a new intake arriving every six months, and a time-expired group of roughly equal numbers leaving at the same time. Units, many of whom were under-strength anyway, lost their most experienced 25 per cent which were replaced by completely green recruits who required further training. As was pointed out to me, this was one of the reasons why Soviet units had so small a proportion of their men available for active operations away from their bases. A regimental commander could seldom, if ever, put his entire regiment in the field. He would have one battalion resting and being used as a training unit, another manning static defensive posts, with only his third available for deployment. On examining the figures, I doubted whether more than 10-12,000 Soviet troops from their 85,000 inside Afghanistan could have been committed to active operations at any one time. Even these men were in scattered formations, not all concentrated in one area for a major offensive.

Although I treated the horror stories of deserters or prisoners with a degree of scepticism, there appeared to be a basis of truth in what they said, if only because so many told the same thing. By and large the average man from an MRD detested the war, had no enthusiasm for his task, was concerned only with surviving and going home. Living conditions were harsh. Even in Kabul camps were often tented, with forty men living in each throughout the winter, packed around a single stove in the centre. Those in the middle roasted, those on the outside froze. Lack of hygiene and bathing facilities caused sickness, as did a vitamin-deficient diet. Many Soviets went hungry for much of the time. Their rations were insufficient in quantity and lacked variety. Rarely did they eat fruit or vegetables.

These deprivations were accentuated by a lack of cash. A conscript private with no qualifications or experience received roughly the equivalent of five dollars a month. Usually this was spent at once on more food. As well as being bleak and brutal, the existence of many was also boring. The same troops could man the same hilltop outpost for months on end, freezing in winter, baking in the summer. The daily grind of sentry duty, bad food and boredom caused many to seek solace in drugs or alcohol. Hashish was cheaper and easier to obtain than drink, vodka being a luxury reserved for officers. A Soviet soldier from Estonia was quoted as saying, 'Often regular

Afghan Army soldiers exchanged their Russian arms for food and drink from the peasants. So we did the same thing, because in the chaos of war to explain the loss of a weapon is easy.... We used to buy all kinds of food and drink, and even bread in exchange for our weapons.... Some soldiers got hashish and other drugs. Our Asian soldiers were very often drug addicts because hash and other things grow on their land.'

For money the Soviet soldier would sell anything, including weapons and ammunition, despite draconian punishments if the offender was caught. It was hardly surprising, therefore, that these conscripts were reluctant warriors. Often they were loath to quit the comparative security of their bases, or to dismount from behind armour plate in the field. Their preferred tactics seemed to be to leave the fighting to the Afghan Army, make maximum use of firepower, both ground and air, and stick to the roads as much as possible, only venturing out on foot when the area had been thoroughly strafed and pounded by shells, bombs and rockets. It was my impression, which I retained throughout my tour, that the Soviets were excessively casualty-conscious. This was reflected in the tactics of the senior commanders as well as the actions of individual soldiers.

There were exceptions. The paratroop (air assault) units fought much more aggressively. These men were all jump-trained before arriving in Afghanistan; their NCOs had all done six month courses. Their units had better equipment and their officers were normally of a higher calibre than those in MRDs. In the months following my arrival the Soviets committed more Special Operations Forces to the conflict. These Spetsnaz (Soviet Special Forces) troops were highly trained and motivated. Although the soldiers were conscripts they were the cream of the national intake. In Afghanistan they eventually deployed seven battalions, each of around 250 men, five of which were located in the east and two in the south of the country. I noticed there was a high proportion of paratroops in the Soviet order of battle, indicating that it was these units that would play a key role in offensive sweeps away from the roads. This was invariably the case, although they deployed to battle in helicopters rather than by parachute.

Although the Soviets were my principal target, and it was their withdrawal that was our ultimate goal, most of the time the Mujahideen would be fighting the Afghan Army — Afghan against Afghan. At the start of the resistance movement against the communist government in Kabul in 1978-79, the Afghan Army, trained and equipped by the Soviets for many years, was divided against itself. When the government had announced a compulsory literacy campaign for all women in early 1979, it provoked nationwide protests. This was against all the traditions of Afghans. On 15 March, 1979, a mob of armed protesters had assembled in the city of Herat. The demonstration rapidly turned into a general uprising of the townsmen and an assault on the prison to release political opponents of the regime. On the 17th soldiers from the garrison joined in, shooting some of their officers. That day the entire Afghan 17th Division mutinied, led by Captain Ismael Khan from the anti-aircraft battalion (he subsequently became a leading Mujahideen Commander in the Herat area). It was the only occasion that a complete division went over to the resistance with its weapons. In the ensuing chaos the people vented their hatred on the Soviet military advisers and their families in Herat. Some fifty or more were rounded up, tortured, cut to pieces, and their heads stuck on poles for parading round the city. Government armoured reinforcements from Kabul and heavy bombing subsequently retook Herat and smashed the resistance at a cost of 5,000, mostly civilian, lives. It was the start of what I would term the 'revolving door' period of the Afghan Army.

This period lasted two years, during which it was common for whole units to defect to the Mujahideen. As fast as the Kabul government rounded up recruits, even greater numbers deserted — hence the likeness to a revolving door. In 1980 the situation was so desperate that the 9th Division was down to little more than 1000 men. Commanders confined their men to their bases, or within defensive posts, as to take them out on an operation was tantamount to sending them over to the Mujahideen. Wire and mines were laid to keep defenders in as much as attackers out. The Soviet invasion had given the guerrillas what was to prove their largest recruitment boost of the war as thousands of civilians and soldiers joined what had become a Jehad. The arrival of the infidels gave the resistance a cause, transformed the guerrilla fighter into a crusader, a Mujahideen, with all that that implied. From 100,000 men the Afghan Army shrivelled to a mere 25,000.

Right up to 1987, when I left ISI, I believe the Afghan Army had an annual loss due to desertion, demobilization and death, of around 20,000. Recruitment had to be maintained by press-gangs. In theory conscription was for men aged 18-25 for a period of three years, but in practice those from 15-55 were often taken. The problem was that the manpower pool from which to take recruits had been cut dramatically by the war. Kabul found it impossible to tap the rural areas outside their control, which only left the larger cities which could provide conscripts. By the end of 1980 severe penalties were imposed to keep men in. For ignoring call-up papers up to four years' jail, for absence without leave up to five years and for desertion, conspiracy against the revolution and a long list of other offences, fifteen years or execution. Later the period of service was extended to four years, which sparked off several mutinies. I heard of men conscripted twice, even three times. Once conscripted a private had to exist on 200 afghanis ($2) a month, whereas if he had volunteered he would have got 3000-6000 afghanis. Everywhere he went he was watched, an escort accompanied him to the toilet, and sometimes it was two months before he was allowed a weapon at night, or ammunition for his rifle.

This was the force that the Soviets had expected to go out and fight the guerrillas; more often it had to be locked in to prevent its men joining them. This situation threw the Soviets' initial plan out of gear. I believe now, looking back on it with the benefit of hindsight, that 1980 was the year in which the Mujahideen could have won the war. It was the period in which they received the most recruits from a population nine-tenths opposed to communism; it was the period in which the Soviets found themselves ill-equipped, ill-trained and disinclined to mount counter-insurgency operations (and they were also under immense international pressure as aggressors); and it was the time that the Afghan Army was almost totally useless as a military force. In combination, these factors could have proved fatal to the communists. They did not, for two reasons. Firstly, the Mujahideen did not combine quickly to take advantage of their enemy's weakness. Secondly, they were not being supplied with sufficient weapons designed to engage tanks, APCs and aircraft. The supply pipeline through Pakistan was not yet functioning at anything like the capacity of the mid-1980s. The Soviets, and the Kabul government, were given time to put their house in order, which they partially succeeded in doing. Thereafter, success for the Jehad was that much more elusive and time-consuming, but still far from impossible.

By 1983 the Afghan Army was functioning again as a viable force. Its dispositions down to divisional level are shown on Map 3, but none of them exceeded 5000 men, making them at best brigades as far as numbers were concerned. One division, the 7th in Kabul, could only muster 1000, while battalions of 200 were not uncommon. Nevertheless, the total strength of the Army had climbed back up to 35,000-40,000 men. It was being utilized in the field to a limited extent and the Soviets were using it to fight the war along the Pakistan border. All the minor posts and garrisons in the east were manned by Afghans. In theory the Afghan High Command worked alongside the Soviets, there supposedly being a partnership to run the war. In practice this was nonsense, as all strategic and most tactical decisions were made by the Soviets. A Soviet military adviser looked over his Afghan opposite number's shoulder from the headquarters of 40th Army in Kabul down to every isolated company post throughout the twenty-nine provinces. An Afghan officer disregarded his adviser at his peril. There seemed to be a widening rift between Soviet and Afghan commanders, with the former regarding the latter as a second-rate, even expendable, ally. I was later to read transcripts of intercepted radio messages in which Afghan officers complained that they were being ordered to undertake risky, dangerous missions, while the Soviets remained secure in base. I was certain there was little love lost between the two, although both parties realized neither could survive without the other, so they kept up a pretence of fraternal cooperation.

I was especially keen to understand what was happening in the air. Airpower was assuredly the enemy's greatest asset. It bestowed not only unlimited firepower, but also mobility. Used correctly, these two could be combined on the battlefield to defeat the guerrillas tactically, if not strategically. The problem from the Mujahideen's point of view was not so much that they had no airpower of their own, but that their means of striking back at enemy planes and helicopters was restricted to a few outdated SA-7, shoulder-fired, surface-to-air missiles (SAMs). I will discuss this deficiency, and the air war, in detail in a later chapter but I would make the point here, as it was made to me on my arrival at ISI, that this lack of an effective and suitable anti-aircraft weapon was the most serious defect in the Mujahideen's armoury. This situation was not to be remedied for another three years.

Discounting at least four helicopter regiments, the air map depicted Bagram Air Base as having the largest concentration with 54 fighter and fighter-bomber aircraft. Next was Shindand in the west with 45, and then Kandahar with 15. These planes were outnumbered by those stationed in the Soviet Union, but which regularly carried out sorties over Afghanistan. At that time our intelligence was showing 195 such aircraft based at Mary North, Karshi Khanabad, Kokayty and Chirchik — this latter being 350 kilometres north of the Amu (see Map 5).

As was explained to me, the Soviet fixed-wing aircraft were being used to attack villages which might be serving as Mujahideen bases. Close air support, that is attacking guerrillas in contact with communist ground troops, was limited. This task was invariably given to helicopter gunships rather than fighter-bombers. Heavy use of bombing in localized areas was a common way of exacting reprisals after a successful guerrilla ambush. Indiscriminate bombing was causing great destruction of villages and inflicting hundreds of civilian casualties. It did not normally do much harm to the Mujahideen, but it was the primary cause of the torrent of refugees flowing into Pakistan. I suppose this in itself was counted as a success by the Soviets, as the refugees became a growing source of discontent in Pakistan.

The Mujahideen feared the helicopter rather than the MiG or the SU-17, because he could not hit back at it. It had become a personal enemy, spitting shells at him from a few thousand feet with comparative impunity. The M1-24 Hind gunship was the Soviet's battlefield workhorse of the war. Its armaments could include 12.7mm machine guns, 57mm rockets, HE, white phosphorus and incendiary bombs, air-dropped minelet pods, cluster bombs or chemical canisters. By late 1983, working in pairs, they could be seen providing close air support, rocketing villages, flying as convoy escorts and patrolling and destroying whatever they could find moving below them. As a transport helicopter, the Mi-8 or Mi-17 of the Hip series predominated.

Map 5

SOVIET AIR FORCES OPERATING IN AFGHANISTAN DEC 1983

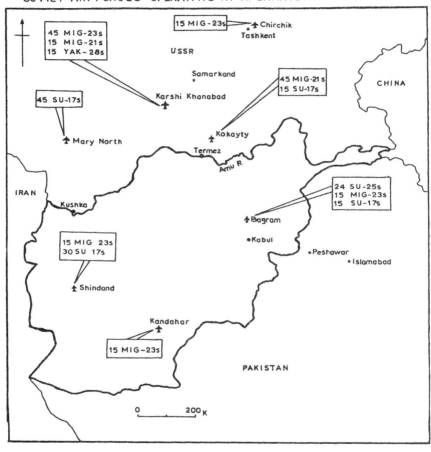

They were beginning to be used more effectively to air-land troops into blocking or cut-off positions during the larger sweep operations.

By mid-November I felt more confident that I was beginning to understand the Mujahideen and their enemies. It was time to consult General Akhtar on an overall long-term strategy for the war. We needed to decide priorities, to agree how best to improve the ability of the Mujahideen to defeat a superpower.

CHAPTER FOUR

Another Vietnam

'There were 58,000 [US] dead in Vietnam and we owe the Russians one.... I have a slight obsession with it because of Vietnam. I thought the Soviets ought to get a dose of it.'
Congressman Charles Wilson, formerly an avid supporter of US assistance to the Mujahideen, as quoted in the *Daily Telegraph*, 14 January 1985.

I ARRANGED Wilson's visit into Afghanistan in 1987 It was something he had always wanted to do, as he had been an energetic and persuasive spokesman for the Mujahideen cause inside the House of Representatives for a number of years. He had proved a good supporter of the Jehad, and was well known to President Zia, to whom he had casually let slip that he was going inside Afghanistan. Zia, who was not aware that this had been arranged, kept a straight face but later sought out General Akhtar and forbade it. He did so for political reasons, in case news of it were to leak, and because of the slight risk of his becoming a casualty, or, much worse, taken prisoner. Zia wanted the water warm, not boiling hot. Wilson had also arrived with a lady friend who he had hoped would accompany him, but this would have proved embarrassing and risky to arrange.

Wilson had arranged his visit directly with Khalis' Party, and we were unaware of it, as was the President. Although Zia vetoed the visit, he was adamant that Wilson should not know that he, or ISI, had prevented it. We concocted a plan whereby Wilson be allowed to approach the border, and then be stopped by Mujahideen on the pretext of inter-tribal fighting in the vicinity. This worked, and I went to Peshawar to escort him back to Islamabad. When he saw General Akhtar he was told that if he came back secretly arrangements would be made to get him into Afghanistan. Wilson duly returned and visited the Mujahideen base at Zhawar, some five kilometres into Afghanistan, opposite Miram Shah (see Map 1). There he enjoyed himself, being photographed on a white pony dressed as a Mujahideen, with a bandolier of bullets across his chest. He was most excited when he came under spasmodic shellfire, although nothing landed closer than 200 metres. Because we had several Stingers with us we tried to tempt a helicopter to come within range, as the Mujahideen wanted to show off their skill, and Wilson was equally enthusiastic to see one brought down. Unfortunately, they kept well away. On his return he was furious that the US Embassy had, somewhat thoughtlessly, arranged for him to fly home via Moscow. He made a monumental fuss and refused to board the aircraft, so another flight had to be found for him. I still have his letter of thanks for this covert trip to the war.

I mention this now because Wilson epitomized the attitude of many American officials that I met that Afghanistan must be made into a Soviet Vietnam. The Soviets had kept the Viet-Cong supplied with the hardware to fight and kill Americans, so the US would now do the same for the Mujahideen so they could kill Soviets. This view was similarly prevalent among CIA officers including, particularly, the Director, William Casey. I could see they were deeply resentful of their failure to win in Vietnam, which had been a major military defeat for the world's leading superpower. To me, getting their own back seemed to be the primary reason for the US backing the war with so much money. I have no doubt that the State Department had many valid strategic and political reasons for US support, but I am merely emphasizing that many American officials appeared to regard it as a God-given opportunity to kill Soviets, without any US lives being endangered. General Akhtar agreed with them that the war could be turned into a Soviet Vietnam. He had convinced the President it was entirely feasible, and now it was my job to see it carried out.

Certainly it seemed there were numerous similarities between the two wars. At the political level both involved superpowers fighting in a foreign country on the Asian continent; in both cases they fought to prop up a government that was corrupt and unpopular with the majority of the population; in both Vietnam and Afghanistan huge, modern, conventional forces fought, at least initially, a guerrilla force; and in both instances the superpower fatally underestimated their enemy, considering, at the outset, speedy victory within their grasp.

Strategically the terrain favoured the guerrillas in both countries, with the jungle-covered mountains of Vietnam, and the high, barren, rocky mountains of Afghanistan providing refuge and cover from the air to the insurgents. Both the US and Soviet Union relied heavily on airpower to compensate for their inability to meet their enemies on equal terms on the ground. For the conventional armies it was primarily a defensive war on land, with each trying to retain control over cities, communication centres, towns and strategic military bases, leaving the rural areas to the guerrillas. Both wars saw the use of terror and the indiscriminate bombing of villages which were supposedly sheltering the enemy. The guerrillas in Vietnam could obtain reinforcements, supplies and sanctuary across the borders in Laos and Cambodia, while the Mujahideen sought the same in Pakistan.

At the tactical level the superpowers depended heavily on firepower, rather than infantry manpower, to destroy their elusive opponents. Both re-learned the lesson that this tactic on its own does not defeat the guerrilla. The Americans coined a new military phrase, search and destroy, which became synonymous with surrounding a village or locality, then pounding it from the air and ground, irrespective of who was inside the cordon. Afterwards, there was a body count and the units claimed another victory. The Soviets copied this type of haphazard slaughter with great zeal, although they were not so adept at the cordoning. Neither America nor the Soviet Union could have survived as long as they did without the helicopter; but even then this wonder weapon could not give either the victory they sought. The attitudes of the soldiery of both superpowers developed along remarkably similar lines. Both were largely conscript armies, whose men fought with great reluctance — in order to survive. They had no interest in the war, no cause with which they could relate. This resulted in poor performance, particularly at small-unit level. Morale dropped alarmingly, and many resorted to alcohol or drugs in order to forget. With the Americans it led to widespread 'combat refusals', and over a thousand cases of fragging (soldiers murdering their own officers). With certain notable exceptions, the average US and Soviet infantryman proved, at best mediocre, at worst useless. It was the inevitable result of their governments expecting reluctant conscript troops to fight in a war in which they could see no purpose.

Interestingly, the career officers of both armies saw the war differently from their men. It was, for them, an opportunity to further their careers. Many did this, 'punching their ticket' with (for the Americans) a six-month tour to gain combat experience. Something like 60,000 Soviet officers went through the Afghanistan war, thus qualifying for the 'Afghan Brotherhood', membership of which was so often rewarded with promotion and medals.

I was now cast in the role of overall guerrilla leader. I ran over in my mind the recognized criteria normally necessary for an armed resistance movement to succeed: first, a loyal people who would support the effort at great risk to themselves, a local population, the majority of whom would supply shelter, food, recruits and information. The Afghan people in the thousands of rural villages met this requirement. Second, the need for the guerrilla to believe implicitly in his cause, for him to be willing to sacrifice himself completely to achieve victory. The Afghans had Islam. They fought a Jehad, they fought to protect their homes and families. Third, favourable terrain. With over two-thirds of Afghanistan covered by inhospitable mountains known only to the local people, I had no doubts about this. Fourth, a safe haven — a secure base area to which the guerrilla could withdraw to refit and rest without fear of attack. Pakistan provided the Mujahideen with such a sanctuary. Fifth, and possibly most important of all, a resistance movement needs outside backers, who will not only represent his cause in international councils, but are a bountiful source of funds. The US and Saudi Arabia certainly fulfilled this role. General Akhtar had been right; the ingredients for military victory were all there. I needed to give careful thought to where, and how, to apply the thousand cuts to bring down the bear.

It was important for me to understand the military geography of Afghanistan and how it related to the bases and lines of communication of both sides (see Map 6). No army, not even a guerrilla one, can fight a prolonged campaign without bases with lines of communication leading from them to the troops in the field. There are two types of base — the main strategic base of supply and the operational bases. The main bases of supply in this case were the Soviet Republics of southern Central Asia, from the borders of Iran in the west to China in the east, and for the Mujahideen the western border areas of Pakistan. Behind these frontiers were the depots, stores, training camps, main ammunition dumps, staging areas and, in the case of the Soviets, airfields that supplied the forces in Afghanistan. In both cases they had so far been immune from serious attack. Units could return for resting and refitting, and reinforcements could assemble unhindered. These were extremely long frontiers, each stretching several thousand kilometres. The Pakistan — Afghanistan border was mountainous for 90 per cent of its length, and in western Baluchistan there was desert. This frontier followed bleak and formidable barriers. Because of the excessive length of both borders, these bases of supply were developed around two towns in each country. In the Soviet Union Termez saw 75 per cent of supplies destined for Afghanistan pass through it, while the remainder went via Kushka. For the Mujahideen, Peshawar was the centre of their supply organization, with Quetta the secondary one in the south.

Operational bases were different. They were tactical bases inside Afghanistan, upon which formations or units were dependent for their immediate battlefield needs on a day-to-day basis. They were also usually the locations at which the units were stationed, and from which they sallied out on operations. After a sweep operation the Soviets would normally withdraw to their operational base; similarly, the Mujahideen would retire to their local base area after an ambush or rocket attack. For the Soviets the main operational bases were the larger cities and airfields such as Kabul, Bagram, Kunduz, Jalalabad, Shindand, Kandahar, and the newly built depot just south of Pul-i-Khumri. The Mujahideen used the hundreds of small villages and valleys scattered all over Afghanistan. Every Commander had his operational base.

A secure base of supply in which you can stockpile all the necessary weapons of war is useless unless the items can be delivered to the units in the field. For that lines of communication are essential. They are the arteries

65

Map 6

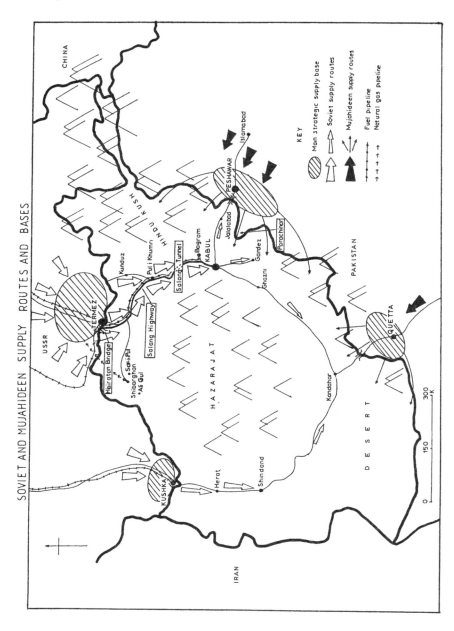

SOVIET AND MUJAHIDEEN SUPPLY ROUTES AND BASES

KEY

Main strategic supply base

Soviet supply routes

Mujahideen supply routes

Fuel pipeline

Natural gas pipeline

CHINA

PESHAWAR

Islamabad

Jalalabad

Gardez

Parachinar

PAKISTAN

KABUL

Ghazni

QUETTA

Kandahar

DESERT

Bagram

Salang Tunnel

Salang Highway

Pul-i-Khumri

Kunduz

HINDU KUSH

TERMEZ

Hairatan Bridge

Sar-i-Pul

Shibarghan

'Ali Gul

USSR

HAZARAJAT

KUSHKA

Herat

Shindand

IRAN

0   150   300
K

and veins of an army. Just as a human heart pumps blood along these veins to all parts of the body, so a strategic base must pump supplies to all parts of an army. Block a minor road for a short period and a unit is inconvenienced until the route is cleared, just as a cut finger will bleed until bandaged. Neither are serious injuries. But sever or block an army's main line of communication and it must be retaken or the army will die, just as surely as a patient with a severed artery will die without immediate attention.

Map 6 indicates the Soviets' ground logistics system. They were able to airlift supplies to most of their garrisons or operational bases if necessary, and they did so, particularly in emergencies when a post was surrounded. But air supply could not replace ground lines of communication, the scale of their needs was so immense. If the Termez base of supply was their heart, then Kabul was the head of the Soviet forces inside Afghanistan. Here was their forward headquarters, here was the centre of the communist government, and whoever sat at the centre controlled the country, at least as far as the outside world was concerned. The artery, the main line of communication, that kept Kabul functioning was Highway 2, the Salang Highway. It stretched for 450 vulnerable kilometres. It had been, and was to continue to be, the scene of some of the most successful Mujahideen ambushes of the war.

From Kabul other routes led forward to the limbs of the Soviet forces. Highway 1 led south to Ghazni, and then to Kandahar 500 kilometres away to the SW. Route 157 went due south to the garrison at Gardez 120 kilometres away, and the eastern arm of Highway 1 led to Jalalabad, and thence to Peshawar via the Khyber Pass. Each of these roads was important. If they were cut it was painful, and possibly incapacitating for a while, but it was not fatal.

In the west the secondary base around Kushka fed the forces at Herat and Shindand. In comparison to the east and the north this was a backwater of the war. Its importance lay in acting as a buffer against Iran. To get from Shindand to Kabul, by the southern route, necessitated taking the great 'ring road' via Kandahar. One thousand kilometres of tortuous, back-breaking, blistering motoring, every one through hostile provinces, and much of it across the Desert of Death.

The more I examined the map the more I understood the Soviet's problems. Their main lifeline, the Salang Highway, and its extension for 500 kilometres further south to Kandahar, was comparatively close to and, most importantly, parallel to, the Pakistan border. The Mujahideen's main base, with all its jump-off points, was within striking distance of the Soviets' principal north-south line of communication for over a distance of 1000 kilometres. The Parachinar (Parrot's Beak) peninsula pointed directly at Kabul. From its tip the centre of communist Afghanistan was only 90 kilometres away. By a strange coincidence a similar peninsula, also called the

Parrot's Beak, had jutted out from Cambodian territory only 65 kilometres from Saigon in South Vietnam. This gave us a great strategic advantage. Not only did the Soviets depend on one single highway in the critical eastern portion of the country, but it was excessively long, passed through Mujahideen-held areas and across the Hindu Kush mountains, but it was exposed throughout its length to the enemy frontier (Pakistan). We, on the other hand, had many routes into Afghanistan from the border bases, and they were comparatively short to the eastern provinces, and certainly far less exposed to attack.

As I well knew, the longer an army's line of communication the weaker the forces in the field. This is because such an army must deploy a high proportion of its troops protecting supply lines. The longer the route the more guards required, and the weaker the field force. This was the case with the Soviet and Afghan Armies. It was a major factor in limiting their ability to gather together a sizeable force for prolonged operations in the rural areas. I would estimate that 9 out of 10 of the enemy soldiers were committed to static defensive duties, garrisoning posts protecting roads or logistic bases, convoy escorts and administrative tasks.

The Soviets were sensitive to threats against their main supply line because they really only had one in the part of the country that mattered. They could not switch to another line if the Salang Highway was blocked. It was also their line of retreat. Eventually, when in 1988/89 the Soviets withdrew, it was up this road. In terms of military strategy theirs was an awkward position. Their forces had been compelled, by the relative positions of their supply base and Pakistan, to 'turn front to flank'. In other words their army had marched south for several hundred kilometres to the Kabul area with their supply route trailing behind them. Then, to get to the critical eastern provinces and face the enemy frontier, they had to turn left (east). Their front was now facing towards what had been their flank, but their line of communication was still running north-south, and so much more exposed to attack. The Mujahideen did not have this problem.

Despite these advantages, I had to be careful to remember that the Mujahideen were a guerrilla force and could not, in 1983, confront their opponents in a conventional stand-up battle. Our strategy must remain one of a thousand cuts. There is a great deal of difference between a stroke that cuts a major supply route and keeps it severed and a raid that is a fleeting attack which causes losses but does not block the route for a long period. To achieve the former on the Salang Highway would require a substantial force, able and prepared to hold on to the blocking position in the face of the inevitable massive air and ground counter-attack. Such a strategy was, I believed, beyond the capacity of the Mujahideen, even had I been able to get sufficient concentration and cooperation. The better strategy would be the raid, the ambush, the stand-off attack, but made with such frequency and ferocity that the loss of blood from these multiple cuts would seriously weaken the enemy's ability to continue. Such pressure on the supply lines would have the added benefit of compelling the Soviets to tie down an ever higher proportion of their men in static security duties. The initiative would be retained by the Mujahideen, with all that would mean in terms of their morale, and in convincing their backers to keep supporting them.

During my early weeks I met with General Akhtar several times to discuss an overall strategy for the war. In his view 1984 would see the Soviets continue to adopt their generally defensive posture, with emphasis on protecting important political centres, lines of communication and key installations, such as airfields, dams, industrial sites and hydro-electric plants. He foresaw the enemy confining any major operations to those necessary to increase security to the above vulnerable points. These would be likely in areas close to the Pakistan border to disrupt the Mujahideen supply routes, and in Mujahideen operational base areas close to important cities or air bases such as Kabul and Bagram. The Panjsher valley (see Map 7), which had so often been the springboard for attacks on the Salang Highway, and which had already been the target for no less than six major sweep operations in the first three years of the war, was considered the likely location of another Soviet offensive.

Akhtar also anticipated a build-up of air and artillery violations across the border into Pakistan. He saw the desire to create a widening rift between the local Pakistani population and the refugees as a crucial part of Soviet strategy. Sabotage and subversion would continue to be used to destabilize Pakistan, and this would include the provision of arms and money to tribes in the frontier areas that had always been hostile to the central government at Islamabad. If a breakdown of law and order could be fomented then it would put further pressure on Pakistan, which at this time meant President Zia, to withdraw its support for the Jehad. We both agreed that the Soviets seemed wedded to a military defensive strategy in Afghanistan, aimed at holding what they had got, coupled with a sabotage offensive in Pakistan, aimed at making support for the Mujahideen too expensive politically for Zia. The Soviets seemed disinclined to raise the stakes with large-scale reinforcements, hoping that in the long run the inability of the Mujahideen to capture key towns and the progressive destruction of the villages and rural infrastructure would make them give up the struggle through sheer war-weariness.

Our plans for 1984 were modest in their scope. They envisaged concentrating attacks on Kabul, which General Akhtar saw as the centre of gravity of the communist regime and army. It should be subjected to every type of assault and harassment to gain a political and psychological edge in the international press and media. Operations against the enemy's main line

Map 7

THE PANJSHER 7 OFFENSIVE APRIL– MAY 1984

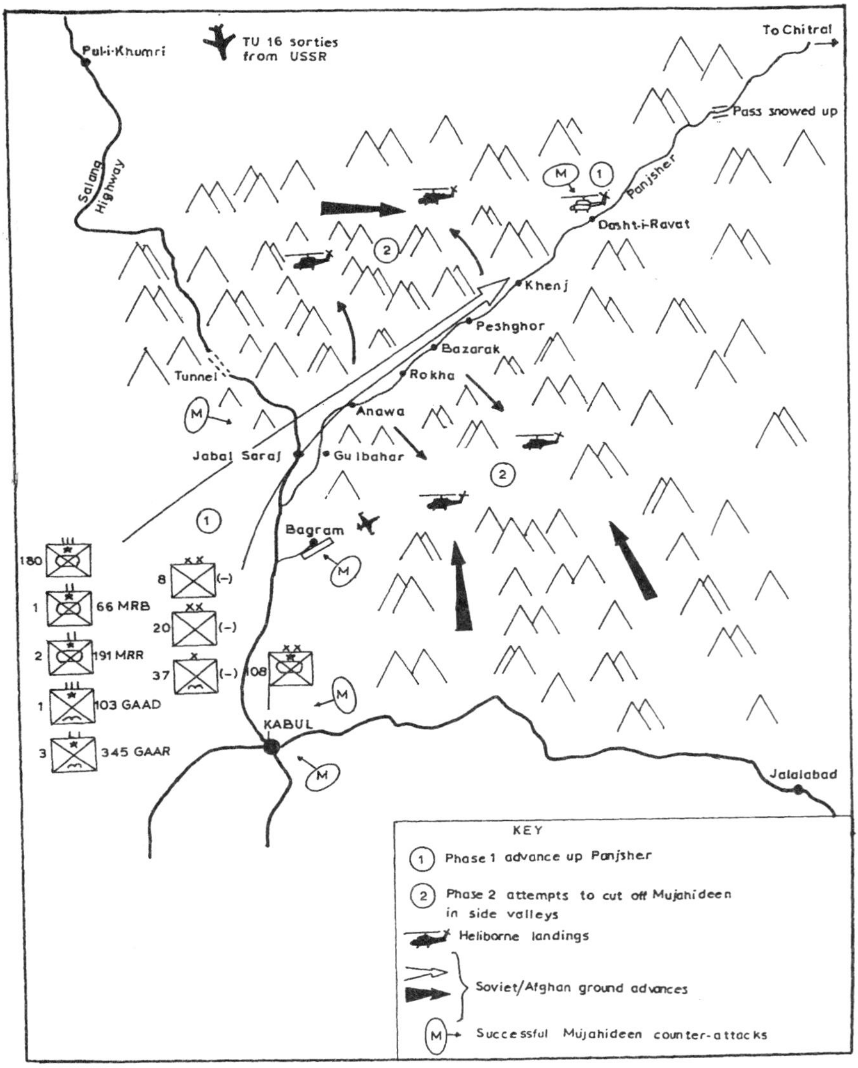

To Chitral

Puli-Khumri

TU 16 sorties
from USSR

Pass snowed up

Salang Highway

Panjsher

M 1

Dasht-i-Ravat

2

Khenj

Peshghor

Bazarak

Rokha

Tunnel

M

Anawa

Jabal Saraj

Gulbahar

2

M

2

1

Bagram

M

180

8 (-)

1 66 MRB

20 (-)

2 191 MRR

37 (-) 108

M

1 103 GAAD

KABUL

3 345 GAAR

M

Jalalabad

KEY

1 Phase 1 advance up Panjsher

2 Phase 2 attempts to cut off Mujahideen
in side valleys

Heliborne landings

Soviet/Afghan ground advances

M Successful Mujahideen counter-attacks

of communication and airfields were to be intensified and attempts should be made to lure small garrisons out into the field so that they could be caught at a disadvantage.

This was not an ambitious strategy. But, as I was quickly to appreciate, it took account of the limited capabilities of the Mujahideen at that stage of the war. There was still no real unity among Leaders; the Alliance was only just being set up; the Military Committee was in its infancy; the number of Mujahideen who had received training was tiny and they possessed no effective answer to the helicopter gunship. It was only during that year that Chinese 107mm rockets started to arrive; until then the Mujahideen's artillery had been the 82mm mortar.

Before I could do much to implement these decisions a major offensive was launched up the Panjsher Valley. It was the seventh such attack and illustrated the critical importance of this valley to both sides. Map 7 makes clear its significance. It takes its name from the river that rises in the heart of the Hindu Kush, amongst ice-capped peaks 20,000 feet high, and it points like a sword at the Salang Highway. The tip of the blade almost touches the road at Jabal Saraj. This valley contained the operational bases of the Mujahideen Commander Ahmad Shah Massoud. Massoud had agreed a ceasefire in the valley during 1983, but had refused to renew it for 1984, and this is what sparked the offensive.

The winter of 1983/84 had been a hard one and we did not expect any large-scale offensive until May. Nevertheless, we started receiving reports via our informers in Kabul that a major attack was coming in the Panjsher Valley. I held hurried discussions with my staff and the Military Committee as to how we could best assist Massoud. Our problem was that the shortest supply route to Panjsher was through the northern passes of the Hindu Kush from Chitral, but these were snow-bound, and on the other routes Commanders from different Parties to Massoud would not allow supply trains through their area. It was my first experience of how these inter-Party feuds could jeopardize operations. Massoud belonged to Rabbani's Party, so I put a lot of pressure on Rabbani to swallow his pride and ask the others to assist and cooperate. Reluctantly he did so, and I was relieved when Hekmatyar agreed, as his men were strong near the mouth of the valley overlooking Jabal Saraj and Gulbahar where we wanted to counter-attack as the offensive moved up the valley. I also hurriedly briefed and trained as many Mujahideen as were available in Pakistan, before despatching them to undertake diversionary attacks on Kabul, Bagram and in the Pakistan border regions. It was not much, but time was against me and there was no way I could coordinate any response to prevent the offensive getting under way.

The Soviets achieved surprise with the timing, strength and scope of their attack. Although we at ISI had insufficient time to organize an immediate response to the warning, Massoud was able to blunt the expected blow. He evacuated hundreds of villagers from the mouth and lower part of the valley into the side valleys; he laid mines along the road up the valley and he sprung a highly successful ambush on the Salang Highway in which some 70 fuel tankers were destroyed. He also blew up two important road bridges. The next day, 20 April, he started to pull back his men, who numbered up to 5000, into the mountains and side valleys.

On the same day the aerial bombardment started (see Map 7). Thirty-six TU-16 high-altitude bombers (Badgers), together with numerous SU-24 bombers (Fencers), had been pre-positioned from other parts of the Soviet Union to airfields at Mary North and Termez. The ground advance was to be preceded by high-level carpet bombing of the valley. The Badgers would be so high as to make them inaudible and invisible. On the people in the Panjsher it suddenly started raining 500 and 1000lb bombs. As the Americans had found with their massive B-52 raids over Vietnam, and the Allies in N.W Europe in 1944/45, aerial bombardment can be disappointing if its aim is to kill people or break their will to fight. So it was in the Panjsher, where Massoud's forethought reduced casualties, while the poor weather hampered the Fencers and forced one Badger to fly into a mountain. The narrow, steep-sided valleys offered excellent shelter from aerial attack. The mountains rose up to 19,000 feet in places, the tiny valleys twisted and turned, often becoming gorges rather than valleys, making such attacks extremely hazardous, if not impossible. In these areas attacking aircraft could not make proper approaches to the target and high-level bombing was usually wide of the mark. It was a lesson worth learning, and I made a mental note of the value of mountains against air attack.

For the Soviets this was their most ambitious offensive to date, reflecting the importance they attached to the Salang Highway, and the Panjsher as a threat to its security. It is likely that Major-General Saradov, the commander of the 108th MRD, was in charge of the operation, with a senior general from the General Staff flown in from Moscow to advise and report on progress. An airborne command post was set up in a four-engined An-12 Cub, which was packed with Soviet staff officers and nicknamed the 'Flying Kremlin'. Under command were some 10,000 Soviet and 5,000 Afghan troops.

The attack was in two phases. The first lasted from 22-30 April and was largely confined to the Panjsher valley, with armoured columns crawling slowly up the road, taking casualties from mines and Mujahideen spoiling attacks from the flanks. A rolling barrage of gunfire and rockets preceded the advance, while heliborne units were landed behind villages in front of the attackers to act as stop groups. It took the force eight days to get to Khenj, a small village some 60 kilometres up the valley. Here they halted, although a battalion was helicoptered into Dasht-i-Ravat, 20 kilometres further on, where it was mauled for its audacity and isolation. Phase two now started, as the upper reaches of the Panjsher were still secured by the snow.

This was the boldest part of the operation, as it involved several units outside the Panjsher Valley joining in an attempt to squeeze the Mujahideen between the forces approaching up the side valleys, and others coming over the passes behind them. These units formed an outer cordon, while battalion-sized units of paratroops would be landed in dominating positions to form an inner cordon (see Map 7). Again a battalion was cut up when it landed too far ahead of the ground troops.

By 7 May the second phase was over, and our activity around Kabul was being felt. A highly successful Mujahideen attack on Bagram Air Base demolished several aircraft on the ground. The attackers pulled back from the side valleys and from Dasht-i-Ravat, which was the furthest they had penetrated. As the Soviets withdrew to their bases at the end of June they left behind Afghan garrisons in permanent posts at Anawa, Rokha, Bazarak and Peshghor.

It had been a partial success for the Soviets. It also gave me further insight into future Soviet tactics and capabilities, as well as underlining some obvious Mujahideen weaknesses. The Soviets seemed to have improved their techniques since the previous, small-scale offensive up the Salang Highway that had occurred shortly after my arrival. This attack was better coordinated, with much more use being made of helicopters to position units in cordon positions. But once again there had been a *déjà vu* feeling about the operation. US Vietnam veterans, and their South Vietnamese comrades, would have found little difficulty in relating to the problems facing the Soviets and their Afghan allies, trying to destroy an elusive enemy who could turn from fighter to farmer in a few moments. Search and destroy missions are much the same whoever undertakes them.

I had had a sharp reminder of how inter-Party jealousies had the potential to cripple the best laid plans. I had seen how difficult, if not impossible, it was to mount a quick operation. I had received the warning of an impending attack several weeks in advance, but the lack of communications, the lack of any sort of mobile reserve force which could be despatched to a critical point, and the lack of a willingness among Leaders and Commanders to cooperate, had negated this advantage. Our efforts were belated, and therefore only partially succeeded.

On the other hand I had been shown how hard it is for aircraft to kill guerrillas in the mountains, and I knew for certain that the jugular vein of the Soviets in Afghanistan was the Salang Highway.

The Salang Highway had been constructed by the Soviets in the sixties as part of their development aid. Its primary purpose was to link Kabul to the Soviet Union and to establish a permanent, all-weather route over the Hindu Kush so that there could be a free flow of goods and people in both directions. Certainly its military significance had been appreciated, if not openly discussed. It effectively joined northern to southern Afghanistan, something that had not been achieved before, cutting the journey time from weeks to hours. While the Soviets had concentrated on this strategic link, the Americans struggled to build the 'ring road' to the south of the inhospitable mass of mountains, the Hazarajat, that sat in the centre of the country.

If the base area around Termez was the heart, which pumped supplies along the Salang artery to the head of the war effort at Kabul, then the choke point at the neck, 120 kilometres from Kabul, was the Salang Tunnel. Also built by the Soviets in 1964, the tunnel is a masterful piece of engineering. Located just east of Mount Salang, at 11,000 feet up, it is the highest tunnel in the world. It was blasted through solid rock for nearly five kilometres at the point where the Hindu Kush is at its narrowest. It is expected to remain open throughout the winter but this is only possible with the extensive use of bulldozers clearing snowdrifts and rock falls on the approaches. Although lit inside with power from its own generators, the journey through was seldom pleasant. In winter Soviet soldiers recall the intense cold, trucks slipping on ice, filth, the stink of fumes and the claustrophobic feeling as they disappeared into the mountain. The horror of being entombed remained with many until, after some 15 minutes if all went smoothly, the fresh air and freedom at the far end was reached.

Entrapment was not an unreasonable fear. In 1982 a series of landslides of snow and boulders blocked the road, bottling up a large convoy inside. The dense clouds of exhaust fumes quickly built up a poisonous concentration of carbon monoxide in the confined space, causing several Soviet deaths, much sickness and total chaos. This incident was erroneously reported as being a Mujahideen ambush and the number of deaths was exaggerated. It resulted in more ventilation shafts being bored through the roof. Stringent security was enforced at the tunnel. At each end permanent company posts were built to guard the entrances from close attack. Check points and barriers were in operation, with security troops or KHAD officials scrutinizing documents and searching suspect vehicles.

To me it was probably the most alluring target in Afghanistan. It cried out for attack. To destroy the tunnel would cause staggering logistic difficulties for the Soviets and be a Mujahideen triumph of the first magnitude. But, as I was to appreciate more and more, selecting a target was easy, hitting it was the problem.

Nevertheless, I determined to try. First there were the technical calculations of the quantity, type and positioning of the explosive. On the advice of a CIA expert it was established that several tons were necessary, which meant using a truck. Then, I was told one truckload would only cause damage that could be cleared in two or three days, so three trucks positioned at intervals inside would be needed.

There was a complication with the type of truck. Vehicles were liable to search on entering, so packing explosives into an ordinary lorry was impossible. We opted for a fuel tanker. With modification these vehicles could be filled with explosives, while a cursory inspection would still reveal fuel. Afghan government tankers would be ideal, so one was purchased for examination and testing. Another difficulty arose. A full tanker must enter the tunnel from the north end as only empty ones came up from Kabul in the south. The trouble was that the only road from Pakistan into Afghanistan ended up in Kabul. How to get three tankers packed with explosives positioned north of the tunnel was probably the most baffling of our tasks. They would have to travel up empty, and somehow the explosives would be carried in on horses or mules to a suitable rendezvous for loading.

We had to find several volunteer drivers to be trained and briefed. This proved difficult. It involved high personal risk and was not the sort of operation popular with the Mujahideen, who preferred the glamour and glory of the battlefield to clandestine sabotage activities. In practical terms the vehicles would need to be driven into the tunnel, have some sort of mechanical breakdown at the appropriate positions, the timing devices started, and then the drivers must get out. Motor cycles, or another vehicle leading the way, were possibilities, but a lot could go wrong. Breakdowns always caused chaos inside, plus an immediate reaction from the security units at either end. The tankers would need to be disabled in such a way that they could not be quickly towed clear. Both a remote-control exploder and a timing device were to be used. A timing mechanism was important in case the remote control one did not work. If all went well, the remote control would be used as soon as the drivers got out, in the hope of catching the Soviets inside attempting to clear the breakdowns. This they would try to do at once, with their suspicions aroused by three tankers stalled simultaneously. The timers would be set for about half an hour, long enough for the drivers to escape, but not long enough for the vehicles to be recovered, or the explosives found and defused. To obtain the maximum effect the operation was scheduled for the winter when Kabul would be short of supplies and clearance hampered by the weather, with bulldozers battling ten-foot snowdrifts on both approaches.

It would have been a magnificent Mujahideen triumph, but sadly it was not to be. Several times Commanders agreed they would do it, but always after a few months I would get word that it was impossible to find the men. Perhaps it was too ambitious, although I personally do not think so. It had all the makings of a classic guerrilla attack. History would surely have recorded it as the supreme example of a single act of sabotage crippling a modern army for weeks.

The Salang Highway was the most closely guarded road in Afghanistan. From the newly built bridge at Hairatan, just west of Termez, to Kabul, troops were deployed at scores of posts, large and small, each sited for mutual support. At intervals of about 20 kilometres large garrisons would be positioned with a mobile reserve force, artillery, armoured vehicles, tanks, and often Air Force ground controllers. They seemed not so very different from the fire support bases that the Americans built all over South Vietnam to protect supply routes, or support search-and-destroy missions. At places where the ground favoured an ambush the smaller posts would usually be sited on high ground overlooking the highway. Each post would be surrounded by wire and minefields, and was linked to its sector headquarters by radio. Mines were frequently strewn off the road at potential ambush sites, while any trees or scrub that might provide cover were cut down.

Not only did 75 per cent of all ground traffic to support the war travel down this road, but so did all the fuel oil. Only a few feet from the highway, above ground, ran the oil pipeline from the Soviet Union. It followed the road throughout its length to the air base at Bagram and was another tempting target for the Mujahideen.

Apart from the road, the pipeline, the convoys, the bridges and the tunnel, there were two major bases located close to or on the highway. One south of the Hindu Kush was at Bagram which was the most important air base in the country. To the north of the mountains, just south of Pol-i-Khumri, was the largest Soviet/Afghan logistics depot in Afghanistan, divided into two parts, one for fuel and the other for ammunition and vehicles. Although on a grander scale, Cam Ranh Bay and Da Nang had served similar purposes in South Vietnam.

To turn Afghanistan into a Vietnam, and by that I mean forcing a Soviet military withdrawal, so that the Mujahideen were only left with the Afghans to deal with, was by no means the impossibility I had once thought. 1984 was, for me, to be a year of learning from experience what could or could not be achieved. It was to be the year in which training facilities were dramatically increased, the year in which operations against Kabul were stepped up and coordinated, the year in which my first request for the Stinger SAM was rejected, and it was the year in which we made the first tentative moves along the Amu River, aimed at Soviet soil. Those first twelve months confirmed me in my belief that the Soviets were casualty-shy. Many times they would not leave their armoured vehicles, or at the last moment push forward an assault to clinch a victory. They were also scared of night operations. Everything stopped at night. There were no convoys, no movement, no attacks, and very few patrols during darkness. This was due to the reduced effectiveness of air cover. Our enemy was frightened to do anything without helicopters hovering nearby, or on immediate call – a trait which mirrored many Americans in Vietnam. My impression was that both these superpowers had been geared up to wage a conventional, or even nuclear, war in Europe, but never a counter-insurgency campaign in Asia. Other things being equal, it is the infantryman on the ground taking the war to the guerrilla that wins, not sitting tight in static posts and blasting the countryside with bombs and rockets. In simple terms both the capitalist and communist governments had asked the impossible in expecting conscripts, for whom the war meant nothing, to take on such a task.

I had to fight a guerrilla war of a thousand cuts. I knew my enemy's sensitive spots — the Salang Highway, aircraft on the ground, the power supply, the dams, the bridges, the pipelines, the isolated posts or convoys and, at the centre of them all, Kabul. I knew where to wield the knife, but knowing what to do is a far cry from doing it. Selecting a target, deciding a particular move would be effective, or pinpointing an opponent's weakness is the easy part of generalship. The hard part is assembling your force in sufficient strength; getting it well trained under reliable leaders; ensuring it is adequately armed, equipped and fed; making certain it understands the plan; and then moving it, covertly, to the right place at the right time. This is the real test of generalship.

As I was about to discover, nothing moves, in peace or war, without money. The Mujahideen could achieve nothing without financial support. No matter how brilliant my strategy might be, the implementation depended on the availability of a vast reservoir of cash with which to arm, train and move my forces. Almost half of this money originated from the US taxpayer, with the remainder coming from the Saudi Arabian government or rich Arab individuals.

CHAPTER FIVE

The Role of the CIA

'Give us the tools, and we will finish the job.'
Winston S. Churchill, broadcast addressed to President Roosevelt, 1941.

IT was always during darkness that the aircraft arrived. Usually at around 9.00 pm or just before dawn General Akhtar and I, along with the local CIA staff, would be waiting at Chaklala Air Base for the huge black C-141 Starlifter to taxi up to a secluded part of the terminal. No US Embassy personnel were ever present, either at the planes' arrival or departure. In order to distract attention it was normal practice on these occasions for the Ambassador to arrange a diplomatic dinner at the Embassy. Although the control tower guided the aircraft in, no Air Force personnel were involved with its reception on the ground. None of the passengers would be subjected to any form of immigration or customs formalities; even the baggage would be handled entirely by the Americans.

The aircraft had flown non-stop from Washington, some 10,000 miles, with KC10 tanker aircraft based in Europe or the Middle East intercepting it for mid-air refuelling. The crew were always in civilian clothes, as were all the passengers. Apart from the US markings on the outside there was no way of identifying the plane. Inside, the enormous transporter had been transformed into a flying hotel and communications centre. Up front, the VIP area was luxuriously appointed with couches, easy chairs, beds and washing facilities – super first class. The rear portion contained the ultra-sophisticated communications that allowed the occupants to speak securely to Washington, or anywhere else in the world. The aircraft was protected by the latest electronic jamming devices and radar to counter incoming missiles. When on the ground, a US crew member was always on board on a 24-hour basis. While in Pakistan the ISI would provide an armed outer perimeter guard, but our personnel could not enter the aircraft.

As the plane came to a stop the waiting cars would creep forward in single file, while outside the base an ISI security vehicle would patrol the route the cortege was about to take to the US Ambassador's residence in Islamabad. The vehicles were lined up – ISI escort, US security car, VIP car, US security car, ISI escort, and then the others. The man descending the steps was tall, very old, and was nicknamed 'Cyclone' in recognition of his propensity for anti-communist outbursts, or the 'Wanderer' from the frequency of his flights to CIA stations around the world. He headed the intelligence organization of the most powerful nation on earth. William Casey was President Reagan's principal adviser on intelligence matters, Director of Central Intelligence reporting to the National Security Committee (NSC), Chairman of the US Intelligence Board, and Director of the Central Intelligence Agency (CIA). He was arriving on one of his annual two-day visits to Pakistan for discussions with General Akhtar and myself on the situation in Afghanistan. Occasionally either his wife or daughter accompanied him. Sometimes his deputy would come, but always he would bring the head of the Afghanistan and Far East desk at CIA headquarters. This man, who is still serving so I will call him Mr A, had been in the US Special Forces and I found him to be one of the very few senior CIA officials whose military knowledge was sound, and to whom we in ISI could relate.

For the next 48 hours security for our guest was a major headache. His two-man advance party would arrive several days beforehand to discuss the arrangements, check the route and test their communications. Mr Casey's visits were the only time I saw CIA officials 'flapping' or badly agitated. Keeping his stay under wraps was far from simple and involved many men, much forethought and meticulous planning. We even went to the extent of referring to our visitor as 'Mr Black' in conversation or in writing.

The following morning the CIA and ISI would confront each other across the conference table at the main ISI headquarters in Islamabad. Casey would be flanked by the US Ambassador on one side and Mr A on the other, with the rest of his team, including the local CIA chief and various analysts, on either side. Opposite were General Akhtar, myself, a staff officer and analysts from ISI. I would watch Casey closely. At times he appeared to be dozing while the analysts droned on, but once a topic of importance was mentioned he came alert at once. He had a quick brain, with a bold and ruthless approach to the war against the Soviets. He hated communism. In fact, like many CIA officers, he regarded Afghanistan as the place where America could be avenged for its defeat in Vietnam. The Soviets must pay a high price in blood for their support of the North Vietnamese was his oft-repeated view. 'Those bastards must pay,' summed up his philosophy on the war, and he appeared none too squeamish about the methods to be used. Probably his years making millions as a New York businessman had added that callous, combative streak to his character.

Whatever his personal motivations, the result for us was always positive. He would often turn on his staff, who were perhaps disputing some request of ours, with the words; 'No, the General [Akhtar] knows what he wants'. For myself I found his visits stimulating, and I developed an admiration for his industry, dedication and unwavering determination to defeat communism.

He had little patience with politicians. He headed an agency with the fastest growing budget among all the executive branches of the US government. In 1987 the CIA received funds totalling $30 billion, a 200 per cent increase over 1980. With Reagan backing clandestine operations in Nicaragua and Angola as well as Afghanistan, Casey was on the crest of a wave. He was contemptuous of Congress's right to know what was happening in covert operations. He fought ferociously with the Senate Intelligence Committee, withholding information if he possibly could, and reporting only sporadically. His ridicule of rules and regulations worked to our advantage. Once, when one of his staff tried to explain that the delay in our obtaining sniper rifles was due to some obscure edict classifying them as terrorist sabotage weapons, Casey yelled, 'To hell with politicians, we're fighting a war.' It was good to have him on our side.

Casey had a flair for innovation, for bright ideas, for the James Bond unorthodox approach. As an ex-OSS man from World War 2, he seemed at times merely to have substituted the Soviets for the Nazis. His detractors called this his 'night parachute drop syndrome', but he had, along with Mr A, the rare ability within the CIA hierarchy of being able to discuss military matters sensibly. He understood strategy and the practical problems of fighting a guerrilla campaign.

Casey always flew out of Islamabad as he had arrived, at night. Invariably he was on his way to Saudi Arabia to meet his opposite number, Prince Turkie, for discussions on that government's financial contribution to the Jehad for the coming year. Although the security burden was lifted, I was normally sorry to see him go. He was a powerful and practical ally in the American camp, who understood both the abilities and shortcomings of the Mujahideen. He was prepared to listen to, and frequently accept, our arguments or reasoning on operational matters. He did us the courtesy of respecting our professional judgement as soldiers with an intimate knowledge of what could, or could not, be done in Afghanistan. If only some of his subordinates had done the same, countless millions of dollars and not a few lives might have been saved.

My first meeting with Casey was in early 1984 and I was to meet him again on several occasions during the coming months. As I quickly appreciated, the chances of success in Afghanistan were dependent on the quality and quantity of the arms we received. In this regard we were beholden to the CIA, and through it to our financial backers, the US and Saudi governments. My experiences with the CIA were spread over the four years I was with ISI, but I have gathered together the highlights in this chapter, as I believe this to be the best way for the reader to judge the real significance of its activities.

The foremost function of the CIA was to spend money. It was always galling to the Americans, and I can understand their point of view, that although they paid the piper they could not call the tune. The CIA supported the Mujahideen by spending the American taxpayers' money, billions of dollars of it over the years, on buying arms, ammunition and equipment. It was their secret arms procurement branch that was kept busy. It was, however, a cardinal rule of Pakistan's policy that no Americans ever become involved with the distribution of funds or arms once they arrived in the country. No Americans ever trained, or had direct contact with, the Mujahideen, and no American official ever went inside Afghanistan. To my knowledge this last was only broken once for Congressman Charles Wilson (R. Texas), as related previously, against the explicit orders of President Zia. To admit Americans directly into the system of supply and training would not only have led to chaos but would have proved the communist propaganda correct. All along, the Soviets, and their Afghan agents in KHAD, endeavoured to subvert the Mujahideen supporters and families by claiming they were not fighting a Jehad, but merely doing the dirty work of, and dying for, the US. Their assertion that the Afghans had no real quarrel with each other but were pawns in a superpower conflict would have been impossible to refute if Americans became overtly involved inside Pakistan. A high proportion of the CIA aid was in the form of cash. For every dollar supplied by the US, another was added by the Saudi Arabian government. The combined funds, running into several hundred million dollars a year, were transferred by the CIA to special accounts in Pakistan under the control of ISI. This money was quite separate from, and additional to, that used for arms purchases. Nevertheless it was critical to the war effort. As was to be continually brought home to me, without money nothing moves − particularly in Pakistan (see p.82).

I was not personally involved with the distribution of all these funds. This was the responsibility of General Akhtar and his Director of Administration. Nonetheless, I was well aware that lack of money was a never-ending anxiety, with the usual monthly allocation for recurrent expenditure seldom lasting more than two weeks. When one considers that there was a month-in, month-out requirement to meet the needs of tens of thousands of Mujahideen it is not surprising that the logistic requirements soaked up cash as a sponge does water. Take vehicles as an example. CIA money was used to purchase hundreds of trucks for ferrying arms and ammunition up to the border. Often the Parties used vehicles for taking supplies into Afghanistan, so they too needed their own transport. Every vehicle needed fuel and maintenance, so for this alone the bill was huge. Add to this the purchase, or hire, of thousands of mules, horses and camels, plus their fodder; add again the need for building materials, tools and equipment, for the construction of warehouses, bases, training facilities, then add

THE MONEY FLOW

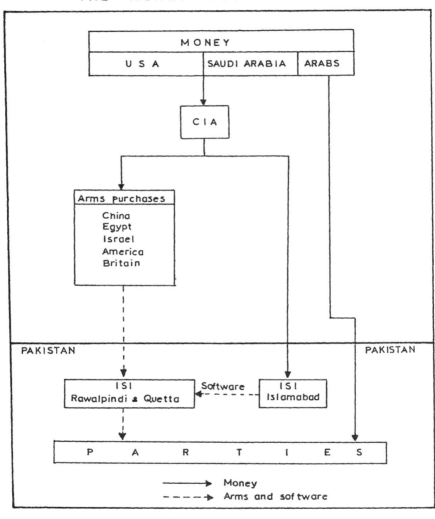

tentage, clothing, winter equipment, rations and medical expenses, and the magnitude of the problem becomes clear. As an example, in 1987 some 30-35 million rupees ($1.5 million) were required monthly for the movement of stores inside Pakistan and Afghanistan.

All this was money spent in Pakistan or Afghanistan, but the bulk of the CIA/Saudi Arabian funds was spent outside these countries, buying arms and ammunition. The system worked like this. In advance of the US annual budget allocations the CIA would give us a suggested list of types and quantities of arms that they considered we needed. I would examine this, but as I was never told either the amount of money available or the cost of the various weapons, it was impossible to alter the lists other than by guessing whether the changes were within, or over, the allocation. If we overshot we had to review our needs again. More time wasted.

A never-ending source of friction between ourselves and the CIA arose over their apparent total ignorance of military logistics. At times even basic common sense seemed lacking. Invariably we wasted days, if not weeks, going through their lists pointing out errors and inconsistencies. They seldom related our ammunition needs to the weapons. For example, it was agreed that as a rule twenty rockets would be provided for every RPG-7 launcher purchased. In 1985 we were to receive 10,000 RPGs along with 200,000 rockets, but our CIA friends in Washington failed to take into account all the RPGs we had already received since 1980 (less an annual wastage rate of 15 per cent). It had not occurred to them that we needed ammunition for them as well. Similarly with anti-aircraft ammunition, the CIA lists were often woefully inadequate as no account was taken of the very high rate of fire of these weapons. So much time and effort could have been saved had the CIA given us a ceiling on funds, some idea of costs, and left us to prepare our annual requirements taking into account existing stocks, operational needs and wastage. Alas, that was not to happen.

Having agreed what was wanted, it was up to the CIA to provide it. They had to purchase all the items and get them by ship to Karachi or, for a small proportion, by air to Islamabad. Until 1985 it was a firm policy that only communist block weapons could be bought. This was part of pretending that the West, and America in particular, were not backing the Mujahideen with material assistance. So the CIA buyers with their shopping lists were limited as to sources. During 1983 approximately 10,000 tons were received, rising to 65,000 tons in 1987. The type of weapons purchased ranged from small arms through to anti-tank and anti-aircraft (AA) rocket launchers and guns.

The great bulk came from China, Egypt, and later on from Israel. I had no idea that Israel was a source until quite recently, as, had it been known, there would have been considerable trouble with the Arab nations. It would not have been acceptable to wage a Jehad with weapons bought from Israel.

These were weapons that had been captured in large quantities during Israel's invasion of the Lebanon and which they were delighted to sell. That the Americans spent funds in Israel is not surprising, but they were careful to conceal the source from us.

The CIA would arrange and pay for shipment to Karachi, notifying us of arrival dates. Once the vessel docked the ISI took over storage and distribution. It has often been stated in the world press that China supplied arms overland via the Karakoram highway, the old Silk Route. This is not so. Not one bullet came that way, although that was the route used to bring us hundreds of mules. On occasion arms would be flown to Islamabad in Chinese, American, Saudi or PAF planes. For some reason Saudi aircraft never kept to their schedules and caused endless problems for our planes going to pick up cargo in Saudi Arabia, so we were forced to stop all such flights and rely on the USAF. Not that Saudi Arabia actually supplied weapons, but it was at times used as a trans-shipment point. I believe that the Americans later switched to Cairo, which was used by some aircraft when carrying Egyptian arms.

During my years with the ISI I met a large number of CIA officials, from the director down to his personal security guards. I discerned three types of CIA officer. The largest group were those who joined the Agency fairly young and had made it their career, gaining balanced experience between field and headquarters posts. The second category included those recruited in their thirties or forties from outside the service for their particular expertise. They were the technical experts and analysts. To me these people's opinions and recommendations seemed always to carry great weight with the decision makers. They appeared to be able to reach higher grades more quickly than the field operators. In most cases these officers had a strictly limited military background, yet they often played a key role in military matters. The third group was drawn from the Armed Forces, normally at the major level. Some were on attachment to the CIA, while others belonged permanently. They were usually the weapons experts, or trainers, and I noticed a deep-rooted professional jealousy between them and the others. There was, at Islamabad certainly, a mutual lack of trust and confidence within the CIA. I believe that much of the problem stemmed from the fact that these former military officers could see only too well the error of their seniors' military decisions, but their advice was seldom sought and, if given, ignored. I remember asking one of these officers why the 'civilians' were for ever trying to dictate to us how to run the war in Afghanistan. He replied, 'General, in the United States, CIA is getting all the credit for anything good happening in Afghanistan and you [Pakistan] are getting all the discredit for anything going wrong.'

Two examples of CIA incompetence, or possibly corruption, will serve to illustrate the avoidable waste of millions of dollars and the serious

1. General Akhtar: "a cold, reserved personality, almost inscrutable, always secretive". (p.22)

2. The author (right) with Gul Badin Hekmatyar, "the best-known and the most controversial Fundamentalist Leader". (p.40)

3. The author briefing Mujahideen Commanders on forthcoming joint operations.

4. "Strategically the terrain favoured the guerrillas . . . the high rocky mountains providing refuge and cover from the air." (p.63)

5. "I arranged Congressman Charles Wilson's visit into Afghanistan in 1987." (p62). Here he poses in a BMP in Zhawar.

6. The author *(centre)* visiting the administrative tunnels at the Mujahideen forward base at Zhawar, just inside Afghanistan.

7. "The artery, the main line of communication that kept Kabul functioning was the Salang Highway." (p.67). Looking South from the Salang Tunnel.

8. "It was the scene of one of the most successful Mujahideen ambushes of the war." (p.67)

9. A daylight rocket attack on Kabul, using 122mm rockets on improvised bases.

10. The rockets heading for Kabul.

11. A Mujahid examines a partially exploded bomb. Note the ruined building in the background.

12. A Mujahid with a Chinese-made 7.62 RPK light machine gun. Note the Afghan pony used for transport.

13. The Stinger "fired an infra-red, heat-seeking missile, capable of engaging low-altitude, high-speed jets". (p.175). Mujahid with Stinger in Afghanistan.

14. Ali Khel village under rocket attack in 1985. (see Map 9, p.111)

15. The results of a successful Mujahideen ambush in the Panjsher Valley, 1987.

implications of these failings on the battlefield. Both concern the deliberate purchase of old, outdated arms on the basis that these were good enough for the Mujahideen. The sellers were delighted to get rid of these otherwise worthless weapons at a profit. The CIA spent the US taxpayers' money to provide third-rate, and in one instance totally unserviceable weapons, for use against a modern superpower.

Until 1984 the bulk of all arms and ammunition was purchased from China, and they proved to be an excellent supplier, completely reliable, discreet and, at a later stage, even providing weapons as aid as well as for sale. But in 1985 the CIA started buying large quantities from Egypt. I shall never forget the first shipment. When the boxes were opened the weapons were revealed as used, rusty and in many cases quite unserviceable. They dated back to the days when the Soviets had equipped the Egyptian Army. Rifles were rusted together, barrels were solid with dirt and corrosion, some boxes were empty, while in others the contents were deficient. Rarely was ammunition properly packed; rounds that were supposed to be boxed or belted came in heaps of loose rounds. I did not have the manpower to check every crate before it was forwarded to the Mujahideen, so the extent of the problem did not become apparent until I got reports from inside Afghanistan. To my horror, no less than 30,000 82mm mortar bombs were found unusable on the battlefield as the cartridges had swollen in the damp and would not fit the bombs. The Egyptians had cobbled together arms that had been lying exposed to the atmosphere for years in order to make a substantial amount of money. Nobody in the CIA had done a spot check before shipment; either that or they had been a party to the deal. I had photographs taken and sent to the US, while I protested vehemently to the CIA. At first they seemed disinterested, but eventually an official came out to see for himself. Thereafter Egyptian purchases were marginally better, but the Mujahideen never trusted their supplies in the future.

The next incident, or rather incidents as one concerns .303 rifles and the other .303 ammunition, involved both India and Pakistan. In the middle of 1984 an enormous shipment of 100,000 .303 rifles arrived at Karachi. When we protested that we had not requested this amount, and that we had no storage space, the CIA advised that they represented the 1985 supply in advance, as well as those for the current year. When pressed as to storage space we were told in confidence that they had been bought at a rock-bottom price from India. When I queried how and why the Indians sold weapons that they knew would be used against their friends the Soviets, the CIA officer replied 'The Indians are mean bastards, not trustworthy at all. For money they would even sell their mothers'.

With the ammunition, a Pakistani arms merchant pulled a

once-in-a-lifetime deal with the buyer. He persuaded the CIA to purchase 30 million rounds of .303 through his overseas office, without revealing the true source of the ammunition. At about 50 cents a round the dealer was a happy man. Unknown to the CIA, the ammunition came from old stocks of the Pakistan Army which no longer used this weapon. A ship was duly loaded, sailed out from Karachi for a few days, turned around, and we were notified by the CIA that our ammunition had arrived. When some crates were opened at Rawalpindi every round was found to have POF (Pakistan Ordnance Factory) stamped on it. There was no way this could be fired in Afghanistan without giving irrefutable proof that Pakistan was arming the guerrillas. Every round had to go back to the POF so it could be defaced, a task that took three years and cost a lot more money. Again the losers were the US taxpayer and the Mujahideen.

It was the same story with Turkey. In 1984 the Turkish authorities made an offer to supply weapons, so General Akhtar instructed me to visit Turkey to finalize the arrangements. Once in Ankara, the Turks seemed hesitant when I asked to see the arms they were sending. Anyhow, I insisted, and to my dismay found them all to be weapons withdrawn from the Turkish Army 30 years before. Their date of manufacture was 1940-1942. I was at a loss for words, as I did not want to offend my hosts who were pressing for agreement to shipping dates. I went to our Ambassador to explain that these weapons were not worth the shipment and distribution costs, which we would have to pay. He was most upset. As far as he was concerned there was no question of causing a diplomatic row by refusing this 'generous' offer. On my return I urged General Akhtar against acceptance, and he spoke either to the President or Foreign Minister, but to no avail. In the end 60,000 rifles, 8,000 light machine guns, 10,000 pistols and over 100 million rounds of ammunition duly arrived. Most were badly corroded or faulty and could not be given to the Mujahideen.

Perhaps the most frustrating aspect of my dealings with the CIA was the way in which the Mujahideen were so often fobbed off with unsuitable weapons. There were, I believe, three reasons for this. Firstly, the attitude among some Americans that the Mujahideen did not deserve, and would not be able to use, modern arms. This was later proved totally wrong with the Stinger, but for a long time this feeling that they were second-rate soldiers so they could make do with second-rate weapons existed. Secondly, there was financial greed. A number of countries, and many people, saw the guerrilla resistance as a splendid opportunity to sell off arms that nobody else wanted, weapons that were obsolete or obsolescent, even ones that were dangerous to fire. I have strong suspicions that at least one weapon system was forced on us because a US congressman had a lot to gain if the sale went ahead. Finally, so many CIA officials connected with the arms procurement programme in the US were not soldiers, never had been soldiers and had no idea what it was like fighting inside Afghanistan. They did not begin to comprehend the Mujahideen's needs.

Again and again we in the ISI fought hard against accepting weapons we knew were unsuited to our guerrilla war. In only one case were we successful. The so-called military experts of the CIA seemed to feel we should be grateful for every gun. If we queried its value on the battlefield we were labelled obstructionists. No doubt politicians were having their say, and undoubtedly people were getting rich along the line, but at the end of the day I was responsible for getting the best arms and equipment I could to the Mujahideen. They paid for mistakes with their lives.

In mid-1984 the CIA came up with an offer of the Swiss-designed 20mm Oerlikon anti-aircraft guns. General Akhtar and I requested further details of their characteristics, which the CIA had somehow forgotten to include. After much discussion within ISI we said it was not suitable for Afghanistan. We explained that the weapon weighed 1,200 pounds and was therefore far too heavy. It would require some twenty mules to transport a section of three guns; it would impede the Mujahideen's mobility and was more suited to positional defense of strong points. There was no way mules could use the steep mountain trails, making its deployment so restricted as to make the weapon more of a liability than an asset. We also pointed out that the long, heavy, cumbersome barrel could not be loaded lengthwise along a horse's or mule's back. It had to be positioned across the animal, making it impossible to go through narrow defiles, where it snagged on every bush. Then we pointed out that this weapon had a high rate of fire, needed to be deployed in threes, and the Mujahideen's lack of fire control would mean excessive ammunition expenditure. With bullets costing $50 each, and a rate of fire of 1000 rounds a minute, I thought this would be a telling point for cost-conscious Americans. Finally, it was explained that the Oerlikon crews would need lengthy special training.

Our objections were overruled. I was told that ten guns had already been purchased. General Akhtar told the CIA that that was their problem; the weapons should remain in the US. Reluctantly, he was then informed that it was now a political issue, that a congressman who was a vocal supporter of the Mujahideen had insisted on the Oerlikon purchase, so to cancel it now would cause too much embarrassment all round. We eventually received between forty and fifty guns which had to be deployed in threes in a triangular pattern near border bases in a static role. It was popular with some Commanders as a prestige weapon, but was not particularly effective in action.

Next it was the Egyptian mortar. This weapon had marginally longer range that our plentiful supply of 82mm mortars, but it fell far short of that of our rocket launchers (RLs). It was of no value to us. We had a good mortar, we had RLs, and the last thing we needed was the added complication of a different calibre weapon with different ammunition, different training and more logistic problems. As usual our protests fell on deaf ears, although I succeeded in preventing its induction until after I left ISI.

Perhaps the best example of politics and money overruling military judgement was with the British Blowpipe surface-to-air missile (SAM). The CIA was well aware that our overriding requirement was for an effective, manportable, anti-aircraft weapon. In mid-1985 they offered us Blowpipe. Once again we objected on practical grounds. Although the Blowpipe is able to destroy attacking aircraft head on as it does not need to seek a hot exhaust pipe as a heat source, the firer stands up to engage the target. This might be acceptable on the battlefield for a few brief moments, if the system is what the military call a 'fire-and-forget' weapon. This means you aim, fire and take cover while the missile homes in on its target. With the Blowpipe the firer must remain standing to aim, fire, and then guide the missile optically on to the target using a thumb control. We knew it had been a disappointment to the British in the Falklands war, and that it was obsolescent, as it was being replaced by the Javelin, with a much improved guidance system. A British artillery officer explained that a major problem was that it had not been designed to take on targets moving across the firer's front, only those approaching head-on, or disappearing tail-on. Nor is it manpackable over any distance, due to its awkward shape and excessive weight. Another significant disadvantage was the lengthy training time needed. We did not want to put so much effort into training on a weapon that was being phased out by an army that had found it ineffective on the battlefield. On top of this, Blowpipe operators required refresher training every six months on the simulator — utterly impossible for the Mujahideen.

I believe the CIA must have done a deal with the British to buy this system as they insisted on their team coming to Pakistan later in the year to demonstrate the Blowpipe. It was a disaster. Even without the stress, excitement and fear of battle, the CIA experts obtained miserable results at gently descending parachute flares. Still they insisted we must accept it. They eventually got their way by bypassing General Akhtar and going to President Zia personally. He took the political view that acceptance of the Blowpipe would involve the UK directly as a supporter of the Jehad, and thus the Mujahideen cause would gain internationally, so we were compelled to accept several thousand of these missiles. Once again the Mujahideen were the losers while others, many miles from the fighting, made millions.

This fiasco dragged on for months. We found that with the first batch of Blowpipes half of them would not accept the command signal, so the missile would go astray immediately after firing. The CIA were called in to watch. Then a British expert was flown out. He agreed that something was indeed very wrong, so all the missiles and launchers were flown back to the UK. Eventually, after modifications, we began receiving our Blowpipes, but still there was too high a proportion of firing failures. The first four were captured by the Soviets when the Mujahideen firing party were compelled to withdraw in a hurry. They were later shown on Soviet television screens. During the rest of my time with ISI I do not recall a single confirmed kill by a Blowpipe in Afghanistan.

Our solitary success in stopping the induction of a weapon system that we felt valueless occurred in late 1986. This involved the Red Arrow, a Chinese anti-tank, wire-guided missile. Once again the CIA were insistent that it would be effective, although they deliberately delayed sending us detailed characteristics of the weapon, urging us to take it on their assurances. After this deadlock had continued for some time, the information on Red Arrow arrived. We rejected it immediately. The wire guidance system, whereby the firer steers the missile on to the target by sending signals down a thin wire attached to the missile, had not worked well with the Pakistan Army in its wars with India. Obstacles between the firer and target, such as bushes, trees or rocks, tended to prohibit its use, but above all the training was long and, like the Blowpipe, frequent refresher training was necessary. By this time the Chinese had joined the CIA to get their weapon accepted. Tremendous pressure built up from Washington for us not to reject this missile. We conceded that a Chinese team could come and train Pakistani instructors and that, depending on the results, a final decision would be made after the course. The training lasted for eight weeks and was unique in that the Chinese brought an attractive young woman as their weapon-training interpreter. Despite her charm and efforts the results, watched by the CIA, were poor. Red Arrow was not bought.

These are all examples of senior CIA officers, with no knowledge of battlefield conditions, let alone conditions pertaining in Afghanistan, succumbing to political and financial pressures. As one put it to me, 'General, people sitting in America have no idea how the war is being fought by the Mujahideen.' The CIA staff showed little understanding of military logistics or battlefield time and space problems. Every two years their civilian logistics man would change over so there was a period when the newcomer was completely cold and inexperienced with regard to Afghanistan. They never seemed to grasp that April, when the snows melted, was always a critical time for us, as we needed to rush supplies forward in bulk. Invariably the CIA failed to meet our needs. Their system was such that they never knew what their allocation of funds would be in advance, and neither could they hold back a reserve to meet the Spring demands. I am sure these bureaucratic snarl-ups would not have been accepted had it been US troops in the firing line.

Bright ideas were forthcoming about other things as well as weapon systems. One concerned sabotage. A CIA expert flew in to advise me on fuel contamination. He was of the opinion that Mujahideen sympathizers working at workshops or airports should be given this contaminent to mix with the fuel in vehicle or aircraft tanks. I explained that this would not kill many people or destroy equipment, and that the Mujahideen would never regard this as a way of fighting a Jehad. They demanded immediate results, preferably visible and noisy ones. Their idea of fighting involved much shooting, the inflicting of casualties, the opportunity to show off their courage and the possibility of war booty. It was hard enough for me to get them to blow up a pipeline covertly, let alone get them to pour a liquid into a fuel tank. It was not their way. If a person could put a contaminent in an aircraft's fuel tank he could just as easily destroy the plane with a magnetic charge. To the suggestion that it could be put into fuel storage facilities, my response was to ask how the saboteur was to manhandle the drums of contaminent needed. There was no practical answer. Neither this suggestion, nor his second one of putting another chemical in vehicle batteries, were relevant or practical for the type of war being fought in Afghanistan.

Neither was the suggestion that supplies be parachuted direct to the Mujahideen in Afghanistan. This was a serious proposal to speed up the system and bypass Pakistan. No consideration had been given as to whose aircraft were to be used; if American, then the President was directly involving the US in operations against the Soviets. Had the proposers considered how many flights would be needed to dump 20-30 thousand tons at a time? Were they prepared for combat losses, or for up to 50 per cent falling into Soviet hands? What about overflying permission from Pakistan? It was a nonsensical idea, but it refused to go away for about six months.

The headlines in the *Washington Post* of 8 May, 1987, typify the half-truths that so frequently became accepted as fact. 'AFGHAN REBEL AID ENRICHES GENERALS — The Central Intelligence Agency has spent $3 billion on arms for Afghan rebels — half of it put up by the US taxpayers. Yet not a single American decides who gets the weapons.'

Regarding the allegations of corruption, I can only speak with authority on my own office and staff. I am certain that there were no deals struck, no arms sold, and that allocations were strictly in accordance with operational priorities, the agreed percentage allocation to each Party, and combat effectiveness. General Akhtar was utterly ruthless on this. Although corruption is a way of life in Pakistan, the military is perhaps the only organization in which it is minimal; but I cannot speak with certainty on what happened once supplies left ISI control.

If the sum spent was $3 billion then half would have been Saudi Arabian government money. Many additional millions were contributed by Arab organizations and rich individuals, mostly from Saudi Arabia. These funds were channelled directly to the Party of the donor's choice, usually a Fundamentalist one. The allocation policy is discussed further in the relevant chapter, so I would merely emphasize here that the ISI distributed in accordance with strict criteria of military effectiveness and the overall campaign strategy. The *Washington Post* was correct in stating that no American decided who got the weapons, and was close to the mark when the writer concluded 'that the opportunities for diversion and corruption are far greater before the arms get to Karachi than after'.

Relations between the CIA and ourselves were always strained There was never really a feeling of mutual trust. I, and my staff, resented their never-ending probing to interfere in the allocation of weapons, accusations of corruption and pressing to take over both the training of the Mujahideen and to advise on operations. They were anxious to set up their own operations office alongside mine at Rawalpindi. This they were never permitted to do; in fact I resorted to trying to avoid contact with the local CIA staff as much as possible. I never ever visited the US Embassy, and only went to the CIA safe house three times during my four years.

One of these visits illustrated some CIA officials' infuriating inability to grasp the basic elements of how the guerrilla war was being fought. In early 1984 General Akhtar's staff officer rang me at midnight to say that the CIA wanted me urgently at their safe house, on a matter that could not be discussed on the telephone. I said I would be there in half an hour (I never spoke personally to the CIA on the telephone). My driver was late coming so I decided to drive myself, but could not find the safe house in the dark, so it was over an hour before I finally arrived. The message was that the Soviets had spotted a Mujahideen supply convoy in the Helmund Province of western Afghanistan and had laid an ambush for it. What was I going to do? I was flabbergasted. Helmund was over 1000 kilometres from Rawalpindi; as the CIA were well aware, I had absolutely no means of communicating with Mujahideen groups in Afghanistan by radio because they didn't have any, nor had I the faintest idea which group was about to be attacked. I did not wait to hear the CIA officer's suggestions.

I could not, however, prevent the ceaseless stream of CIA-sponsored visitors from Washington who arrived with commendable regularity every two weeks. They appeared to have a never-ending supply of officials, experts, technicians and analysts, who all felt they could help win the war. Some did make valuable contributions – but not all. I remember one man who spoke at length on the benefits of the use of electrical power by the Mujahideen in their bases in Afghanistan. He felt it was valuable for the radios. He showed no knowledge of the environment, no comprehension of the lack of repair facilities for generators, shortages of fuel, the effects of winter on operations, or the total absence of trained technicians in the field.

The CIA had two officers on post in 1983 but these increased to five by the time I left. These were the permanent and acknowledged staff, which excluded the visitors, and the countless paid agents operating within the Mujahideen, the Parties, the Military Committee, and even, I suspect, within

ISI staff. Like any intelligence organization they were invariably devious in the way they went about things. It amused me that after we had refused to accept a particular weapon, within a week or so a Party, or a member of their Military Committee, would suddenly start pressing for its induction and extolling its virtues, although the CIA never met them face to face.

Part of the problem was that the CIA were under great pressure from Washington, from Congress, and ultimately from the American public whose money they were spending. Like their Director, they resented political constraint, tending to blame politicians when things went wrong. In this vein a senior CIA official alleged to me that President Carter had been briefed with the aid of aerial photographs on the Soviet's impending invasion of Afghanistan. 'But the bastard refused to accept the evidence because he did not want to react — if he had you would never have had this problem.' One thing I was never in doubt about was their single-minded determination to make the Soviets suffer in Afghanistan. 'We must make the bastards burn,' was a favourite CIA catchphrase.

Another interesting activity of the CIA, and indeed of the Western intelligence organizations from the UK, France, West Germany and elsewhere, was their scramble to buy captured Soviet weapons or equipment. In 1985 the new AK74 rifle was being used by Soviet troops. It is smaller and lighter than the old AK47 and fires a 5.45mm bullet, which tends to tumble inside a body, thus giving extensive internal injuries and a large exit wound. The first one captured was sold to the CIA for $5,000. Then the rush started. Weapons, armour plating, avionics equipment (particularly from M1-24 gunships), cipher machines, tank tracks, even binoculars, all had a commercial value soon appreciated by the Mujahideen. Embassy staff cars used to go up to the tribal areas near the border on buying trips, until General Akhtar protested to the embassies that this must stop and that they should channel their requests through ISI.

From 1984 onwards the CIA had been trying, through their agents, to get an Afghan pilot to defect with an M1-24 Hind helicopter gunship. They had made contacts in Kabul and time after time I would be told at short notice that the helicopter was arriving, so would I identify a suitable landing place, warn the PAF to receive it, not shoot it down, and ensure it was not destroyed on the ground by Soviet aircraft once it had landed. Needless to say, the plane never came and I gave up alerting the Air Force for these disruptive false alarms. The problem was that the CIA expected the pilot to conform exactly to some prearranged date and time schedule for his escape. They found it hard to understand that such a plan must be simple and allow the defector complete freedom to chose the time and place. The opportunity, when it came, would be fleeting and had to be seized at once without telling the CIA in advance. In the end it was our plan that gave the CIA not one, but two, M1-24s.

I merely explained to the Party Leaders that we needed to acquire such a helicopter. They simply let it be known in Kabul that a defector would be welcome. One afternoon in mid-1985 I received a call telling me that two Ml-24s had landed at Miram Shah, just inside Pakistan. Apparently, on arrival, the startled border security force officer had explained to them that they had made a mistake and landed in Pakistan; if they so wished he would turn his back while they took off again. They stayed; although one co-pilot had no idea that his captain was defecting when they took off from Kabul. Within hours we started receiving congratulatory messages; every embassy wanted to examine the helicopters. For two weeks they were kept securely at an air base before experts from the UK, West Germany, France and China were permitted to examine and photograph them. After a few weeks they were transported to the US, as, eventually, were four of the six crew members. There were other defections by Afghan pilots. The first was an MI-8 helicopter pilot early in the war. This was followed by a light aircraft. During the flight the pilot had told the co-pilot that he was heading for Pakistan to defect. The co-pilot objected violently, so the captain pulled out his pistol and shot him dead in the cockpit. The CIA also got their hands on a SU22 fighter aircraft through the defection of an ace Afghan pilot, Captain Nabi, who for some time fought as a Mujahideen commander until petty bickering with his Party led to his opting to go to the US.

The richest military contribution of the CIA to the Afghan war was in the field of satellite intelligence through photographs. Nothing above ground was hidden from the all-seeing satellite. The pictures, taken from such enormous height, showed up tanks, vehicles, bridges, culverts and damage caused by bombing or rocket attacks with a clarity that amazed me. It made both the planning of operations and the briefing of the Mujahideen Commanders a comparatively simple business. It enabled me to select priority targets for rocket attacks, choose alternative firing points and consider the various routes to and from the target. I was able to ask the CIA for photographs of a particular area and within a short time they would be brought to my office for study. The CIA would then transfer all the details on to a map which we could retain. A typical example of such a map upon which an operation was planned is that of Sherkhan on the Amu River on page 196. With every photograph or map we would be supplied with a list of possible targets, a description of each, together with recommended approaches, enemy dispositions, likely reactions to attack and possible counter-attacks. This information, in conjunction with the local knowledge of the Mujahideen, considerably enhanced our ability to conduct effective operations.

I was always fascinated by the Americans' technical ability. In the communications field this was truly astounding. I was told, for example, that in the US their computers would record the conversation of a Soviet pilot in his aircraft on flights around Moscow. Seemingly all pilots have certain recognizable ways of speaking, either of accent, pauses, words used or expressions. It is their signature. The Americans would give each pilot a code number, so if pilot X was later picked up speaking in Kabul, intelligence would know that either the individual had been posted or his squadron had moved. It was a simple matter to establish which. In such a way an updated Soviet Air Force order of battle in or near Afghanistan was maintained.

We also used their technical expertise when assessing how best to destroy a particular target, be it a bridge, a dam, a fuel dump or a pipeline. The CIA would supply the photographs and a demolition expert would give us advice on the type of explosive, the amount required, the best method of detonation and the precise location at which to place the charges, together with the likely extent of the damage. Again, invaluable information for planning.

The CIA also contributed substantially with the installation of wireless interception equipment. I was not involved directly with this type of aid, although I know it was generous and gave me a reliable, up-to-the-minute source of both Soviet and Afghan intercepted radio messages. This was high-grade tactical information on the movement of units, and sometimes their intentions. Often the messages would be tense and dramatic, as when we heard operators under attack yelling their orders, or frantically calling for help. It was listening in to some of these exchanges that confirmed the high level of mistrust that existed between the Soviets and Afghans. Once the Mujahideen had acquired Stingers we would hear Afghan pilots objecting to being sent on risky missions, while the Soviet helicopters remained at base. In one instance a Soviet headquarters was threatening to court-martial a junior officer who was insisting he must withdraw from his post. It was also radio interception that gave us feedback on the success or otherwise of some of our Mujahideen attacks in terms of damage caused or casualties inflicted.

In the summer of 1985 I visited the CIA headquarters at Langley, Virginia, not far from Washington, after repeated invitations to do so. I was keen to go, feeling I would learn a lot from the experience. Unfortunately, I gained little professionally from the trip. In reality it turned out to be more of a holiday break, but one from which I returned with my personal regard for the CIA greatly diminished.

I understand the need for the CIA to surround their activities and facilities with a sophisticated security system. Nevertheless, I was at first surprised at the lengths to which they went, and then hurt and affronted by their applying petty rules to somebody who was an American ally and himself a senior officer in a friendly intelligence organization. My surprise came when I was taken to the CIA headquarters and was ushered into the director's own special lift. On my entering, the lift operator smiled at me and his face seemed familiar. On the way down the same man asked if I did not recognize him, as he was a member of Mr Casey's personal security team. It surprised me that even the director's lift had a personal security guard manning it at all times, even, as was the case then, when he was out of station.

I was hurt on my visit to the CIA's sabotage school a short distance from Washington. We flew there, although I think this was designed to convince me that its location was a long way from the capital. I am certain the aircraft circled round a lot more than it need have done to use up time, while the curtains of all the windows were tightly drawn. I was not to be allowed to catch a glimpse of where we were going. On the ground it was the same. Our car was completely closed, making it impossible to see out. I might just as well have been blindfolded from the outset. I regarded this as insulting. It was explained that my hosts had to abide by the regulations, but I was not suspect, and whenever the CIA visited my training camps in Pakistan they were never subjected to this kind of treatment. They came in broad daylight in open vehicles, with no attempts at concealment of the route or the camp's location.

It was during this visit also that my suspicions that the CIA gave undue weight to the opinions of desk-bound analysts were verified. Firstly, I was ushered into a conference room to be briefed on Afghanistan. I had never been briefed by a woman military analyst before, so my attention was immediately captured. The poor woman was nervous and shaky, reading from her notes — a sure way of alienating her audience, but a practice many Americans seem to adopt. It is a sign that the speaker has not mastered the subject. And so it proved on this occasion. When she had finished I asked what she meant when she had stated that the Mujahideen had suffered heavy casualties in a particular battle. What percentage did she consider heavy — 10 per cent, 20 per cent, or 50 per cent? She was immediately flummoxed. She was similarly confused when I pressed her for the numbers who actually fought in the battle. Her male companions attempted to come to her rescue. Later, I was told she had been working on Afghanistan since the Soviet invasion and had obtained a Master's Degree in war studies before joining the CIA. Of course she had no practical experience of war, and never would have. Without this experience, or first-hand knowledge of conditions on a battlefield, even the best analyst is apt to draw the wrong conclusions from his facts and figures.

The next example involved a man considered to be an expert on Soviet tactics. After listening for a while to his discourse on what seemed to me to relate to how the Red Army would advance across the north European plain, I queried the relevance of what he had said to the terrain in Afghanistan. This seemed to upset him because he didn't speak again.

To sum up: the CIA's tasks in Afghanistan were to purchase arms and equipment and arrange their transportation to Pakistan; provide funds for the purchase of vehicles and transportation inside Pakistan and Afghanistan; train Pakistani instructors on new weapons or equipment; provide satellite photographs and maps for our operational planning; provide radio equipment and training, and advise on technical matters when so requested. The entire planning of the war, all types of training of the Mujahideen and the allocation and distribution of arms and supplies were the sole responsibility of the ISI, and my office in particular.

I stress that the CIA's strength was in their access to sophisticated technology. If it was possible to solve a problem by technical means they would get the answer, but if military decisions had to be made on the basis of experience, military knowledge, or even applied military common sense, then, in my view, few CIA officers could come up with workable solutions.

A lot of money was wasted, and probably still is, on the war in Afghanistan. Some of it was undoubtedly due to corruption or mistakes in Pakistan and Afghanistan, but I believe a larger proportion has disappeared into the pockets of unscrupulous governments, arms dealers, politicians and CIA agents, who through incompetence or dishonesty bought or sold millions of dollars worth of worthless or inappropriate arms and ammunition.

Let me finish on a positive note. Notwithstanding all I have said, on balance the CIA's contributions have played a vital role in the conduct of the Afghan Jehad. Without the backing of the US and Saudi Arabia the Soviets would still be entrenched in that country. Without the intelligence provided by the CIA many battles would have been lost, and without the CIA's training of our Pakistani instructors the Mujahideen would have been fearfully ill-equipped to face, and ultimately defeat, a superpower.

What happened once the weapons arrived in Pakistan was our responsibility.

CHAPTER SIX

The Pipeline

'We have found that the CIA's secret arms pipeline to the Mujahideen is riddled with opportunities for corruption. The losers are the poorly equipped guerrillas fighting the Soviets in Afghanistan, and the American people whose congressional representatives have been betrayed by the CIA.'
Washington Post, 8 May, 1987.

THE above is an extract from the text of an article on the supply of arms and ammunition to the Mujahideen, written by a journalist who had spent some weeks in Pakistan trying to unravel the complexities of a system that stretched half way round the world, involved six countries other than Pakistan and Afghanistan, and was costing, by 1987, over a million dollars a day. Perhaps, not surprisingly, Mr Jack Anderson's comments were largely guesswork, but in this case not too far from the mark. As I have explained in the previous chapter the CIA has much to answer for with its wasteful purchasing system. Nevertheless, it was not the CIA's pipeline that provided weapons to the Mujahideen. As soon as the arms arrived in Pakistan the CIA's responsibility ended. From then on it was our pipeline, our organization, that moved, allocated and distributed every bullet that the CIA procured. But even the ISI did not actually give the guns and ammunition to the Mujahideen who were to use them in battle. The last stretch of the line into and across Afghanistan was in the hands of the seven Parties and the Commanders in the field. To understand how the arms reached the battlefield from places as remote from Afghanistan as the USA or Britain it is necessary to know that the pipeline was divided into three distinct parts. The first part belonged to the CIA, who bought the weapons and paid for their delivery to Pakistan; the second stretch was the ISI's responsibility, getting everything carried across Pakistan, allocated to, and handed over to the Parties at their headquarter offices near Peshawar and Quetta; the third and final leg of the journey belonged to them. The Parties allocated the weapons to their Commanders, and distributed them inside Afghanistan.

When a Mujahid dropped a bomb down the barrel of his mortar it was the end of a journey that had involved being loaded, or off-loaded, at least fifteen times; being moved many thousands of kilometres by truck, ship, train, truck again, and pack animal, before being carried to the firing point by the mortarmen themselves. Seldom, even in guerrilla operations, can a line of communication have been so tenuous and fraught with frustrations long before any item reached hostile territory. A British general once said something to the effect that, for every thought that a commander bestows upon his enemy, he probably directs a hundred anxious glances to his own supply line in his rear. I would endorse that comment.

As far as I was concerned my major headache was logistics – getting sufficient supplies forward, in time, to the right people, and at the right place. Everything else was of secondary importance. My difficulties were compounded by the fact that I only had direct control over the centre section of the pipeline, both ends being in the hands of others (see Map 8). With the CIA and the Parties I could only plead, explain, cajole or persuade. I could not intervene directly when things went wrong and I could not use my own resources to put matters right. The task of my logistics colonel was certainly the most unenviable within my bureau, if not within the entire ISI organization. His was the daily grind of keeping supplies moving, of worrying about ship or aircraft arrivals, lack of manpower, late supply of railway wagons, insufficient vehicles, mechanical breakdowns, and above all security – preventing any leaks as to what we were doing getting to the public, or over-inquisitive foreign journalists and enemy agents. What he achieved was a minor miracle, as the system was never exposed, never disrupted by sabotage inside Pakistan, during the period 1984-87. In 1983 some 10,000 tons of arms and ammunition went through the pipeline. By 1987 this amount had risen to 65,000 tons, all of it handled by 200 men from the Ministry of Defence Constabulary (MODC) with four fork-lift trucks, working seven days a week, month after month.

At the CIA end of the pipe it was not just that we often received inappropriate and outdated weapons systems that we did not want, but their scheduling of shipments frequently took no account of our capacity to handle the huge quantities involved. It was usually a feast or a famine situation. I repeatedly stressed that we needed a smooth, regular flow of arrivals at Karachi port, of about one or two ships a month. This we could manage. Such a steady build-up would prevent bottlenecks when our stores were overflowing, or periods when they were virtually empty. Perhaps I was asking the impossible, because sometimes three, or even four, ships would arrive within a month, or there would be a long period when nothing came.

A small proportion of arms arrived by air at Rawalpindi (Chaklala Air Base). Until 1986 many of these deliveries were the cause of increasing friction between ISI and the Pakistan Air Force (PAF). The trouble seemed to stem from Saudi Arabia, where the CIA had arranged to dump supplies

Map 8

THE ARMS PIPELINE

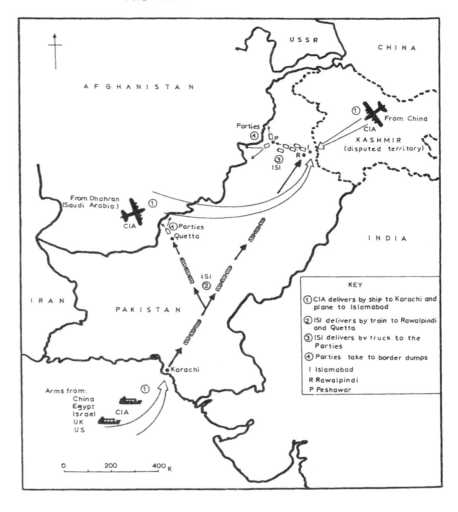

at Dhahran Air Base either for onward delivery by Saudi aircraft or collection by the PAF. For some reason unknown to me, these flights always seemed to go wrong. The CIA provided the liaison, but even when they had an agent at the Saudi airfield invariably our planes were not allowed to land on schedule, or were even turned away. When Saudi aircraft flew to Pakistan they did not arrive on time, or came completely unannounced, causing the PAF to go on unnecessary alerts. After nearly two years of this I managed to get the system stopped and USAF planes used, but our relationship with the PAF was badly soured.

Once the arms arrived on Pakistani soil we took over. I should explain that the supply system had been established before I arrived at ISI and that overall security of our methods was greatly enhanced by our operating under martial law. The military was in complete control. They were both the makers and executors of the law. For example, the normal bureaucratic stream of paperwork was suspended as far as we were concerned. Until later, when the size of the supply system expanded so enormously, nothing was committed to writing. Officials in government agencies or departments that had to be involved in keeping things moving were briefed verbally on what they had to do. If they became too curious they were told that the consignment or work was related to the widely publicized, but 'secret', project of making a nuclear bomb. This was normally enough to get cooperation.

At Karachi the port authorities were paid their dues in cash, the ship's manifest merely stated 'defense stores' and the customs department was not involved. From the ship the crates were loaded on to between ten and twenty freight wagons for the journey by rail to my warehouse at Ojhri camp or, for a small proportion, direct to Quetta. The wagons were accompanied by armed MODC escorts. This rail movement was a daily event. Ten wagons would take about 200 tons, although I could cope with up to 400 as a maximum. If several ships arrived in quick succession the system broke down, with a build-up of stores at the docks as my men toiled to shift them, while my colonel contended with the railway functionaries for more rolling stock.

At Rawalpindi we had a fleet of 200 vehicles, mostly five- or ten-ton trucks with false and frequently changed number plates, with which to move the weapons further down the pipeline. All the boxes had to be brought to the camp from the railway station to be separated, checked and stored in the warehouse. Everything had to be taken on charge and stock lists updated daily. I insisted on having this information on my desk early every morning.

Next came the business of breaking bulk, and dividing up the weapons and ammunition into consignments for the Parties at Peshawar. This was done in accordance with the allocation priorities that I will describe later. Arms and ammunition is useless sitting at a depot, it needs to be in the hands of the user, so I made it a point of honour to keep the flow moving towards Afghanistan. I preferred an almost empty warehouse to a full one — it was also a much less tempting target should a saboteur obtain knowledge of its location, or in the event of an accidental fire. We were, after all, sitting on a potentially very large bang, close to a built-up area. At least 80 per cent of all arms and ammunition used in Afghanistan passed through my warehouse at Ojhri, yet I believe our secret was kept. Despite the daily volume of traffic and activity to and from the camp, we never experienced any incident that suggested security had been breached during those four years.

Every morning, at times varying from 5.00 am to noon, a convoy of trucks with MODC drivers in civilian clothes would leave for Peshawar. It was a 150-kilometre drive, which had to be completed by evening so nothing could leave Rawalpindi later than noon. Every afternoon empty vehicles from the previous day's delivery arrived back. Our workshop staff were kept frantically busy on maintenance.

To call these vehicles convoys is perhaps misleading, in that the 50-60 trucks did not follow one another in a long column — far from it. We sent them off in small packets of two or three lorries at intervals of five to ten minutes. They merged with the civilian traffic, with the man riding shotgun in the cab having his weapon concealed on the floor. Once, when travelling from Peshawar with the local CIA chief, I challenged him to try to spot any of our vehicles. He failed to do so.

Our main worry was the possibility of road accidents. An officer always travelled with the leading truck and another at the end of the convoy, and we included one or two empty vehicles in case of breakdowns. General Akhtar refused to countenance the possibility of accidents, although he knew our difficulties and that the law of statistics made a few inevitable. He remained adamant that they were not to happen, so I was forced to increase the number of officers on convoy duties to the detriment of training and operational requirements.

In 1986 I calculated that my trucks travelled well over a million kilometres. With such distance accidents happened. The most unfortunate was when a truck hit a car head on. By the time the officer at the rear reached the scene the casualties had been evacuated, and despite enquiries at the nearby hospital he failed to locate the car passengers. It turned out that the car occupants were Army officers and that two had died at the military hospital. There was a lot of unpleasantness as the Army blamed the ISI, despite witnesses testifying that the car was at fault.

At Peshawar the Parties took over. Their consignments were off-loaded at their warehouses while the drivers overnighted before the return journey next day. This was the system I used for the great bulk of arms and ammunition. There were a few exceptions, apart from those going direct to

Quetta from Karachi. These involved rocket launchers and SAMs, weapons that were scarce and were needed in particularly critical operational areas such as around Kabul, or airbases, or along the Salang Highway. Everybody wanted to shoot down helicopters or launch rocket attacks from 10 kilometres from the target as this added to a Commander's prestige, but I insisted they must be deployed in accordance with the overall guerrilla strategy. With these weapons I insisted I deliver them direct to the Commanders from those key areas, but in consultation with the Parties. Similarly, if there was a special operation being mounted, such as the sinking of barges on the Amu that required limpet mines, or a coordinated large-scale attack on a large enemy garrison, then I would also arrange a direct issue to the Commanders involved, again with the Parties' concurrence.

Despite the allegations of corruption levelled at those involved with the arms pipeline, I remain totally convinced that as far as my organization was concerned nothing much went astray. The middle section of the pipe was virtually corruption-free. The beginning section under the CIA was riddled with opportunities for fraud and, as I have shown, there was ineptitude and probably dishonesty as well.

I should explain that there were also charges that the ISI diverted arms to the Pakistan Army. These were correct to the extent that some 200 14.5mm machine guns, RPG-7s and SA-7s were given to the Army to be deployed in emergencies on the western border when the Soviet/Afghan forces stepped up their air and artillery violations into Pakistan. I can say with absolute authority that no other weapon was so diverted. It was foolish of us to do it without taking the CIA into our confidence, as I am sure they would not have objected. As it was, they found out, so there was a flurry of accusations and denials which damaged our relationship unnecessarily. Perhaps more detrimental, and increasingly so as time went on, to our association with the CIA was the endless bickering over their persistent demands for control over the allocation of all arms and ammunition entering Pakistan.

During General Akhtar's eight years as Director-General of ISI it was the policy, on which he rightly remained unmoveable, that ISI decided who got the weapons, how many, and what types. By this I mean that, after the formation of the Alliance, the detailed allocation to each Party was our responsibility. It bears repeating. No one outside the ISI, including President Zia, had any say or control over the allocation of arms, ammunition and allied logistic stores from our warehouses at Rawalpindi and Quetta. It was not only the CIA who criticized us over this matter. The US Ambassador was often outspokenly disapproving, as were the US Congress, foreign journalists, senior generals in the Pakistan Army and the Parties themselves. They all thought they knew best. They all had their own political and personal motives for knocking the system, so they took every opportunity of pressuring ISI to alter allocations. Parties and Commanders routinely clamoured for more, for bigger and better weapons, while the Americans insisted we favoured the Fundamentalist Parties, particularly Hekmatyar. It was a never-ending source of friction, in-fighting and frustration.

The US felt that as they were paying for at least half of all the arms they should have a say in who used them. As the war progressed, and especially when the Soviets started talking about withdrawing, US officials started becoming more and more concerned that the next government in Kabul might be an Islamic Fundamentalist one, possibly with Hekmatyar becoming another Khomeini. This fear was eventually to lead to a deliberate US policy of withholding support to prevent a Mujahideen victory, but during my tenure it manifested itself in mounting allegations of partiality over arms allocations.

My job was to apply military pressure inside Afghanistan to get the Soviets out. I was a professional soldier, with a soldier's ambition to win on the battlefield. With these as my motives I decided who got the means to win — the weapons and ammunition — on the basis of maximum combat effectiveness. I had to implement a campaign strategy to influence operations without the ability to issue orders to subordinates, without any military infrastructure to sustain or implement decisions. I had to coordinate attacks on strategic targets and maintain the initiative over an area of 260,000 square miles by exhortation, supported by animal pack trains and, for most of the time, a system of messengers that had not much changed since Alexander's days. Concentration and cooperation are two immutable principles of war. Success in battle is often dependent on both being applied simultaneously at the right time and place. The only way I could influence the Parties and Commanders, get them moving in the right direction, was through the allocation or withholding of supplies and training.

As I have emphasized before, weapons have always played an important part in an Afghan's life. The more modern the rifle that a man owns the higher his standing. For Mujahideen the possession of heavy weapons and plentiful ammunition was a common goal, for which they were willing to show some flexibility, some inclination to listen, or to follow instructions. My giving assurances that a certain operation would be backed up with extra weapons or more missiles, and that success would lead to further supplies, was sometimes the only way I could obtain cooperation. I had a carrot to offer. My stick was to withhold the weapons. Had the ISI not retained this prerogative my task would have been hopeless.

Eighty per cent of all arms and ammunition was allocated to the Parties for onward distribution. Commanders had to belong to a Party in order to get weapons, the only exception being when they came for training for special operations, but, even though they were then given the weapons direct, they came from their Parties' allocation. Our American allies favoured giving arms direct to Commanders. This had been the system before I took over, when the supply was a trickle, before the Quetta incident described previously, and prior to the formation of the Alliance. By the mid-eighties such a policy was unworkable. It was daunting enough trying to get results dealing with seven Parties; to attempt to do so by direct contact with hundreds of rival Commanders, each anxious to enhance his own reputation, was to invite chaos.

Every three months an operational conference would be held between General Akhtar, myself, and my officers of lieutenant-colonel or above. A key matter for discussion and decision was always the arms share and any modifications needed to existing arrangements. Because it was such a critical and controversial matter, I spent many hours before the conference going over the problems with my staff. I needed their opinions before making firm recommendations to the General. Frequently this subject would generate long debate at the conference and, although the final decision was Akhtar's, he seldom overruled our recommendations. For planning purposes we worked on a rough percentage basis for each Party. These were not permanently fixed; they varied slightly for operational reasons, and sometimes they were deliberately reduced if a Party was seen not to be pulling its weight in the field. Such reductions were normally gradual and followed a verbal warning to the Leader.

The criteria we used in drawing up these rule-of-thumb percentages were all related to battlefield competence. The numerical following of a Party as such was not a factor. For example, Khalis' Party was comparatively small but its combat effectiveness was greater than a large Party like Mujaddadi's. The location of Commanders of each Party in Afghanistan was an important consideration. The majority would not fight outside their own area, even their own valley, so it was pointless pouring arms down the pipeline to a Commander far removed from strategic targets. Any Party strong around Kabul could rely on a higher percentage, likewise those operating against sensitive spots such as airfields, or main lines of communication. By using the word 'strong' I do not mean large numbers of Mujahideen at a given place, but the frequency of successful attacks in the area. To assess this I was indebted to the radio interception service which often provided me with confirmation of activities claimed by Commanders and Parties. Similarly, we used the CIA's satellite photographs to establish the validity of damage claims. I, and my officers, well understood the Mujahideen's inclination to exaggerate. Debriefing of individuals, the CIA and MI-6 weekly intelligence reports and the careful sifting of all information from various sources were important ways of verifying who was actually fighting and who was not.

Then we looked at the Parties' control over such dubious activities as the illegal sale of arms. I had a Major working fulltime on gathering this information. If a Party could not control its Commanders in this respect then their share would be cut. Nevertheless, I should qualify this condemnation of the sale of arms by the Mujahideen by saying that it is my belief there is probably no Commander in Afghanistan who has not, at some time, sold or bartered weapons. So long as it was done in Afghanistan between Mujahideen, for the Jehad, we never penalized them. Sometimes, in an emergency, it was the only way to obtain food, evacuate a casualty, or secure urgently needed ammunition. If the sale took place in Pakistan for the Commanders' personal enrichment or comfort, then we treated the offence as serious. Several Leaders were lax with their Commanders on this, and these tended to be the Moderates, part of the reason being that they were always short of funds. These Parties employed permanent staff, often Western-educated men who were not satisfied with the meagre $100 a month salary paid by the Fundamentalists. They demanded, and got, three times this amount, plus free housing. There was an ever-present temptation to sell weapons they had been given at 100 per cent profit to make up cash shortfalls.

The final factor we considered was the general efficiency of the Party and their own logistic system, which I shall describe shortly. A sure way of judging a Party's competence was to visit their warehouse regularly. If my officers reported a warehouse was always full, sometimes for months, it meant that the Party was less than enthusiastic at prosecuting the war, and as such never qualified for an increased share of arms. Nabi's Party was a prime culprit in this respect. Despite having great potential, with some fine Commanders in the field, plus a numerous following, together with a former Afghan general as his military representative, Nabi and his officials never seemed able to improve their efficiency. In marked contrast was Sayaf, whose warehouses invariably held the minimum of stocks, although I must admit he had the singular advantage of receiving generous extra financial aid direct from rich Arab supporters.

In 1987 the broad percentages allocated to the Parties were Hekmatyar 18-20 per cent, Rabbani 18-19 per cent, Sayaf 17-18 per cent, Khalis 13-15 per cent, Nabi 13-15 per cent, Gailani 10-11 per cent, and Mujaddadi trailing with 3-5 per cent. Certainly the Fundamentalists came out on top with 67-73 per cent, much to the CIA's chagrin, but using strictly military criteria it could never be otherwise. My critics were taking into account political considerations and biases which, as a soldier, I was fortunately able to ignore.

I wish I had calculated the total cost of getting a weapon or bullet from the seller to the firer; it would have been a staggering statistic; shipment costs, rail and truck movement to Peshawar, followed by carriage over the border deep into Afghanistan, multiplied the purchase price a hundredfold. Probably the most expensive leg of the journey was the last sector of the pipeline from the Parties to the Mujahideen who would use the weapons. In some cases, where the supplies were going to Kabul or the eastern provinces, this was the shortest part of the journey, in which case the costs were more manageable, but charges to get arms to the crucial northern provinces were constantly rising, and by 1986 were little short of extortionate. By this time the going rate was $15-20 per kilogram. This meant the cost of moving a mortar from the Pakistan border to the Mazar-i-Sharif area was approximately $1100, while just one bomb cost around $65. Little wonder that the monthly expenditure by the Parties on transport and allied expenses was $1.5 million.

The CIA placed funds each month in the ISI-controlled bank account. This money had to pay for Party offices, construction and maintenance of warehouses, purchase of software (rations, clothes), subsistence allowance for Leaders, salaries for Party officials/employees, and transport. This latter included buying vehicles, and paying contractors to carry all supplies forward into Afghanistan, but not the purchase of mules from China (or later of horses from Argentina) which the CIA did themselves. Normally every Party had exhausted this source of money within 10-12 days. Without cash, supplies got stuck in the pipe, which meant in Party warehouses at Peshawar or Quetta. I recall how horrified I was when I first visited their warehouses in Peshawar, which at that stage were merely houses within the city. There were no proper storage or security arrangements as they were run in the most casual and unmilitary fashion. In one warehouse the 'storeman' was sitting on an upturned anti-tank mine cooking his meal over an open fire. Things did improve marginally and I managed to get funds to move all seven warehouses several kilometres outside the city, but there was little I could do to make up cash shortfalls.

Parties and Commanders did have other sources of finance. Until late 1984 local taxes were levied by Commanders in their valleys in Afghanistan, but as the Soviets progressively pounded the villages, smashed the irrigation systems, burnt crops and drove survivors into refugee camps, these taxes became impossible to collect. Captured weapons were used, sold or bartered. According to Islamic law war booty must be divided so that a fifth goes to the state (Party). I know Mujahideen sometimes found it cheaper to buy weapons or ammunition from Soviet or Afghan posts. I can vouch for this happening on a small scale on numerous occasions.

It was largely Arab money that saved the system. By this I mean cash from rich individuals or private organizations in the Arab world, not Saudi government funds. Without these extra millions the flow of arms actually getting to the Mujahideen would have been cut to a trickle. The problem was it all went to the four Fundamentalist Parties, not the Moderates. Sayaf, in particular, had many personal religious or academic contacts in Saudi Arabia, so his coffers were usually kept well filled. This meant the Moderates became proportionately less efficient, lack of Arab money being one of the causes of their inability to match the Fundamentalists in operational effectiveness. Their income was less, their administrative and bureaucratic expenditure greater, thus making it harder for them to come up to our allocation criteria.

When my vehicle dumped the arms and ammunition at the Party warehouses responsibility for its distribution to the Mujahideen passed to the Parties (except for certain special types, or that earmarked for special operations). If some Commanders failed to receive their supply, or they felt their share was insufficient, there was little I could do about it. Each Party had its own method of deciding allocations to its Commanders. Sometimes it was on a fixed percentage basis — a hopelessly ineffective system which allowed Mujahideen in quiet areas to receive the same as those where fighting was frequent. At times supplies were sent to a single Provincial Commander for further distribution, on other occasions it was several Commanders who shared out between their sub-Commanders. Now and again all Commanders in a province would come to collect direct from the Party bases at the border.

How did the Parties move their supplies? It was one of the most complicated, chaotic and time-consuming operations of the war. Trucks and tractors, carts and camels, mules and horses all played their part, as did the backs of the Mujahideen themselves.

The larger Parties owned up to 300 vehicles of all types. These were civilian-pattern trucks which blended with the normal cross-border traffic. A number were Afghan vehicles purchased in Kabul, which were used for the longer journeys by road. They were more numerous than ISI's transport as often these vehicles undertook journeys of several days or more, with no possibility of returning empty on the second day. A truck could be absent from the Party pool for weeks. It was sometimes possible to drive all the way to the northern or western provinces, journeys of over 1000 kilometres, while on other occasions only pack animals could be used. Inside Afghanistan deals were often struck with local Afghan commanders for the use of Afghan Army transport. One of the peculiarities of the war was that on occasion the Mujahideen could have their arms delivered to them in their enemy's trucks. This occurred more often with sabotage operations in Kabul or other important cities, and included KHAD vehicles as well as military ones. At times, such activities were provided free, but normally money would have to change hands.

It was by lorry that the Parties moved their freight forward along the next stage of the pipe to the frontier. Here, some fifty-five border bases were located just inside Pakistan, mostly clustered around the main entry points near Parachinar and Chaman, NW of Quetta. To reach them the vehicles had to travel through the restricted areas of NWFP, Baluchistan, and the Tribal Areas (see Map 2). Throughout these regions the Pakistan Army, Border Scouts and Police were always on an active-service footing. Passage was controlled and subject to permits, check points, or vehicle search. To facilitate progress ISI issued all trucks with a 'let go vehicle' permit which gave all details of the lorry, except its cargo. Check points en route were given lists of the trucks expected to pass through in advance. These vehicles were immune from search on the outward journey only, as a precaution against smuggling drugs or arms into Pakistan. Most of the time the system worked, but it was far from perfect. At times police check points would exact a 'fee' to avoid delays. Pay a bribe and the barrier was raised at once; refuse, and all sorts of excuses and telephone calls to non-existent or absent superiors could halt vehicles for hours.

I had an amusing personal experience of exactly this sort of difficulty when I took Congressman Wilson to the border prior to his secret visit to Afghanistan. I had sent an officer ahead to tell the police posts that our car was not to be delayed. At the first checkpoint a civilian official refused to let us proceed without 'clearance'. I showed him my Army identity card, but he insisted he would have to check back. His telephone call conveniently found his superiors out of office – more waiting. After 15 minutes I exploded. I told the official that if he did not raise the barrier I would get my three escorts, who were armed with AK-47 rifles, to empty their magazines into him. They cocked their weapons and the barrier was forcibly raised. Later, I told the officer who had gone ahead what had happened, and that I was not impressed with his 'smoothing' of our route. On the return trip the same officer was travelling in a second vehicle. At the checkpoint this officer ordered his men into the post, and had the unfortunate individual dragged out at gunpoint. Shrieking protests, he was bundled into the vehicle to be driven off. I am sure he thought his end was near. After driving about 15 kilometres, during which time the wretched man was weeping and apologizing pathetically, he was dumped at the roadside to fend for himself. He had picked the wrong person from which to try to extract a 'sweetener'.

Close to the border, especially around Parachinar, Miram Shah and Chaman, everybody was involved in the war in some way or other. There were tens of thousands of refugees in their camps, the bases teemed with Mujahideen, hundreds of transport contractors milled around with their animals, and scores of trucks were being loaded for their final journey to the end of the supply pipeline. Every day of every month, winter permitting, arms and ammunition were on the move. These areas contained the main jump-off points from the Mujahideen's base of supply. The Durand Line was to the Mujahideen what the Amu River was to the Soviets. Here Commanders came to collect their supplies, here the trucks from Peshawar and Quetta were off-loaded, and here the pack trains of animals assembled and loaded up.

In the early days a Commander would arrive in Pakistan with his own horses, perhaps a hundred, to collect his weapons, but as the quantity of stores multiplied and horses were lost, this system became totally inadequate. Thousands of animals were needed, and they became casualties like the men, so a reliable replacement organization was necessary. The answer was the contractor, although costs were high and climbed steadily every year. The contractor was a businessman, he owned the animals, he accompanied them into Afghanistan and he fed them. As it was his livelihood, he looked after his beasts, taking away this responsibility from the Mujahideen. Our CIA comrades did not like the system. They advocated specially formed animal transport companies operated by the Mujahideen. I did not agree, as the Mujahideen would not own the animals, would not have a personal financial interest in their care and half the animals would be needed to carry fodder. From experience I knew such companies would be as expensive, but less efficient, than the contractors.

The animals used were camels, horses and mules. The camels were usually employed on the long routes to the southern provinces where the land was arid. Horses were by far the most numerous pack animals. The Afghan pony was ideally suited to the task, having been reared in the country over the centuries for precisely this type of work. The horse tended to be the long-distance, strategic carrier of supplies from the border to the operational bases in the provinces. As more and more died or were killed, we resorted, in the later stages, to importing Argentinian horses. There were far less mules than horses. The mule was not bred in Afghanistan. There were some in Pakistan, and China had mule farms which provided an additional source of supply. These animals were usually to be seen as operational, or tactical, carriers. Normally it would be mules that packed the mortar, the heavy machine gun or the SBRL and its ammunition to the actual firing point, or very close to it. The mules, together with some horses, were given to Commanders to keep at their operational bases as what the military would term 'F' Echelon transport − transport that carried weapons on to or near the battlefield. The CIA would buy the animals, then give them to the Parties to issue to their Commanders. They were quite separate from the contractors' animals.

Apart from the branch from Karachi to Quetta there was really one main pipeline via Rawalpindi and Peshawar to the border. From then on numerous branch lines spread out into Afghanistan. I would liken our system to a tree. The roots represented the ships and aircraft bringing supplies from various countries to Pakistan. The trunk lay from Karachi almost to the border, at which point the main branches lay across the frontier. These branches divided into hundreds of smaller ones inside Afghanistan, taking the sap (arms and ammunition) to the leaves (the Mujahideen). Lop off a small branch, even a large one, and the tree survives, and in time others grow. Only severing the roots or trunk kills the tree. In our case only the branches were subject to attack. Unlike the Soviets, whose lines of communication were confined to main roads, ours made use of scores of tracks and trails through the mountains and valleys. If a road was blocked a route round could always be found.

There were six main routes leading into Afghanistan (see Map 9). Starting in the north, from Chitral a high route led to the Panjsher valley, Faizabad and the northern provinces. This was the shortest, cheapest and safest passage to these regions, but it was closed by the snow for up to eight months every year. We could only use it from June to October. Next came the busiest route. From Parachinar (the Parrot's Beak) via Ali Khel into Logar Province was the gateway to the Jehad, through which some 40 per cent of our supplies passed. This was the shortest route to Kabul, only a week's journey away. We also used it for journeys north over the mountains to the plains around Mazar-i-Sharif, although this could take a month or more. The disadvantage lay in the strong enemy opposition that tried to bar the way. When the Soviets wanted to decrease pressure on Kabul it was in the eastern provinces that they launched their largest search and destroy missions.

A little further south, the third route started around Miram Shah via Zhawar, again into Logar Province. Supply trains could either swing south near Gardez or Ghazni, or north to join the second route over the mountains. This was another busy route, but enemy interference was relatively light.

The fourth route started in Quetta, crossed the frontier at Chaman, before leading towards Kandahar and nearby provinces. There was much open country which meant vehicles were required to shift the bulk of the supplies quickly. We aimed to get trucks to their destination in one day's or night's fast driving. Suspicious vehicles were subjected to enemy ground or air attacks.

Over 400 kilometres further west, on the southern border of Helmund Province, was the smaller and unpopular base at Girzi-Jungle. It was used to replenish Helmund, Nimroz, Farah, and Herat Provinces. It was unpopular as vehicles were so vulnerable to attack. Seldom did we send in a convoy without incident. It was an arid, open area, sparsely populated, with little possibility of early warning of attack. Trucks travelling north were easily spotted from the air and were often shot up by gunships or ambushed by heliborne troops pre-positioned ahead of them. To reach Herat by vehicle took a week.

Finally, the sixth route was via Iran. A glance at Map 9 will show that to get supplies quickly and safely to Farah and Herat Provinces a long drive west along the Baluchistan border to Iran, then another 600 kilometres north from Zahedan in Iran to the Iran-Afghanistan frontier opposite Herat, a three-day journey, was the answer − in theory. In practice it was very different. Although we did use this route it took up to six months for the Iranians to grant a special permit, then only small arms could be carried,

Map 9

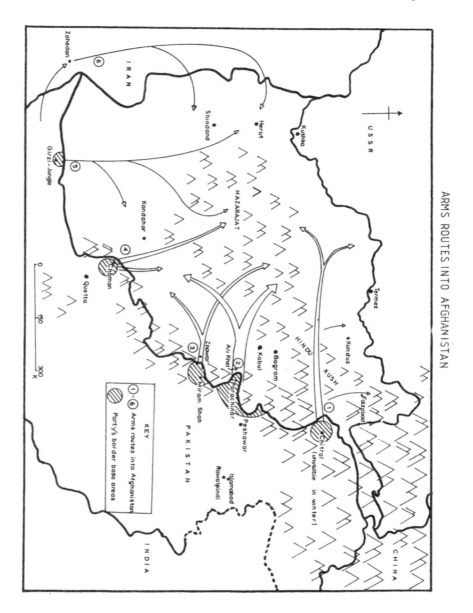

ARMS ROUTES INTO AFGHANISTAN

while every convoy was checked, inspected and escorted by Revolutionary Guards. It was the same when our empty vehicles re-entered Iran.

Such was our pipeline. For all its complexity, cost and length, somehow it worked. Of course there was much bellyaching from aggrieved Commanders, who protested bitterly that they were starved of supplies. In some cases they did go short, but I know of no battle that the Mujahideen lost for lack of ammunition, certainly not during the years 1983-87. Most often it was Commanders whose Parties were inefficient, or who operated in areas remote from strategic targets, or who lacked vigour in the fighting, who had cause for complaint.

My problem was in getting the right type of weapon and sufficient ammunition to the right Commander, at the right place, at the right time. If I achieved this it was usually the prelude to operational success. It involved thinking months ahead. Up to nine months were needed to organize operations in the north. It was this inescapable time lag between the conception of a plan and its execution that outsiders, such as the CIA, so often failed to comprehend.

CHAPTER SEVEN

Training and Tactics

'To lead an untrained people to war is to throw them away.'
Confucius, *Analects*, XIII (c.500 BC)

In EARLY April, 1989, *The Times* carried a short article describing the trial of two alleged Pakistani spies in Kabul. One was said to be an Army intelligence sergeant, the other a Special Branch corporal. Both had been captured in Kandahar. They had supposedly confessed to their espionage or sabotage activities under torture, although the report indicated that their confessions were unconvincing and contradictory. Nevertheless, they received 18- and 16-year jail sentences respectively. Such a sentence in the infamous Pol-i-Charki prison outside Kabul would be a living nightmare; for many an execution would be preferable. The Pakistan Embassy had, inevitably, disowned them, while our foreign minister described the affair as a 'propaganda stunt'.

I have no way of knowing whether the charges were true or false, but I know for certain that we at ISI were sending Pakistani military personnel into Afghanistan from 1981 through to 1986. I know, because it was part of my job to select the individuals, and brief them as to their tasks. It is quite likely that these highly secret activities were resumed after I had left the Army. I must make it clear, however, that the men we sent into Afghanistan were not spies, they were soldiers from the Pakistan Army, serving with the Afghan Bureau of ISI. Their mission was to accompany Mujahideen on special operations, they acted as advisers, assisting the Commander in carrying out his task. This assignment could range from blowing up an oil pipeline or mounting a rocket attack on an airfield to laying an ambush. During my time there were usually two Pakistani teams in Afghanistan at the same time throughout the period May to October. Depending on the distance, a team could remain in the field from one to three months. No team ever knew the other was operating. They were at their peak in 1984, when no less than eleven such teams operated, seven against Kabul, two against Bagram airfield and two around Jalalabad.

All these Pakistanis were volunteers from my staff at ISI. Officers and

NCOs were posted to ISI from all branches of the Pakistan Army and General Akhtar sent them to the various Directorates, reserving the best for the Afghan Bureau. They came to me for a 2-3 year tour, and I decided whether they would work on training, operations or logistics. I would always ask if anyone was willing to go inside Afghanistan, and from those who agreed I would carefully select those most suitable for special missions.

Normally a team would consist of an officer (usually a major), a JCO and an NCO, one of whom had to be a Pushtun speaker. I would have to make it absolutely clear to each individual the risks he would be taking. Under no circumstances must he allow himself to be captured, as this would expose the Pakistan government's clandestine support for the Jehad. Of course we would deny everything, disown them, but they would certainly be subjected to the most vile and prolonged torture. As every man has his breaking point, eventually some information detrimental to our operations would be extracted, with the likelihood of a show trial and much publicity and propaganda. Nobody was encouraged to kill himself to avoid capture, no suicide tablets were issued, as to take one's own life is forbidden to Muslims. It was repeatedly stressed that they were to escape from tight corners, or as a last resort to die fighting. If this occurred the Mujahideen with him had to do their utmost to retrieve the body. Similarly, if a Pakistani was wounded he had to be got out — somehow.

All my men going into Afghanistan had plenty of time to prepare themselves and the Mujahideen they would be accompanying. Once a mission had been decided, and a Commander selected, then the team would be responsible for the training of that Commander and his Mujahideen, although they never knew their instructors would be going with them until the end of the course. By this time the trainers had grown beards, were dressed as Mujahideen, so that they were indistinguishable from their guerrilla companions.

These officers and NCOs had to live and fight as the Mujahideen, enduring the same privations and hardships. There was none of the military back-up support to feed them or evacuate them if wounded. They became akin to special force advisers. Their duties included giving guidance on all aspects of military operations or duties to the Commander, training the Mujahideen in their operational bases, assisting with defensive measures for the bases, helping the Commander to plan and carry out his special tasks and, if necessary, fighting. Additionally, I relied on them for information as to what was happening in the field. They were a vital part of my intelligence organization, not only on enemy activities, but on the performance of the Mujahideen and their Commanders. I could rely on these men not to exaggerate, not to ignore Mujahideen weaknesses or gaps in their training. The information they brought back was invaluable in planning fresh operations, selecting suitable Commanders, or devising future training programmes. But I had to wait until they returned to Pakistan before any debriefing, as none of these teams ever carried long-range radio sets for fear of enemy interception.

I must admit that when I first took over I was not in favour of Pakistanis being involved in actual operations in Afghanistan. I felt the risk of capture was too high and that, should it happen, the damage it would do to Pakistan, and therefore to the Jehad, outweighed the tactical advantages. I recall several heated discussions with General Akhtar on this, but I was overruled. I had to accept that it was a part of my duty to organize these teams, so I resolved to do so to the utmost of my ability; in fact I set about increasing the number. During all those six years from 1981-86 they performed admirably, nothing ever went seriously wrong, and nobody was captured or killed. These men were a great credit to the Pakistan Army. Although they each received an award, roughly equivalent to the US Silver Star or British Military Cross, for their professionalism and daring, this is the first time their contribution has been made public.

Let me demolish a myth that has been built up by Soviet propaganda and many journalists. Up to the Soviet withdrawal from Afghanistan in early 1989, no American or Chinese instructor was ever involved in giving training on any kind of weapon or equipment to the Mujahideen. Even with the heavier and more sophisticated weapon systems such as the Oerlikon anti-aircraft guns, and later the Stinger SAM, it was always our Pakistani teams who trained the Mujahideen. This was a deliberate, carefully considered policy that we steadfastly refused to change despite mounting pressure from the CIA, and later from the US Defense Department, to allow them to take it over. From the start the Americans wanted to be directly involved with the distribution of the weapons, the operational planning of operations and the training of the guerrillas. From the start, until the last Soviet soldier quit the country, we successfully resisted.

We did so because the Parties were strongly opposed to direct dealings with Americans. They knew that such activities would be widely propagated, thus reinforcing Soviet and KHAD propaganda that the war was not a Jehad but merely part of the global capitalist-communist struggle. We also had every confidence in our Pakistani instructors. This was fully justified by events on the battlefield.

I well remember a visit by Mr Casey to some of our training camps in 1986. In all, three camps were visited, and the CIA delegation was most curious in its questioning of trainees. One senior US official, who spoke Pushtun, repeatedly asked individual Mujahideen at random how long had they been on the course. Had they ever been in the Afghan Army? Had they ever fired these weapons before in Afghanistan? The truth was that they had all been under training for eight days, and yet they were firing heavy machine guns, mortars, RPG-7s and recoilless rifles with the confidence and accuracy of experienced soldiers. Casey was most impressed. At dinner with President Zia that night he expressed his admiration for the high standards achieved in such a short time. Within a month Zia came to see for himself. He too was amazed by what he saw, and as good as accused me of selecting the best shots to demonstrate the weapons. I told him he could select anybody to fire, as what he had seen was the average standard. He declined to do so, but at the end of the day he remarked, 'I only wish our Army had half this standard of shooting.' We had no need of American instructors.

The US did, however, have a role in training our Army instructors. In the case of new weapons, particularly anti-aircraft weapons. that were not on issue to the Pakistan Army, American trainers ran courses for our instructors; they then trained the Mujahideen.

Soon after taking over, General Akhtar and I discussed the importance of improving training at great length. By the end of 1983 only 3,000 Mujahideen had received any formal training at the two camps that had been established in Pakistan. We agreed that this was totally inadequate and set a target of 1,000 trainees a month completing courses. It was a target many thought impossible to hit.

As experienced soldiers, General Akhtar and I both understood that without proper training we would indeed be throwing away the Mujahideen. As the variety and quantity of arms grew, so did the demand for training, but with the guerrilla campaign in Afghanistan there was more to it than that. In a war over which we had no direct or formal control, training, like the supply of weapons, was a key to our being able to influence what went on on the battlefield. If we issued weapons such as MBRLs, or demolition charges, from a Party's allocation to specific Commanders for a particular type of operation in their area, it followed that it was these Commanders, and their men, who must have priority with the training. We had worked out our overall strategy, we had selected sensitive targets for attack, we were providing the arms, so we had also to provide the training to get the tasks carried out.

Commanders, being Afghans, seldom missed the chance of enhancing their own prestige by fair means or foul. We exploited this by offering training and weapons to those who undertook specific operations in their area. If they succeeded they got more training and bigger and better weapons, thus boosting their status as Commanders. Our policy was as simple as that. As we were never able to issue orders direct to our forces in the field, this manipulating of the supply of arms, and training in their use, was the only effective way of getting an operational strategy implemented.

It was fundamental to our system that training should be mission-orientated. By this I mean that if we wanted the oil pipeline destroyed the course would be solely concerned with demolitions suitable to this end. The Commander would receive instruction on the tactics of where best to place the charges, of how to approach the pipeline, how to distract or cover nearby enemy posts, where to lay mines to catch any repair parties, and on the likely Soviet reaction. His men concentrated more on the actual use of explosives and methods of detonation. At the end of the course they would leave, their missions having been discussed in detail with the course officer, and the explosive charges made up ready for use, but without the detonators in place.

In order to increase our capacity our courses were all 'hands on' practical ones, with little theory or peacetime drills. From day one the trainees started handling the weapon and quickly progressed to live firing. We cut the length of the courses, but increased the daily training time. Courses never stopped for holidays as we made use of all 365 days in the year. For the students this was no great burden, but for the instructors the strain was immense, and we had to plan their rest periods with care. We also started running courses for Mujahideen instructors, who had been selected during their attendance at other courses. These men would go back to their bases in Afghanistan to organize courses there. Often we would send a Pakistani Mobile Training Team (MTT) in to help them establish themselves at locations that we had agreed with the Parties. We would also provide a syllabus and training aids. Once these local Mujahideen trainers had gained experience the MTT would merely pay periodic visits to offer advice.

At the end of 1983 we were operating two camps in Pakistan, each with a capacity of 200 trainees. By mid-1984 we were putting over 1000 a month through the system, and by 1987 we had seven camps operating simultaneously – four near Peshawar and three around Quetta. This crash programme necessitated more staff and more money, both of which General Akhtar quickly provided, so the resultant statistics were startling. In 1984 20,000 Mujahideen benefited from our efforts, with 17,700 completing courses in 1985 and 19,400 in 1986. It is no exaggeration to say that by the time I left ISI in late 1987 at least 80,000 Mujahideen had received training in Pakistan over a four-year period, and many thousands more had done so in Afghanistan. I salute my staff; they have never been called upon to work so hard before or since.

Setting up a training camp was never a simple matter of our commandeering an Army camp or using the military's firing ranges. Like all our activities, complete secrecy was the name of the game. Nobody outside the Afghan Bureau was to know what we were doing. The public, the politicians, enemy agents, the Pakistan Army and Soviet spy satellites had to be kept in complete ignorance of the whereabouts of each camp. This necessitated our finding our own sites well away from prying eyes. It was easier said than done.

The camps had to be within a night's drive from Peshawar or Quetta, as all trainees were brought by truck during darkness so they would have no inkling of their location. They had to be administratively convenient and self-sufficient with water. We could not locate them near any Army base or exercise area, nor could we use places to which the public had easy access. Wherever they were sited they had to be concealed from the ground and the air. The latter caused the most difficulty, which we overcame by camouflage and strict track discipline. By this I mean we only used existing roads or paths to, from, or around the camp. Nothing shows up so clearly on an aerial photograph as fresh tracks.

Probably our greatest problem was in finding suitable sites at which we could fire all our weapons. It was not just small arms. We had to fire extensively, on a day-to-day basis, mortars, machine guns, rocket launchers, anti-aircraft guns and SAMs. To anybody within earshot it would sound like a major battle being fought every day, and often at night, with rockets and tracer rounds arching across the sky.

Theoretically we were bound by peacetime safety regulations, but if we had followed them, 90 per cent of our live firing would have been forbidden. We fired and prayed that nobody would find out and that there would be no accident. Allah and General Akhtar were kind, as we got away with it — but only just. Once, when General Akhtar was with us watching the firing of Blowpipe and SA-7 SAMs against illumination mortar bombs floating down on their parachutes, I had to order cease fire when some PAF planes roared overhead. General Akhtar demanded to know why the Air Force was overflying the area. Had they not been warned? He was most upset when I explained the situation, and only with reluctance did he allow the shooting to continue. Within a few minutes more aircraft flew over and we had to abandon the firing. It took a long time to convince General Akhtar that we had no other option. Amazingly we never did have an accident.

We did, however, frequently have to move the camp because we thought its location had been compromised. If civilians wandered into the area we invented some story about an Army exercise with soldiers dressed as Mujahideen. We were gone by the next morning. These hasty moves were most disruptive and we had to have an alternative location already earmarked. Fortunately, the physical effort of dismantling tents was not great, so we could vacate a site quickly.

Another precaution we took was that, until late 1985, none of our training camps had any means of communicating with us. The use of a telephone was obviously totally insecure, and I was fearful of Soviet radio interception being able to pick up transmissions and pinpoint the sites. By the end of that year I had obtained secure radio sets from the CIA so they were installed at the camps. The story of these radios makes for an interesting slight digression.

One of the most vexing aspects of controlling guerrilla forces was the impossibility of communicating, quickly and securely, with scattered Commanders. I knew full well from the use we made of radio interception that insecure communications were worse than none at all. Messages by runner were inordinately slow, but normally they would eventually arrive, uncompromised.

I held many discussions with the CIA experts on this problem before we finally settled for two types of set. The long-range one was known as a 'burst communication' set with a range of over 1000 kilometres; the short-range one was called a 'frequency hopper' having a range of 30-50 kilometres. The technology of the burst sets was impressive. A message of 1000 words would take a few seconds to transmit, making it virtually impossible to decode. Operationally my intention was to locate the burst sets at Parwan (Hekmatyar), Paghman (Sayaf), Mazar-i-Sharif (Rabbani) and Kandahar (Khalis), with about ten frequency hoppers issued to the main Commanders of each Party. This would enable us to get in touch with all groups within 30-50 kilometres of the long-range sets. Other frequency hoppers would be positioned at the training camps. The Leaders agreed, so I pressed ahead. By the time the sets arrived they had changed their minds. Now they refused to pass any messages through another Party. They could not be moved. This forced me to revise the system to an entirely Party one, which was operationally most unsatisfactory.

We initiated long, 20-week radio courses for Party operators part of which included English language instruction. Late in 1985 the first batch went into the field in groups of four, with their sets. Regrettably, the only burst set that functioned was Hekmatyar's, in Parwan Province. For almost three years this radio remained in daily contact with us. Not so the others, who were out of touch for weeks, even months, at a time. There was nothing wrong with the sets, the fault lay with the operators and their Commanders.

There was just no control or discipline. Both operators on duty would absent themselves at the same time, or were too idle to maintain schedules. As we required these men to stay inside Afghanistan for up to a year at a stretch, with the set opened up daily on a pre-arranged schedule, which we knew would be unpopular, we paid each operator 1500 rupees monthly as an inducement. It was futile; only Hakmatyar's Commanders kept communications open. Once again a strongly fundamentalist Party had proved more efficient, so as more sets arrived it got priority, much to the annoyance of the CIA.

It would seem that we were successful in concealing the camps as we never experienced any security incident. Although the Soviet Ambassador to Pakistan went so far as to announce the supposed locations, he was not within 100 kilometres of any of them. They became part of the diplomatic game of denouncements and denials that went on for years, as the Soviets kept accusing Pakistan of supporting the Jehad and our government kept refuting it.

Each camp had a staff of 2-3 officers, 6-8 JCOs and 10-12 NCOs, assisted by about ten soldiers for administrative and guard duties. In most cases the medium of instruction was Pushtun, with a few instructors learning Dari (Persian). The problem of language was accentuated when we had Uzbeks who could not speak either. In this case our trainer taught in Pushtun, which was translated into Dari, and then another Uzbek put it into his own language. Cumbersome, but it seemed to work.

As the months passed our programme expanded to cater for a wide variety of both weapon training and tactical subjects. We set up a two-week heavy weapons course for anti-tank and anti-aircraft guns, and 82mm mortars; there was a mine-laying and lifting course; demolition courses to cover the destruction of bridges, electricity pylons, gas or oil pipelines, and road cratering; urban warfare, which was designed to teach sabotage techniques for use in Kabul or other cities; long communication courses; instructors' courses for Mujahideen and junior leaders courses. Most of these were held at the outdoor, tented camps. When we received the Blowpipes from Britain, and later the Stingers from the US, we opened up indoor facilities, which included simulators, at my headquarters at Ojhri camp. General Akhtar was initially adamant that no visitors should be allowed to any camp; however, the clamour from the CIA and the US was so persistent that eventually he conceded that CIA officials could be admitted. This concession was never given to Chinese or Saudi visitors, nor to US congressmen. The solitary exception was Senator Humphrey who was able to visit the Stinger school in 1987.

Like all our dealings with the Parties and Commanders, training was anything but straightforward. We had two major obstacles. First no Party would agree to joint training at a camp. They refused to allow courses of a mixture of trainees from various Parties, insisting that their Mujahideen should each have a separate course. The problems of planning, administration and waste of resources are self-evident. No appeal to reason could move them. This situation was not rectified until late in 1986.

The second difficulty never went away. It concerned the selection of Commanders for training. Most Party Leaders insisted that they should decide who came, whereas I knew their selection would seldom coincide with operational priorities. General Akhtar tended to support the Leaders in this when they spoke to him directly about their candidates for training. At the end of the argument the Leader would play his trump card, saying, 'I will not accept any responsibility if the Commanders selected by you sell their weapons, or fail to perform the tasks you give them'. I tried to persuade them that, although we should select them, we would not do so without

Party approval. Often this compromise failed to satisfy them as they were under strong pressure from politically influential Commanders for courses that would lead to more heavy weapons, a larger following, and therefore more power. My resources were limited, time was short and I wanted to train men who were reliable, vigorous, and whose area of operation contained suitable targets. It would be worse than useless to train a Commander in the tactics of rocket attacks on airfields, issue him the MBRLs, when his base was in the centre of the Hazarajat with no airfield within reach — but this is what some Leaders would have us do. The issue of weapons, and training in their use, were really one and the same. It resembled the 'chicken and egg' situation. Did we issue weapons and then train the recipients, or did we train selected Commanders before giving them the weapons? It did not really matter which came first, provided the process furthered the overall war strategy. At the end of the day I could never actually refuse to provide training to a Commander, some of whom would be summoned by their Party without my knowledge. They would complete a course but I would not issue them with long-range or special weapons, as I retained personal control over the allocation of these items. By the middle of 1985 my experience had given me the knack of picking a good Commander on our first meeting. I found that the smart, sophisticated and talkative man was seldom reliable, whereas the scruffy fellow in stinking clothes usually made an admirable leader. Not an infallible method of selection, but one I found to work nine times out of ten.

In 1984 we instituted a series of successful attacks on Bagram Air Base during which some twenty aircraft were destroyed on the ground. The story of how one of them was carried out illustrates the system of training and tactics working in practise.

Bagram was a well-protected base with a large garrison (see Map 10). It was primarily a Soviet base, with at least two Fighter Aviation Regiments from the Soviet Union with MiG-21s, MiG-23s, Su-25s and several An-26 transport aircraft. In addition, the Afghan Air Force deployed three fighter squadrons of MiG-21s, plus three fighter-bomber squadrons with Su-7s and Su-22s. The rows of planes parked on the tarmac were tempting targets on which to try out the 107mm Chinese MBRLs that had recently started arriving. Its heavyweight fire (it had twelve barrels) and range of 9 kilometres meant that it could be set up well outside the airfield's ring of defensive posts, with a good chance of hitting the closely parked planes or other vital facilities. It had been under attack earlier in the year as part of our efforts to distract the Soviets from their seventh Panjsher offensive, but this would be the first time we were able to mount long-range stand-off attacks.

Our operational conference agreed that Bagram merited sustained pressure and that Commanders should be selected and trained accordingly. Among the various Party Leaders and officials, I spoke to the Military Committee

Map 10

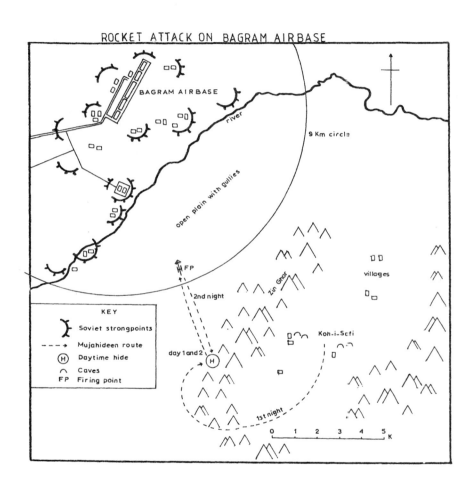

ROCKET ATTACK ON BAGRAM AIRBASE

BAGRAM AIRBASE

river

9 Km circle

open plain with gullies

FP

2nd night

Zin Ghar

villages

Koh-i-Scfi

day 1 and 2 (H)

KEY

) Soviet strongpoints

- - - → Mujahideen route

(H) Daytime hide

∩ Caves

FP Firing point

1st night

0 1 2 3 4 5
K

representative of Nabi's Party, who maintained a Mujahideen base some 15 kilometres to the SE of Bagram, near Koh-i-Safi. Between us we agreed on a suitable Commander who should bring thirty men with him for training. A messenger was despatched to Koh-i-Safi. There was then a wait of about five weeks, which was the time required for the messenger to reach his destination, the Commander to collect his men and for them all to arrive at Peshawar. I was then informed and would normally send my operations staff officer to conduct the preliminary interview and assessment.

My officer wanted to find out as much as possible about the man and his following. The Commander was photographed, he was queried on his Party affiliation, the exact location of his base, the extent of the area in which he operated, the strength of his force, details of the heavy weapons already issued, any previous training, and recent operations. Also, we wanted information on the other Commanders within a 50-kilometre radius of his base, and we asked if he was willing to cooperate with them. We built up a pen picture of the man, with an assessment of his potential. In this case we discussed his likely objective — Bagram — and received a favourable response. As the years passed we built up a library of information on individuals, and in most cases knew far more about the Commanders than their Party Leaders.

This particular commander had up to 400 men at his disposal, based around Koh-i-Safi where maximum use had been made of the numerous caves in the area to provide concealment and shelter from bombing. The base was screened from Bagram by a steep-sided ridge that rose in places to almost 6,000 feet. In this instance the Commander had followed instructions and only brought thirty men. So often they sought to impress us by bringing twice the number, causing grave problems as we could not train them all. On the specified night the Mujahideen were assembled at an RV at Peshawar where they boarded closed trucks to take them to the training camp. On arrival they had no idea where they were. They would remain for the 2-3 week course, before being driven out back to Peshawar in the same manner.

The thirty Mujahideen received intensive training on the handling and firing of the MBRL. The course was entirely practical, starting with assembling and disassembling, preparation of the rockets, estimated ranges, setting the bearing and elevation, loading and firing. They learnt that the MBRL was heavy, its main disadvantage, as it took three men to manpack its three components (wheels, stand and barrels) and this was only practical for short distances. For the Bagram operation mules would be necessary. They learned to make up gun teams of three, one aiming and setting, two loading, cranking (it was fired by a crank handle), and firing (by pressing a button). Although it had twelve barrels the rockets were fired singly, not in one broadside. They had to learn to spot the fall of shot and estimate whether it had gone too far, left or right, or short of the target. For this they used binoculars. Then they had to shout corrections — 'drop 100', 'up 300', or 'left 200' to the crew, so that adjustments could be made. They were becoming artillerymen.

They were also taught to improvise. The rockets could be fired electrically, using a makeshift bipod or support. In the field this usually meant propping them up on a pile of rocks, although against pinpoint targets the chances of a hit were small, but this method could be used against a barracks, airfield or fuel storage depot, for example.

While his men mastered the weapon itself, the Commander spent a lot of time with his training officer discussing tactics. The commander had to know the characteristics of the MBRL, how to divide his men into crews and the OP party, how best to site both so that they were concealed, with the MBRL in dead ground. He was taught that his tactics would normally be to move into a firing position in the dark, fire in the dark and withdraw under cover of darkness to a previously selected hide, if time did not permit a clean break before dawn. This procedure largely negated the Soviet control of the air. Not only were they reluctant to fly at night, but if they did so using flares their firing was always haphazard. The only problem was the near impossibility of spotting the fall of shot, particularly from level ground. Sometimes it was possible to fire a few rockets at night, use the following day to discover whether the target had been hit and, if not, make the adjustments and fire again the next night. Pinpoint accuracy was not so essential with area targets such as Bagram airfield.

Commanders were often surprised at the logistic and transport effort required to move these weapons and their ammunition. The MBRL, with its wheels and stand, could be carried by three mules, with another mule for every four rockets. For a mission involving firing thirty-six rockets (not an excessive number) from one MBRL, simple arithmetic told him he would need twelve mules. With crew, OP party, protection party and mule handlers, just to get one MBRL into action would require twenty to twenty-five men.

On this occasion my training officer and the Commander spent many hours pouring over aerial photographs and maps of the Bagram area looking for likely firing points and good approaches to them. Map 10 makes clear the tactical problems. Koh-i-Safi is 15 kilometres in a straight line from the Bagram runway, with the precipitous Zin Ghar ridge, which dominates the Bagram plain, only 2 kilometres to the NW. Although it gave excellent observation over a huge sweep of country up to the airfield itself, it could only be crossed, using mules, by one or two circuitous and steep footpaths to the west of Koh-i-Safi. The Commander was insistent that he knew this route well, and that the alternative, shorter route around the northern tip of the ridge would mean moving through a more populous area.

They had to get the MBRL to within 9 kilometres of the airfield, so a circle was drawn on the map, much as on Map 10. The firing point had to be inside this circle. Often circles with a 7·5 and 3 kilometre radius were also drawn. The object was to select two or three likely firing-point positions, measure distances and bearings to the target and record this information for the Commander. To my officer neither the photographs or the map suggested any satisfactory positions. The track from the Zin Ghar ridge led into the southern portion of the open Bagram plain, which seemed devoid of cover and sloped gently NW towards the airfield and the Soviet outposts. It was also criss-crossed with a confusion of paths and tracks making night-time navigation problematic. More importantly, the flatness and lack of cover over the area posed a serious security dilemma. Dawn or dusk would be likely to catch the maximum number of aircraft on the ground. If, however, the attack was launched just before first light there was the problem of getting away in daylight. A daytime hide would be needed to allow a full night for the final approach, firing and withdrawal. My officer pointed out that once Bagram came under fire it would be like kicking open a hornets' nest. The Soviets would respond with artillery and helicopter gunships within a matter of minutes. If they did so in daylight the chances of the Mujahideen reaching the cover of Zin Ghar, some six kilometres away, unscathed were remote. Better to take the risk of discovery in their hide by day by some wandering herdsman or traveller. The Commander agreed.

His local knowledge of the area led him to believe that a firing position offering cover for up to thirty men and mules could in fact be found in one of the small gullies that ran north towards the river that separated the plain from the villages and orchards east of the airfield. It would clearly have to be a two-night operation, with probably two days in a hide, one on the way out and another on the way back.

Thus were the planning and tactical problems discussed and decided upon by the Commander and his instructor. I was not gong to insist on a definite timetable for the task, but rather would leave it to the Commander's discretion, allowing him ample time to make a careful reconnaissance. Just before the end of the course, I visited the camp to chat with the Commander to satisfy myself that he was up to the mission. He had been given Bagram airfield as his first priority target, but that was not his only task. Alternative missions of lesser importance had also been planned, including rocket attacks on the airfield's perimeter posts, the garrison at Kalakan (Map 4), and at Mir Bach Kot on the Salang Highway. Initially I decided to give him one MBRL with 200 rockets of which fifty were smoke, for their incendiary capabilities. I assured him that I would increase this allocation if he succeeded with his attack on Bagram.

The Commander and his men should have left for the border at once, but there was a two-week delay while Nabi sorted out funds for the contractor's transport. Something like seventy-five animals were needed to get the

MBRLs, rockets and other ammunition carried in. I do not know the precise cost, but it would have exceeded $30,000.

By the time these men had reached Koh-i-Safi twelve weeks had elapsed since I first arranged for the messenger to fetch them. It would be another three before the attack was made. Four months from a plan's conception to its execution was about average for the distance from Pakistan. There had been no major hitch such as an arms shipment arriving late, a Soviet offensive, winter intervening, or simply not having enough money to keep the system moving.

The whole force had not moved to the operational base together. They had followed the normal tactical procedure of having an advance party moving about two hours ahead of the main body, travelling with the animals, which in turn preceded a small rear party. We advocated the Commander moving with the rear party to ensure the mules did not straggle and that all the weapons reached the base.

The operation took place as planned without mishap, and as shown on Map 10. The results were perhaps not as spectacular as we had hoped, in that only four aircraft were confirmed as destroyed, but it was only a small part of my co-ordinated efforts against Bagram. The highlight of the year came when Commander Niazi (from Hekmatyar's Party), who was later Shaheed, hit the main ammunition depot at Bagram. This went up with a most spectacular series of bangs. Reportedly, over 30,000 tons of ammunition were destroyed. I was able to see the devastation and count the burnt-out buildings on the satellite photograph.

Although the 107mm rocket attack was by far the most common Mujahideen tactic in Afghanistan, we at ISI attached a lot of importance to demolitions. The covert use of explosives is a time-honoured tactic of guerrillas, and we ran many such courses. The main targets, outside of Kabul, were the electricity pylon lines, the oil pipeline along the Salang Highway and the natural gas pipeline from Shibarghan to the Soviet border. When we called in Mujahideen for this type of training their course covered one of these targets only. The Commanders would specialize in destroying a particular facility, partly because this speeded up the training, and partly because few if any Commanders were within striking distance of more than one of these three utilities.

Electricity pylons were obviously vulnerable. The overhead lines formed a large triangle to the north and east of Kabul from the city east to Sarubi Dam, then NW to Jabal Saraj, then back to Kabul (see Map 13). We taught the Mujahideen to topple the pylons. The Soviets resorted to laying anti-personnel mines under them, so we instructed the Mujahideen to throw large stones underneath to set off any mines before laying the charges — a simple, but effective method. Our biggest success was in 1984 when we succeeded in destroying eighty pylons in one night in the Sarubi-Kabul sector. Kabul was plunged into darkness. The operation was filmed by some American journalists and later shown on television under the title Operation Blackout.

In chapter two I explained the reasons why such sabotage was not always popular with the Mujahideen. With the oil pipeline this reluctance was reinforced by the Soviets providing free fuel to villagers in some areas by installing taps on the pipe, which they were allowed to use. Not surprisingly, operations intended to destroy this facility could be unpopular, and no Commander wanted to antagonize his own supporters. Even if he was to operate in another area he could not do so without the authority of the local Commander, which was frequently withheld. Despite this, the oil pipeline was subjected to numerous successful attacks. The explosion would start a fire which could last anything from 1-30 minutes. Unfortunately the controls at the nearest pumping station automatically shut off the supply, thus limiting the damage and fire.

With the gas pipeline we trained the Mujahideen in a different technique. The pipe, unlike the oil one, was buried throughout its length, some three feet underground. It even went under, rather than over, the Amu River. Nevertheless, it was easy to locate as there was a small track on the surface that marked its route. The pipe was exposed by the use of a large manual auger (drill) which made a neat hole down to the pipe. In went the magnetic charge, up went the pipe. Again there would be a fire, but it was usually of short duration as the loss of pressure automatically sealed off the damaged section. In early 1985 I initiated a series of attacks which destroyed the pipe at a number of places. Reportedly, all the industrial units using gas were closed for two weeks. We also used rocket attacks on some natural gas facilities which, on one occasion, set two wells on fire. They burnt fiercely for days and could never be used again.

The scope and scale of what we were trying to achieve is, I hope, emerging. It was a question of deciding on the guerrilla strategy for the war, obtaining the means, the money and arms, and training countless thousands of Mujahideen in the tactics and techniques of a guerrilla battlefield. The task was gargantuan and made that much more onerous by the subject of the following chapter — feuding.

CHAPTER EIGHT

Feuding and Fighting

'Besides a common religion, Islam, only foreign invaders — from Alexander the Great to the British in the 19th century, and the Soviets in the 20th — have united the Afghans.'
Insight Magazine, 9 April, 1990

MY first full year in office, 1984, saw a dramatic escalation of the conflict on both sides. The Soviets launched their corps-sized Panjsher 7 offensive, joint Soviet/Afghan divisional operations were carried out in the Herat area, Paktia, and the Kunar Valley close to the Pakistan border. The growing effectiveness and use of Afghan troops was noticeable, as was the increasing reliance by the Soviets on heliborne manoeuvres. Their use of Spetsnaz special forces became more widespread, and their tactics bolder. Nevertheless, despite the press comments to the contrary, I believe the year ended in favour of the Mujahideen.

Although half of the Panjsher Valley was lost, elsewhere the Mujahideen were stronger, better organized, trained and equipped than in previous years. Those who suggested otherwise failed to grasp the overall military situation, due to a dearth of reliable information. The media coverage of the war was patchy. Unlike the Americans in Vietnam, the Soviets and Afghans did not release their losses to the press. Similarly, the Pakistan government refused to give official coverage of the campaign, steadfastly claiming that Pakistan was not involved. Only the handful of adventurous journalists who sometimes accompanied the Mujahideen in battle could provide authentic information, and even they, as I have pointed out in the Introduction, got it wrong at times. My sources, which included intercepted enemy radio transmissions, indicated Soviet losses in 1984 of between 4,000-5,000 killed or wounded, with their Afghan allies suffering some 20,000 casualties, including defections. Despite our lack of an adequate anti-aircraft weapon, the Soviets and Afghans lost more than 200 helicopters or aircraft (mostly on the ground), together with some 2,000 vehicles of all types, including tanks and APCs.

I felt that we now had the basis of an overall strategy for the prosecution of the war. We had a political Seven-Party Alliance in place. I was working with a Military Committee. The quantity of supplies being handled by the pipeline was increasing, training was expanding rapidly, and we had achieved some noticeable successes in the field. I was sure that we had more than matched the increased aggressiveness of our enemies. It was not the fighting that worried me so much as the feuding. I had now grasped the extent of this seemingly intractable problem and resolved to devote my efforts towards curbing its destructive aspects. At its worst feuding was civil war between the Mujahideen. During the eleven years of the Jehad hundreds of Mujahideen have died at the hands of their comrades-in-arms in different Parties, or under rival Commanders. I believe that getting feuding under some sort of control, although we never came near to eradicating it, by 1986-87 was a major factor in the Mujahideen being on the brink of a military victory when the Soviets withdrew in 1988-89. Now, sadly, internal feuding seems once again to be taking precedence over fighting the enemy. A recent example of the extremes to which feuding can divide and destroy the Mujahideen as an effective force, which involved two subordinate Commanders from different fundamentalist Parties, will illustrate my point.

On a cold, grey morning, with a little mist concealing most of the nearby mountains, a crowd of around 1,000 people had gathered to watch an execution. It was 24 December, 1989; the place was a small park in the town of Taloqan, provincial capital of Takhar, in northern Afghanistan. Four men were about to be hanged. Each had been a Mujahid; each had been found guilty by an Islamic court of murdering fellow Mujahideen belonging to a different Party from their own; each had been specifically sentenced to be hung rather than shot, the usual sentence for a soldier. Their leader was Sayad Jamal, a senior Commander of Hekmatyar's Party. With him walked his brother and two other prominent officers. They went to their deaths quietly. At the final moment they had nothing to say, although it was for them a particularly disgraceful way to die. The relatives of their victims had received special invitations to watch.

The executions were but another phase in a long-standing vendetta between rival Commanders. In mid-1989 Ahmad Shah Massoud, the so-called 'Lion of Panjsher', had been the victim of a bloody ambush by Jamal's followers which had killed thirty-six of his men, including seven of his best leaders and friends. The previous year both groups had attacked and cleared Taloqan, but had then divided the town into opposing camps. By the middle of 1989 a truce had been arranged and sealed by the reading aloud to each other by the Commanders of passages from the Holy Koran. The truce was only temporary. Whether or not Jamal was under direct orders from Hekmatyar to do what he did has never been established. Jamal led his men to Tangi Fakhar, where he positioned them at a gorge through which he knew many of Massoud's men would shortly travel. The ambush was highly successful. Thirty-six men died in a storm of automatic fire. They were the lucky ones. The others, who were captured, were gruesomely tortured before being killed.

Massoud spared no effort in seeking revenge. This was badal on a grand scale. Thousands of his Mujahideen combed the countryside rounding up suspects, but it took the offer of a reward of one million afghanis to produce Jamal and his brother. A tip-off led to a trap door in the floor of a house in Taloqan. In the basement below were the two ringleaders.

One of my first serious experiences of feuding and double-dealing came in early 1984, from a Commander operating in the area between Chaman and Kandahar, through which the main route from Quetta passed. The Commander concerned was a former captain in the Afghan Army called Asmat who had defected with his unit in 1981. He came from the Achakazai tribe located on either side of the Pakistan border, so enjoyed considerable popular support from that area. He had fought hard against the Soviets for a year or so, but then resorted to selling weapons, extortion and robbery to enrich himself. By the time I arrived at ISI we had ceased to supply him, although he still controlled a large force. In 1984 he started to interfere with the passage of Mujahideen supply caravans moving through his domain. His men would ambush small convoys and snatch their weapons, or demand arms in return for a safe passage. Other Mujahideen combined against him and serious fighting broke out as they sought to attack his base. Asmat fought well, casualties mounted on both sides, and it was some time before a ceasefire could be arranged. Asmat then turned his attention to our Pakistani government or embassy vehicles travelling on the Quetta to Kandahar road, demanding that arms supplies to him be resumed, or his men would kidnap embassy staff. This created panic in our Foreign Office and they turned to ISI for assurances of protection. General Akhtar summoned Asmat to Islamabad, where he apologized, professed ignorance of what his men were up to and promised such things would not recur. He was a cunning character, as he extracted a promise of arms supply provided he joined a Party. Gailani accepted him, which was unfortunate as I was at least obliged to give him small arms.

He came to me with a scheme to attack Kandahar airfield if only he could have heavy weapons. I responded that he could have them if his operation succeeded. It never happened. About then we started getting reports, and intercepting radio messages, that indicated Asmat was a KGB/KHAD agent. After long discussions as to what to do, General Akhtar agreed he should be arrested. Warrants were prepared when suddenly the Pakistan Army intelligence unit in the area got wind of what was to happen, and claimed Asmat was their man, playing a double role on their instructions. It must have shaken him because within a few days he disappeared – to Kabul.

This was in 1985. Some time later he reappeared in Kandahar as a brigadier tasked with securing the city from the Mujahideen. He bore a charmed life as none of the attempts by the Mujahideen to kill him succeeded. They tried blowing him up in his vehicle with a remote-control-detonated mine, and they tried mining the landing pad where his helicopter was due to touch down. Four or five plans failed. Even the Soviets soon found him more trouble than he was worth. He was a heavy drinker, which once led to his assaulting a senior Soviet officer in Kandahar. As time went on his men established a covert 'live and let live' understanding with the Mujahideen. Eventually he was recalled to Kabul and stripped of his importance. Never being a man to give up easily, Asmat started sending us messages that if he was pardoned he would return to Pakistan after causing substantial damage of the Soviets. I had absolutely no faith in Asmat's promises, although I had a sneaking regard for the man's gall and could not deny his physical courage.

A year later it was again the Kandahar sector that produced further serious feuding. At this time Hekmatyar's Party predominated in the Provinces of Kandahar, Zabul, Helmand and Farah, but unfortunately major differences arose between some Commanders and their Party representative at Quetta over arms allocations. In their pique, several joined other Parties, which in turn infuriated Hekmatyar who demanded they return all the weapons that he had issued to them. This led to the Commanders concerned, under Mohammed Khan, establishing their own independent base on the border, partly in Pakistan, and waylaying Hekmatyar's supply columns. To counter these activities Hekmatyar set up a strong base inside Afghanistan under Commander Janbaz, and a series of armed skirmishes took place between the two. Some of the fighting occurred in Pakistan which caused us acute embarrassment.

Both Mohammed Khan and Janbaz maintained a following of around 1000 Mujahideen each, which meant our efforts in the area against the real enemy were seriously diminished. Hekmatyar wanted to launch a full-scale attack on Mohammed Khan to drive him out of Pakistan, and we seriously considered using the Pakistan Army to do the same. Both options were equally humiliating. Then came allegations that both Commanders were smuggling drugs into Pakistan to help finance their bases, which was quite likely as Helmand Province is one of the largest poppy-growing regions in Afghanistan.

All our efforts to find an amicable solution failed, primarily because of the covert support Mohammed Khan was receiving from other Parties. It took months before I managed to get this support withdrawn, but by then the damage was done. This feud adversely affected the combat capabilities of Hekmatyar's Party in the Quetta sector. It never fully recovered.

The front line of the eastern provinces was the 100-kilometre Kunar Valley which paralleled the Pakistan border at a distance of 10-12 kilometres (see

Map 11). At its base stood Jelalabad, the headquarters of the Soviet 66th MRB and Afghan 11th Division. Half-way up the valley was Asadabad, with the Afghan 9th Division. At the head, almost within rifle range of the frontier, was Barikot with its Afghan garrison of the 51st Brigade. At all the intervening villages the Afghans had constructed defensive posts. Asmar, some 25 kilometres NE of Asadabad, housed the 31st Mountain Brigade and a battalion of Spetsnaz. Such was the importance of the valley to our enemies.

Although there were large numbers of enemy troops deployed in the Kunar Valley, they were, for the most part, bottled up in their forts. The Mujahideen had the perfect sanctuary of Pakistan within a short distance of the valley road and river, and their border bases completely dominated the valley throughout its length. Most Afghan posts were under semi-siege, with the Mujahideen controlling the road, and thus the movement of supplies by truck to maintain the garrisons. All the dominating heights belonged to Pakistan, and we had reason to thank the colonial administrator, Durand, who had so long ago drawn his line with such tactical insight.

Barikot was a typical example of scores of similar Afghan garrisons that fronted the border. Its ground supply line was in the hands of the Mujahideen, it was surrounded by hostile forces, looked down on from every direction, yet it survived. In theory all these forts could be replenished by air if land links were cut, and indeed some were, but the number of such posts, coupled with their isolation in narrow valleys, effectively prevented this type of supply, except for short periods in real emergencies. So how did they feed themselves? The answer lies in yet another of the perversities of the war — they were supplied by local tribesmen from inside Pakistan.

Many Pakistani tribesmen liked to have a foot in both camps. Thousands participated in the Jehad and supported the Mujahideen, but these same people could just as easily give succour to the enemy if there was profit to be had. They found the war provided a variety of additional ways to make money. One of these was the smuggling of food into Afghanistan for sale to the garrisons of border posts. Pulses, flour, cooking oil, rice and items such as petrol, diesel and kerosene for stoves or lamps were purchased by these isolated posts on a regular basis. They came to rely on this source of supply to survive. Even the concrete bunkers at some forts were constructed with cement and iron bars brought direct from Pakistan. On many occasions they bartered arms or ammunition for the goods. There was little we could do to stop it as the Mujahideen supply caravans had to pass through the tribal area, and if the local people were antagonized they would close these routes. The tribes owned transport which was immune from Mujahideen attack, thus rendering them of great value as vehicles to hire to the Afghan Army. With the passage of time, this hiring by the Afghan authorities of tribally-owned buses and lorries became the accepted way of getting some supplies to the more inaccessible posts. These people also did a brisk trade in the sale of

Map 11

THE KUNAR VALLEY OFFENSIVE - SPRING 1985

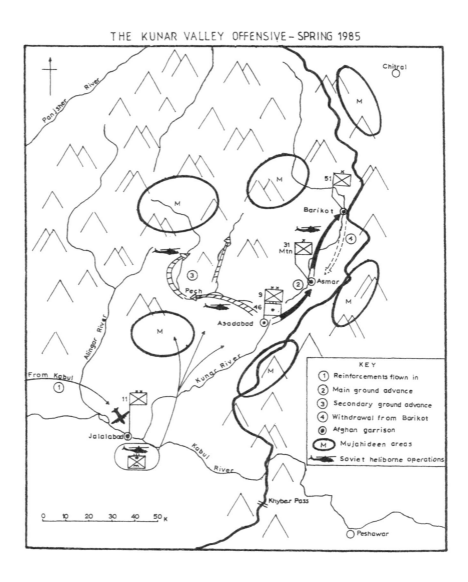

KEY

1 Reinforcements flown in
2 Main ground advance
3 Secondary ground advance
4 Withdrawal from Barikot
⊙ Afghan garrison
M Mujahideen areas
Soviet heliborne operations

arms in Pakistan which they received from KHAD agents, whom they had a habit of harbouring for reasons of financial gain. I would say that these tribes were the people who made the most out of the war, yet they blamed the refugees for ruining their economy.

It was an extraordinary situation in an extraordinary war. On the one hand the Pakistan government was providing full support to the Mujahideen, while on the other thousands of its citizens provided substantial logistic support to its Afghan enemies, enabling them to continue the fight. Militarily, I am convinced that if these Pakistani tribesmen had not sustained our enemy in this way no Afghan post could have endured within 50 kilometres of the frontier.

In January, 1985, we were caught by surprise when the Afghans took to the offensive up the Kunar Valley to relieve Barikot (see Map 11). It was winter, so we had wrongly supposed the Soviets would not take to the field with a major operation, which in turn meant that the Mujahideen bases along the valley, and in the side valleys to the west, were not strongly held. Barikot was still besieged, but with much smaller and less aggressive forces than would have been the case in summer. We had received no warning via satellite.

The enemy task force was under Colonel Gholam Hazrat, the 9th Division commander. He controlled brigades from his own and the Jalalabad-based 11th Division, supplemented by the 46th Artillery Regiment and the 10th Engineer Regiment, whose primary task was road-maintenance and improvement. The Soviet contribution was a single air-assault regiment. The attackers improved on their Panjsher tactics. Armour spearheaded the columns, aerial bombardment flattened the villages to demoralize and disperse the civilian inhabitants, heliborne units seized important heights in advance of the ground thrust, and the same techniques were used up the side valleys such as the Pech. These methods met with success as resistance was thin, a number of small Mujahideen bases were taken, and we could not assemble reinforcements from the refugee camps quickly enough to stop the enemy reaching Barikot.

This offensive was blown up to be a resounding defeat for the Mujahideen. Press, radio and television reports publicized the relief of Barikot as proof that the guerrillas were on the run. Colonel Gholam Hazrat was promoted brigadier.

In fact the Afghans had only remained at Barikot for 12 hours. We rushed reinforcements forward to harass the enemy's lines of communication, particularly around the bases at Asmar and Asadabad. There were several fierce clashes with rearguards, supported by bombers, helicopter gunships and artillery. We kept up the pressure as far as Jalalabad. Nevertheless, I had been disappointed with the Mujahideen's efforts, and I held a detailed postmortem on what had gone wrong, apart from our being surprised. My enquiries revealed that rivalry and feuding were at least partially to blame. The Kunar Valley between Asmar and Barikot was the responsibility of Commanders belonging to Khalis' party, and they had not cooperated in resisting this offensive. In particular, Haji Mir Zaman, who had been tasked with road-cratering and mining operations, had failed to perform, giving, with a look of injured innocence, as his excuse that he needed the valley road open to the enemy so that his men could capture rations and weapons to supplement their own stocks which were low. Some of his fellow Commanders dubbed Mir Zaman as a KHAD agent, so I was forced to investigate his activities thoroughly. Although the charges could not be proved, it was clear that such suspicions and accusations did not augur well for coordinated efforts in the Kunar. The whole episode was typical of the difficulties we faced in conducting joint operations, and the amount of time and effort that was wasted trying to sort out Mujahideen feuds rather than devoting our energies to the fighting.

I quickly found that a large proportion of my time was spent travelling by car or plane. I had to be in Peshawar for several days every week meeting Party Leaders, visiting warehouses, or having discussions with the Military Committee. It was through the members of this committee that I sought to influence events in the field, to get cooperation between Commanders, sort out supply problems, arrange training, or investigate allegations of illegal arms sales.

With this last matter it is of interest to note that the buying and selling of weapons was probably second only to the drug trade as a lucrative business in the border areas. It had been so for 200 years. The town of Darra, south of Peshawar, has what must surely be the biggest open arms market in the world. There are at least 100 shops where a buyer can get anything from rifles to mortars. In 1980 the cost of an AK47 was $1500, but with the glut of weapons brought about by the war it had plummeted to $750 by 1987. Much larger sums would change hands for a modern machine gun, or the latest Soviet AK74 rifle. The temptation to sell weapons supplied by ISI was enormous.

I also had to visit Quetta at least every six weeks, and the border areas and Afghanistan itself as frequently as possible if I was to keep my finger on the pulse of what was happening. Then there were the innumerable trips down the road to Islamabad for conferences or to discuss problems with General Akhtar.

It was mostly through the Military Committee that I attempted to disentangle the feuding or organize the fighting. At the start, committee members themselves were distrustful and silent, refusing to speak on any matters of importance in front of their colleagues from other Parties. Gradually, very gradually, their reserve melted as far as general discussions were concerned, but, despite our efforts, none was prepared to debate their own future plans in our meetings. For that I had to talk to each member separately. Infinite patience would be, I thought, the key to getting things done in Afghanistan. This meant that tact and time were to be the ingredients of success, with no shouting, no anger, no bullying and no threatening. I was careful to treat each representative as an equal, although I usually chaired the formal meetings. At the end of every month each member had to give a résumé of the operations conducted by his Party. In turn we briefed them on the military situation in Afghanistan, based on reports from the CIA and other friendly intelligence agencies, together with intercepted radio messages. I found the fact that representatives had to account for the activities of their Mujahideen in front of colleagues from other Parties had a salutary effect on the accuracy of their reporting. It gave everybody an opportunity to judge the worth of his comrades.

Every four months or so I would receive a message that a 'Grand Bonanza' was to be held on such and such a date. In our language of double talk this meant President Zia would be holding his quarterly conference with the seven Party Leaders. Also in attendance would be General Akhtar, the Foreign Minister (usually), myself, and an interpreter. It was a highly secret meeting at which the top political leaders of Pakistan, with their military advisers, met the men who were responsible for the conduct of the Jehad. In view of the Pakistani government's repeated denials that it was controlling and supplying the war, absolutely no knowledge of these meetings could be allowed beyond a handful of individuals. Elaborate precautions were taken to preserve security.

I would arrange for the Leaders to be brought by car, with ISI officers as escorts, to a safe house in Rawalpindi where cars were changed. They were then driven to General Akhtar's house. Once everybody had arrived, Akhtar personally drove his own car to the President's house, which was only 600 metres away, to fetch him. We had deployed armed guards in civilian clothes in vehicles around the area, as Zia came to these gatherings alone, with no bodyguards, no military secretary and no ADC. He never even told these close personal assistants where he would be.

These occasions were of paramount importance, in that the President would re-emphasize that, although he was committed to supporting the Jehad, it could only succeed with understanding and cooperation by the Parties. Zia always heavily underlined the basic truth that success in the fighting would follow a cessation of feuding. The Foreign Minister would explain progress with negotiations between himself and the Soviet Union within the UN, and seek their views. Each Leader gave a report of his Party's war efforts or difficulties. The meeting normally ended with the President's thanks and dinner.

If a 'Grand Bonanza' was primarily concerned with political affairs, with reassuring the Leaders of Pakistan's political backing and loyalty, a 'Bonanza' was related more to military matters, stressing the importance of tactical collaboration on the battlefield. It was a forum for the leaders to meet with General Akhtar and myself, held every four to six weeks, to discuss a specific agenda. It covered the operational situation, future plans, and the logistics situation. In addition I would aim to meet each Leader individually once every seven weeks. These face-to-face encounters were critical to the build-up of confidence between us, as they all felt less inhibited than at the general meeting.

In the middle of 1984 General Akhtar ordered me to review the prevailing military situation in Afghanistan and to highlight the weak areas of Mujahideen activities. My attention was drawn to the northern provinces. It was quickly obvious that they had not been receiving the attention that their strategic importance merited. These provinces bordered the Soviet Union; the enemy's main lines of communication passed through them, as did the Soviet's oil for the war effort. From Jozjan Afghanistan's natural gas was piped north under the Amu River, and I was alarmed at the Soviet's efforts to exploit the traditional rivalry between the Pushtuns and the Uzbeks and Tajiks of this region. It did not escape my notice that somehow the northern provinces were not getting a share of arms and money commensurate with their operational importance.

Apart from my suspicions that ethnic rivalries were at the root of the problem, there were a number of other explanations put forward. The long distances involved meant higher transportation costs; neither ourselves nor the Parties had detailed information as to the effectiveness of Commanders, or the location of many of their bases; in some areas the terrain was unfavourable and evacuation of casualties to Pakistan was almost impossible, while the Mujahideen had no medical facilities.

At the next ISI's quarterly conference I asked General Akhtar for a special quota of arms for the northern provinces to fill the vacuum, but he did not agree. I was not disappointed for long as within a few days he telephoned me with the go-ahead, so I immediately launched a crash programme for training and supply to the north. It was an ambitious plan which I tried to implement before the onset of winter. This necessitated cutting corners. We were compelled to train, and arm with heavy-weapons, Commanders we knew little about. Some reliable Commanders would not reach Pakistan for training time, and so missed the programme and did not receive the extra weapons. These things created more misunderstandings between Commanders and Parties; feuding and bickering was once again hampering the fighting.

During the next meeting I briefed General Akhtar on what I was doing, but he was far from happy with my sending such a large proportion of weapons to the north. He saw it as detracting from maintaining the pressure on Kabul. Nor did he like my violation of his policy that we should not train Mujahideen in their own bases. I had had to confess to doing both in my haste to produce results quickly. He ordered me to cease using these locations immediately.

General Akhtar had been correct. For one thing, in my rush for results, I had been ignoring security. To train Mujahideen in insecure bases was risking our support becoming common knowledge, as, despite our precautions, these places were full of informers. This was particularly so with the refugee camps.

Refugee camps shelter over three million people. There are more than 350 of them, administered by Pakistani officials with assistance from the UN High Commissioner for Refugees. Camps originally intended to house 10,000 are occupied by 100,000, with one holding 125,000, making it the largest concentration of refugees anywhere in the world. They are squalid places, teeming with humanity. Overcrowding has put impossible strains on rudimentary water, sanitation, and medical facilities. Refugees arrive weak and exhausted, many are sick or wounded, all are virtually destitute. A massive influx of aid in terms of money, food and materials is required to cope with what amounts to half of the world's refugees.

Our interest in the camps was that they provided a safe refuge from the war for the families of the Mujahideen, who could fight in Afghanistan in the knowledge that their relatives were immune from reprisals. They also acted as places to which the Mujahideen could return for a rest and to see their families without compromising themselves. Also, inside these camps was a huge reservoir of potential recruits for the Jehad. Thousands of young boys came to the camps as refugees, grew up, and then followed their fathers and brothers to the war.

But the camps had their disadvantages as well. They became a prime target for Soviet subversion. As they grew in number and size, so did the strain they put on the hospitality of the local population. The refugees took both land and business from tribal owners and traders. Their popularity with many Pakistanis was brief, and the subsequent build-up of hostility was exploited by the hundreds of KHAD agents who infiltrated the camps. It became an important Soviet objective to foster discord between the refugees and the Pakistanis. The more the violence, the more the hatred, the greater the pressure on our government to reduce its support for the Jehad. These camps and their inhabitants were used by our enemies as a means of increasing the feuding within Pakistan. We at ISI sought to use them to sustain the fighting.

Our problems were exacerbated by the rampant corruption in every camp. I will illustrate this through the experiences of a Mujahid called Farid Khan (not his real name) who fled from Kabul with his family in 1984. Their first difficulty was in obtaining registration documents. Without registration there can be no passbook for the head of the family, and without this Farid could receive no aid. Possession of a passbook would entitle Farid to a monthly ration of wheat, oil, sugar, tea, dried milk and, sometimes, a small subsistence allowance of cash amounting to 50 rupees per person, up to a maximum of 350 rupees (about $21). This was where Farid's frustrations started. The slow, bureaucratic process of registration can take months, during which time refugees must hang around the fringes of the camps, the lucky ones relying on relatives who are registered. Some never register at all. The only way to cut the delays is to pay the requisite bribe to one of the Pakistani officials. To be employed in the camps is popular, as the opportunities to lord it over people in desperate poverty and supplement salaries with dishonest practices are legion.

Farid eventually got his passbook, which permitted him to pitch a tent in a camp located on barren waste ground, but, as he quickly discovered, it did not guarantee all his entitlements. For example, the issue of milk, sugar, or tea was somehow always unavailable. If Farid wanted these items, as he bitterly complained, he was obliged to buy them on the black market. It was one of the Pakistanis' perks to be able to withhold rations to sell. This was made easy by officials being able to draw food and money for non-existent refugees.

One particular racket that Farid experienced had a detrimental effect on our recruitment of Mujahideen replacements. If a head of family was absent from the camp for any reason the passbook was cancelled, making the dependants ineligible for further assistance. This happened when Farid went to join the Jehad. While he was away the officials made one of their periodic checks by counting heads. Farid was listed as missing and his passbook withdrawn. It cost his wife 500 rupees to get it back. Of course the camp officials continued to use the confiscated passbooks to draw rations — for sale.

Much of the misery of life was caused by health hazards related to the water supply and pollution. The water ration of 6½ gallons a day per person was seldom available as the tube wells were too few, while the water trucks were often broken down, and always late — unless you kept the driver happy. Diseases are endemic, as sanitation is frequently non-existent, with everybody using the surrounding fields as one vast communal latrine. Malaria, measles, tetanus, typhoid, diarrhoea and tuberculosis are but a few of the sicknesses that plague most camps.

It is the women who suffer the worst. Eighty per cent of the refugees in the camps at any one time are women and children. Many are widows. For the first time in their lives they must fend for themselves when they are suffering from shock, depression and grief. Into these hotbeds of suffering and squalor the Afghan secret police, KHAD, sends its female agents to intimidate and subvert. Farid's wife had first-hand experience of their methods. At first she did not realize the young woman who befriended her was an agent, but slowly it dawned on her that the woman's persistent railing and complaining about the Jehad was aimed at subverting her. Her 'friend' would continually protest at the suffering caused by the war, at the disgraceful conditions in the camps, emphasizing how the Mujahideen were dying while their political leaders lived a life of luxury around Peshawar, driving cars, spending money and seldom exposing themselves to danger. 'We are not fighting a Jehad,' she would say, 'we are fighting each other, Afghan against Afghan. This is not a Jehad, but a war between foreign superpowers. Our men die for America or the Soviet Union.'

Agents would also do their utmost to stir up Pakistanis against the refugees. It was not hard to create hostility, even hatred. They would make a sweeping gesture with their arms, saying, 'Before the war this was your land; now all these foreigners camp on it. They take away your business, your grazing rights, they are the cause of rising inflation. They will soon outnumber you in your own province. It is these wretched refugees that cause the water shortages. Why does Pakistan spend so much to support them? They should return to Afghanistan.'

After a few weeks it became obvious to Farid's wife that her companion was working for KHAD so she reported her to a camp official who in turn had her arrested by the police. The end of the problem? Not a bit of it, as within 24 hours she was back again. She had been well able to afford the 250 rupees which was the going rate for the police to forget the charges.

By the end of 1985, which had seen some of the fiercest fighting of the war, I remained confident that the Mujahideen were still holding their own. Except around Kabul, where the situation was worsening for reasons to be explained in chapter nine, the Mujahideen had not suffered any major setbacks. This was despite greatly increased pressure from the Soviets, and the improved performance of the Afghan Army.

The best-coordinated offensive, and most dangerous to ourselves, was the August/September Paktia operation. It involved an elaborate pincer movement, aimed at the Mujahideen bases just west of the Parrot's Beak, by an armoured column from Kabul moving up the Logar Valley, and another advancing SW from Jalalabad. At the end of August the enemy force around Khost moved against our forward bases at Ali Khel and Zhawar, only a few kilometres from the Pakistan frontier. There was bitter fighting before these attacks petered out. Although this Paktia offensive cost us casualties, and the loss of several supply dumps, we did not suffer as severely as the Soviet propaganda and press would have had the world believe. As in 1984, foreign journalists proclaimed that the Mujahideen were on the run, that the Soviets were coming close to a military victory and that the Kabul régime was secure.

I did not share this view. 1985 had seen some spectacular Mujahideen successes. In June Massoud, in the Panjsher Valley, seized the heavily defended post at Peshghor which was held by a battalion of 500 men, supported by ten mortars, four 76mm guns, two T-55 tanks and five BTR-60 APCs, all protected by sandbagged bunkers, mines and barbed wire. The attackers breached the minefields during darkness, to storm the place at dawn under cover of rocket and heavy machine-gun fire. Resistance was quickly subdued and among the corpses was the Afghan Central Corps Chief of Staff, Brigadier Ahmaddodin. Over 450 prisoners were taken, including five visiting colonels from Kabul.

Also in June we had stepped up our efforts around Kandahar airfield. Rocket attacks on aircraft on the ground were so successful that the Soviets were forced to move the bulk of their planes to Lashkargah and Shindand bases. Lashkargah was developed into their alternative airfield for Kandahar. Our ambushes on the main road leading to Kandahar became so frequent and effective that a by-pass route had to be developed in order to get transport to the city.

In the northern provinces our attacks were gaining momentum, and barges were now being sunk on the Amu River. If our efforts at training, increasing the quality and quantity of supplies and persuading the Mujahideen Leaders and Commanders to spend less time feuding and more fighting the enemy had not been successful, I have little doubt that 1985 would have seen the collapse of the Jehad. Instead, the Mujahideen withstood all that the Soviets could throw at them, despite the grave imbalance in numbers and weaponry. Not that I was overconfident. I was fearful of the effect on our supply system of the Soviets' scorched-earth tactics that deprived the guerrilla of his local source of food and shelter; there was a real need for a light, but long-range rocket-launcher to supplement the heavy MBRLs; the lack of reliable, modern radio communications to important Commanders inside Afghanistan was a major handicap; and without an effective SAM to supplement the SA-7 I despaired of ever being able to defeat the helicopter gunship. But my real worry was Kabul.

CHAPTER NINE

Kabul, the Key

'Kabul must burn.'
Lieutenant-General Akhtar Abdul Rehman Khan, Director of Inter-Services
Intelligence, Pakistan, 1980-1987.

IN the twenty months from April, 1978, to the Soviet invasion of
Afghanistan in December, 1979, Kabul was surely the coup capital of the
world. In that short period no less than three bloody coups took place in the
city. During those months tens of thousands of Afghans died in perhaps the
most murderous purges since Stalin's day. As always Kabul was at the centre
of the bloodbath, with its brand new jail at Pul-i-Charki, 10 kilometres east
of the city, becoming the primary site for executions and torture. Whoever
controlled Kabul controlled Afghanistan, both in the eyes of its people and
the world.

For centuries the palace and throne of Afghan kings had been in Kabul,
until royal rule was abruptly overthrown by King Zahir Shah's cousin,
Daoud Khan, in 1973. But within five years Daoud was showing disturbing
signs of independence from his Soviet masters in Moscow. Things came to
a head in 1977 when, during a visit to the Kremlin, Daoud had a flaming
row with Brezhnev, literally banging his fists on the table, while yelling that
Afghans made the decisions in Afghanistan. Fury showed on the Soviet
President's face. Daoud had signed his own death warrant. At 9.00 am on
27 April, 1978, a group of young Marxist officers led an armoured and air
attack on the Arg Palace in the city centre, where Daoud and his family lived
surrounded by the 1,800-strong Presidential Guard. The coup got off to a
slow, unsteady start at Kabul airport. By afternoon the palace was being
strafed by MiG-21s and Su-7s, but was holding out; that evening Radio
Kabul fell; but not until 4.00 am on the 28th did Daoud die, with his family,
in the rubble of the palace.

The Soviets had to choose who would be the most amenable puppet to
install. The choice was complicated by the fact that the Afghan Communist
Party was split. Like the Mujahideen, these Marxists were first and foremost
Afghans subject to the same propensity for infighting, violence and tribal

rivalries. The Afghan communists were, and still are, divided into two factions. In 1978 the Parcham faction was led by Babrak Karmal and the Khalq group by Nur Mohammad Taraki. Brezhnev picked Taraki as he had met him once and 'was sure he would do a good job'. Taraki's first act was to get rid of his rival, Karmal, by appointing him ambassador in Prague. Then he set about killing Karmal's supporters, many of whom were KGB agents. Afghanistan was now officially a communist state.

Within a month an armed resistance movement started. In Kabul red replaced green as the national colour. A huge demonstration was organized to watch the raising of the red flag and the release of scores of pigeons decorated with red ribbons. Public buildings were painted red, while shopkeepers and householders in Kabul vied with each other to display the largest portrait of Taraki, or have their doors and windows the brightest shade of red. By the spring of 1979 stocks of paint were exhausted. But most Kabulis, indeed most Afghans who professed to be followers of the new faith, were radish communists, red on the outside and white within. Their feverish decorating was inspired by fear rather than political conviction.

The bulldozers were hard at work in the fields outside Pul-i-Charki jail, excavating mass burial pits as execution squads did a brisk business. It was later alleged by witnesses that thirty huge holes were dug. Each was the grave of some 100 prisoners who, with hands tied, were pushed into the pits at night, then buried alive when the bulldozers filled the graves.

In February, 1979, the US Ambassador, Dubs, was shot dead in a Kabul hotel as previously related. The next month saw the mass mutiny of the 17th Division of the Afghan Army at Herat, coupled with the slaughter and dismemberment of Soviet citizens in that city. By then even Brezhnev was having doubts as to the wisdom of picking Taraki. He dispatched the ideological head of the Red Army, General Alexei Yepishev, with six other generals, on a fact-finding mission to Kabul. He was severely shaken by what he saw. The indiscriminate killings were driving the people into the rapidly growing resistance movement, the Afghan Army was on the point of collapse, and Taraki would not listen to his Soviet mentors. A plot was hatched in the Kremlin that Amin, the Prime Minister, should take over the presidency from Taraki. According to KGB sources, this was against their advice as they were suspicious of Amin's student days in the US, at Columbia University, even suspecting he had links with the CIA. Once again Brezhnev overruled them. Taraki was summoned to Moscow for consultations, while in Kabul Amin prepared to pounce. Shortly after Taraki's return, Amin had him seized, tied to a bed and suffocated with a cushion. That was in September, 1979.

Within weeks it was apparent that Brezhnev had made yet another blunder. Amin began to renege on promises made to Moscow. He demanded that Soviet advisers be recalled; he protested against KGB activities; he did nothing to combat the uprising against communism that was taking hold in all provinces. The KGB, who had advised against his appointment, were given the task of removing Amin. An agent, who was at that time one of Amin's chefs, was given the job of poisoning him. But as Amin kept switching his food and drink this method proved difficult. The Politburo lost patience and opted for a full-scale invasion, preceded by a KGB-organized coup that would kill him. In late December, 1979, the Christmas coup took place with Amin dying in Darulaman Palace under the guns of the KGB commandos who had stormed the building. They were under orders' that nobody should survive, and had had a tough, room-by-room fight against Amin's guards. As their commander, Colonel Bayerenov, who was in Afghan uniform, left the palace, supposedly to call up reinforcements, the edgy troops outside shot him dead as well. Soviet divisions were pouring over the Amu and landing at Kabul airport. The invasion was underway, the Jehad was about to start, and Babrak Karmal finally secured his place in the President's palace.

I have deliberately described the events in Kabul immediately preceding the Soviet occupation of the city in some detail, as it is important to understand Kabul's significance to Afghanistan and to the Jehad. Kabul, as the capital, is the hub of political, educational, economic, diplomatic and military activity. Within its confines are the government ministries, the university and technical colleges, foreign embassies and the headquarters of the Afghan Army and its Central Corps. From Radio Kabul and the television studios the ruling régime can manipulate the news, disseminate propaganda and issue its decrees.

Like Rome, in the days of the Roman empire, all roads in Afghanistan eventually lead to Kabul. It sits at the centre of a wheel, whose spokes are the roads and valleys fanning out in all directions. To the north the Salang Highway takes traffic to the Amu, and the Panjsher valley splits the Hindu Kush. In the east Route I carries the traveller along the Kabul River, through Jalalabad, and over the Khyber Pass to Peshawar. Several lesser roads to the SE reach the passes over the mountains into the Parachinar peninsula and, via Gardez and Khost, to Miram Shah in Pakistan. The long 'ring road', built by the Americans, heads south to Ghazni, Kandahar and, eventually, to Herat some 650 kilometres west of Kabul. Even to the immediate west of the city numerous lesser valleys and trails wriggle their way into the mass of mountains that form the Hazarajat. Kabul has great strategic importance. As we at ISI appreciated, so long as a communist government controlled Kabul it controlled the nerve centre of the country. To win the war we had not only to push the Soviets out of Afghanistan, but also to eject the Afghan communists from Kabul. Only with the Mujahideen ensconced in the capital would the world recognize our victory. Such was General Akhtar's belief, such was our objective. In order to achieve it Kabul had to burn.

Kabul's pre-war population was 750,000, but with the ever-increasing Soviet devastation of the countryside refugees poured in. By 1985 some 2 million people were crammed into its confines, or camped in tents on its outskirts. Add to these the influx of tens of thousands of Soviet and Afghan soldiers, and some idea of the resultant strain on all facilities can be imagined. Fifteen people in a 30-square-feet room was common; water and power supplies were erratic; the sewers stank; people lived in constant fear of the midnight knock on the door as KHAD agents abounded; Pul-i-Charki prison, built for 5000, had over 20,000 within its walls.

Everybody had to carry identity cards at all times, every street had its checkpoints at which security personnel scrutinized papers. A curfew cleared the city, except for police and military patrols, between 10.00 pm and 4.00 am, although few people were not home by eight. Movement into and out of Kabul was rigidly restricted. Even diplomats were issued with a map marked with a large red circle with a radius of 10 kilometres from the city centre. This was the furthest they could travel.

Afghan troops in their sand-coloured uniforms and pillbox caps, and Soviet soldiers in olive drab and wide-brimmed floppy hats manned security posts at all government or military buildings. Some installations were sand-bagged, and the Indian Embassy had taped its windows against blast. Telephones were tapped, while at the Post Office everybody was body searched before they could buy a stamp. Huge revolutionary posters were plastered to walls, while loudspeakers in the streets ensured everybody heard the latest political proclamation. Food was always scarce, particularly fruit and vegetables. Staples such as flour, bread, sugar and vegetable oil were sold at subsidized prices, but quantities were limited. The 100 tons of flour distributed daily, half to the bakers and half to the public, did not go far among two million mouths. The price of petrol rose weekly, although communist party officials were cushioned against the soaring cost of living by being allowed to buy at special cheap rates.

Strangely, stores were still full of luxury western consumer goods, which the Soviet troops snapped up if they could afford them. For the average Kabuli, who earned some 3000 afghanis a month, buying such items could only be dreamt about. A small refrigerator cost a year's salary, a colour TV two year's, and a Toyota car 27. Some sought to forget their sorrows in drink. A new distillery had been constructed for vodka, brandy and wine. Drunks in Kabul's bazaars were now common. It was all part of the communists' anti-Islam campaign, which went to the extent of forcing Afghan Army conscripts to drink alcohol.

Well over half the population inside Kabul supported the Jehad, if not in practical ways then at least by their hatred of the Soviets, and indifference to their Afghan allies. Although fear pervaded the city, many of its people were Mujahideen who risked their own and their families' lives daily by carrying out acts of sabotage, passing on information, or giving shelter to those on the run. Despite the tightening of security, despite the use of terror and torture, we always had active supporters in Kabul throughout the war. Our problem was how to bring about the collapse of communism without resorting to a direct military assault, which the Mujahideen could not hope to mount successfully with the Soviet Army occupying the city.

Our strategy had three features. First, there was a concerted effort on my part to coordinate attacks aimed at cutting off Kabul from supplies or facilities coming from outside the city. This involved ambushes on convoys on roads leading to Kabul, the mining of dams that provided its water, or cutting its power lines.

Next was sabotage and assassination from within. I always emphasized that our targets were Soviets, KHAD agents, government officials and their facilities in Kabul. These attacks could range from a knife between the shoulder blades of a Soviet soldier shopping in the bazaar to the placing of a briefcase bomb in a senior official's office. The former were sufficiently successful to force all Soviet troops to move about in armed groups, and for civilians to have military escorts. Markets were eventually declared off-limits to Soviets and their families. The latter included placing a bomb under the dining-room table of Kabul University in late 1983. The explosion, in the middle of their meal, killed nine Soviets, including a woman professor. Educational institutions were considered fair game, as the staff were all communists indoctrinating their students with Marxist dogma. To the Mujahideen this was corrupting the youth of the country, turning them away from the true faith of Islam. I would point out that in 1982 no fewer than 140 Soviet specialists and 105 Russian language teachers taught at the university and Kabul technical colleges. Among other victims were the rector of the university and General Abdul Wadood, the commander of the Central Corps, who was killed in his office. In 1983 seven senior Soviet officers were reported as killed in Kabul. Two such officers were shot dead by a 17-year-old boy whose parents had been killed by the Soviets. He hid a pistol under his blanket and approached them as they were leaving the Soviet Cultural Centre (a cinema), where films were shown for senior officials. Several quick shots and the boy escaped by dashing into the back streets. We later provided him with false identity documents.

We made numerous attempts to kill Najibullah, both when he was head of KHAD and after he became President. In late 1985, for example, a Commander who had the assistance of a KHAD officer in Kabul who was a Mujahideen sympathizer, almost succeeded. Explosives were smuggled into the city, a car purchased under a false name, and a bomb placed in the vehicle. The Commander got details of a planned visit by Najibullah to the Indian Embassy, which was almost opposite the KHAD headquarters in the Ministry of the Interior on Shari Nu Road. He parked the car between the two buildings. As the remote-control exploder had been known to fail at the crucial moment, on this occasion a timing device was used as well. Unfortunately Najibullah was delayed by 40 minutes, so the bomb detonated before its intended victim arrived. The Commander drove off in his get-away car, only to die some months later when he blew himself up preparing another bomb — a not uncommon fate for amateur bomb-makers.

The third way of hitting Kabul was by stand-off long-range rocket attacks. This was by far the most common method. Tens of thousands of rockets have fallen on the city and its environs during the war. Only for brief periods during the winter has a day passed without such an attack. Kabul is a huge place and so is virtually impossible to miss, but I would stress that we never deliberately fired indiscriminately. Our targets were always military, or associated with the Communist government in some way. I am not saying that innocent civilians or Mujahideen supporters were never killed by rockets: they were, but it was unintentional. Regrettably, no modern war can be fought without the innocent suffering. If we had ceased to attack Kabul because of the possibility of hitting civilians it would have pulled the carpet from under our fundamental strategy.

A revealing comment on the unintentional killing of civilians was made to Mark Urban, the author of *War in Afghanistan*, by Abdul Haq, a Commander who operated against Kabul. He said, 'Their [the Mujahideen] target is not the civilians ... but if I hit them I don't care.... If my family lived near the Soviet Embassy I would hit it. I wouldn't care about them. If I am prepared to die, my son has to die for it, and my wife has to die for it.'

My list of potential targets suitable for rocket attack in Kabul ran to over seventy. On Map 12 I have included the important ones. The Soviet and Afghan military installations, barracks and depots were top priority. The Darulaman Palace and Tari Tajbeg Camp, which housed the headquarters of the Soviet 40th Army and Afghan Central Corps; Kabul airport, with its surrounding garrison; Chihilasatoon barracks; the camps opposite Pul-i-Charki prison; Bala Hissar Fort, with its Soviet signals regiment; Khair Khana Camp, housing a massive motor transport depot, and the 108th MRD; Rishkoor garrison, the headquarters of both the Afghan 7th Division and 37th Commando Brigade, plus the 88th Artillery Brigade; and Kargha Garrison, with its enormous ammunition depot and 8th Division headquarters, are examples of purely military targets.

First on the list of Soviet civilian establishments was their Embassy. Hardly a week went by without attempts being made to hit this building. A close second was the Microrayan district of the city. This was a sprawling, prefabricated, apartment development reserved for Soviet advisers, their

Map 12

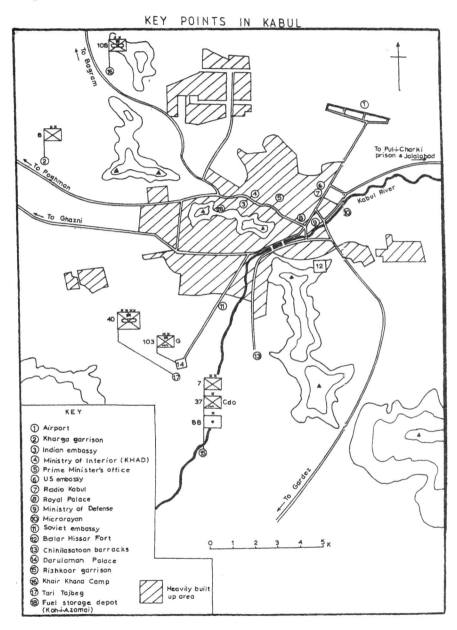

KEY POINTS IN KABUL

KEY

① Airport
② Kharga garrison
③ Indian embassy
④ Ministry of Interior (KHAD)
⑤ Prime Minister's office
⑥ US embassy
⑦ Radio Kabul
⑧ Royal Palace
⑨ Ministry of Defense
⑩ Microrayan
⑪ Soviet embassy
⑫ Balar Hissar Fort
⑬ Chihilasatoon barracks
⑭ Darulaman Palace
⑮ Rishkoor garrison
⑯ Khair Khana Camp
⑰ Tari Tajbeg
⑱ Fuel storage depot
    (Koh-i-Azamai)

Heavily built
up area

families and senior Afghan Communist Party officials. KHAD headquarters buildings, all government ministries, the President's palace, Radio Kabul (which was awkward as it was the neighbour of the US Embassy), television studios, transport pools, power stations and fuel storage tanks, all merited our attention.

Our ability to inflict damage or casualties depended on the weapons we used and their handling by the Mujahideen. With the weapons, it was all a question of range. How far into Kabul would the bomb or rocket fall, and therefore how close to the target must the firing-point be? It was not until early 1984 that we had 107mm MBRLs with ranges of 8 to 10 kilometres. Prior to this our artillery was the 82mm mortar, so we had to get to within 3000 metres of the target which, as the ring on Map 13 illustrates, often meant a firing point inside the city. As time passed, and the Kabul defences were pushed steadily further out from the centre, these short-range attacks became impossible to mount. The arrival of the Chinese MBRL gave us the breakthrough we needed. Although it was a cumbersome and weighty weapon it had the necessary range, accuracy and firepower. With its twelve barrels we were able literally to rain rockets on a target, provided we could hump sufficient ammunition to the firing point. This enabled us to mount truly stand-off attacks throughout the remainder of the war. Some 500 of these weapons were obtained during my time at ISI, of which 75 per cent were deployed against Kabul.

It was not only the range of the weapon that was critical for successful attacks, but the suitability of the ammunition. It was useless to hit a target if it was not damaged, destroyed or casualties inflicted. Often this meant the strike had to cause a secondary explosion or fire. We had a number of disappointments. The largest petrol storage reservoir in Kabul is located in a re-entrant on the northern side of the Koh-i-Azamai feature (see Map 12). It was an obvious objective. Our first attempt was a mortar attack which scored a direct hit, but the fuel did not burn. Perhaps the tanks were not full or there were insufficient fumes to ignite. The high-explosive mortar bomb would penetrate the tank's cover but would not start a fire. A white phosphorous (smoke) bomb could be used for its excellent incendiary effects, but it would not pierce the top of the tank.

The next try involved three Mujahideen creeping to within a hundred metres at night before firing two rockets from a RPG-2 anti-tank launcher into the reservoir and escaping in a car. Again a direct hit, but again no fire. I had long discussions with CIA technicians on this problem, but they could not come up with a direct-fire weapon to do the job. Meanwhile local defences were strengthened, making a close approach impossible. Although it remained a target for long-range stand-off attacks, it survived the war.

By April, 1985, the Soviets had established an outer ring of defences around Kabul that extended up to 10 to 12 kilometres from the centre. This caused us grave problems in mounting rocket attacks, even with the MBRLs. The difficulties were weight and range. The MBRL was too heavy to manpack over long distances, and its range of 9 kilometres meant immunity for most targets deep in the city. As there was, at that time, no prospect of a longer-range weapon, I resorted to self-help to give us a lighter launcher. What was needed was a single-barrel rocket-launcher (SBRL) that could be easily manhandled by one man, at night, between hostile posts.

We obtained a 'tube' from a partially destroyed MBRL which the Pakistan Army converted into a workable weapon – an SBRL. It was demonstrated to the CIA and I asked them to provide this weapon in large quantities. Meanwhile, I met the Chinese military attaché and asked him if he could manufacture this weapon. To my surprise he said that the SBRL used to be issued to the Chinese Army, but that it was now obsolete. It would take some time to get it back into production, but it could be done. The CIA and the Chinese cooperated fully on this project. I placed orders for 500 in 1985, and by early the following year the first consignment was flown to Rawalpindi. We had received 1,000 by late 1987. This weapon greatly enhanced our ability to hit Kabul.

The problem of range was partially overcome when we obtained the Egyptian 122mm rocket launcher which could fire out to 11 kilometres. It was not the complete answer, as, although it only had a single barrel, it was long and unwieldy, making it a difficult horse- or mule-load. Like the MBRL, it was far too heavy for manpacking. Only about 100 were obtained, and I restricted their issue to those Commanders able to fire on Kabul or major airfields.

For two hours from 9.00 pm the sky over Kabul was normally the backdrop for a spectacular firework display, with dozens of rockets roaring through the darkness, Soviet flares and searchlights, and their responding rockets and artillery fire. As most of the city's street lights had long since broken down this duel was the only illumination in an otherwise blacked-out metropolis. By eleven o'clock most Mujahideen firing points had run out of rockets so their firing died away, but not so the Soviets. Their flares and guns kept going until morning. At 5.30 am gunships and fighter bombers would scramble to carry out sweeps over suspected Mujahideen positions. It all became an accepted routine for Kabulis, Soviets and ourselves.

Perhaps our most dramatic success, which was recorded on video film from the roof of the British Embassy, was the strike against the ammunition stockpile at Kharga garrison on the western outskirts of the city. This depot supposedly had the largest storage capacity in Afghanistan, with anything up to 40,000 tons of all types of ammunition, including virtually all the reserve of surface-to-air missiles. I had briefed a number of Commanders to regard this as a priority target, and on 27 August it went up in a spectacular fireball that rose a thousand feet in the air. Missiles flew in every direction, windows vibrated throughout Kabul with each successive explosion, and the fire raged until well into the next day. Scores of Afghan soldiers were killed or injured. The credit was claimed by several Commanders so I carried out an investigation to try to establish whose triumph it was. I examined all the reports, timings, locations and capabilities of the claimants to engage this particular target, before establishing it could have been a Commander from either Khalis' or Sayaf's Party.

Because of our lack of an effective answer to the helicopter gunships we always had to carry out our rocket attacks at night. This meant moving into position in the dark, firing in the dark, and then withdrawing before dawn to avoid the inevitable retaliation from the air. With the increasing number of defensive posts and the ever-widening ring of them around Kabul, it was always a risky operation to infiltrate between them to get within range, particularly with the number of men and mules needed for a large strike. I wanted to be able to hit the city by day as well, but it was not until 1986 that we were able to do so.

The idea was to use free flight rockets. A party of six men, each carrying one rocket, would infiltrate to a firing point in the darkness, set up the rockets using improvised bipods of rocks and connect a delayed-action, electrically-operated firing device. The group would then retire, still at night, and 6-8 hours later the rockets would be on their way. If this was done by numerous groups from different directions, by different Commanders, then Kabul could be under attack at any time, day or night. We successfully instituted this method, but only after some delay, as the CIA could not initially meet our requirement for the special firing devices.

General Akhtar had an obsession with Kabul. He was adamant that attacks on Kabul should have priority over all others. If a Commander made known to the general that he wanted heavy weapons to hit the city, then he was well on the way to getting them, even if I was opposed. Keeping the pressure on the capital was the fundamental theme of our strategy. If Kabul fell we had won the war − it was as simple as that.

Because of its importance the majority of the Pakistani teams of advisers were used against Kabul. As I have indicated before, I was not initially enthusiastic about committing our nationals inside Afghanistan. However, when General Akhtar instructed me to step up the pressure on the city in 1984 I resolved to make the maximum use of them. Of the eleven teams sent in that year seven were used against Kabul. The attacks they led were spread out over the period April to November, and lasted for up to six weeks.

I selected the targets with care. They were to be primarily Soviet installations, the successful attack of which would become well known outside of Afghanistan through foreign embassies and the media. Originally I chose eight objectives, but in the event the last one could not be carried out due to the onset of bad winter weather. The targets were Kabul airfield, Darulaman Palace, Kharga garrison, the Soviet Embassy, Microrayan, Rishkoor garrison, and Chihilasatoon, which was a Soviet barracks area and housed some key officials (see Map 12). Each team had alternative targets.

The team tasked with Rishkoor had an interesting experience with the enemy garrison at one of the posts on their route, which was not untypical. The Commander had been called for training in June for three weeks on the MBRL. The Pakistani major with his two NCOs who were to accompany them were among the instructors on the course. The first that the Commander and his men knew that they would have advisers with them was on the Pakistan border, just prior to their move back into Afghanistan. They were to make for Chakri, some 35 kilometres SE of Kabul, where the Commander had his operational base.

The journey to Chakri (Map 13), via Ali Khel, took seven days, so it was early August before the major and the Commander could start the detailed reconnaissance necessary to confirm the route to a suitable firing point. The three Pakistanis, the Commander and an escort of six Mujahideen spent two days and a night on their reconnaissance. The Commander, who knew the area well, explained that two platoon-sized posts that formed a part of the outer ring of defences would have to be bypassed if they were to get within range.

Back at the base the details of the plan were put together. The Commander had returned with fifty men from the course, all trained on the MBRL, so they would provide the firing party and its covering group, and guide the mules. Another fifty men would be needed as escorts and to man the two 82mm mortars and three machine guns — in total a sizeable force of 100 Mujahideen with twenty-five mules. They wanted to mount a worthwhile attack, so had decided to take sixty rockets, rendering a smaller force impractical.

My major felt that security would be difficult as they crossed the Logar River, as this area was heavily populated, but the Commander knew the people well and was confident they would go unhindered. There seemed to be no answer to the need to pass close to at least one of the guard posts other than a long, laborious, and probably noisy, detour. The Commander's solution was to send a messenger direct to the enemy post to demand safe passage on pain of their position being destroyed. My team thought this somewhat unorthodox and were sceptical when the messenger returned to say that he had to go back in three nights' time as the Afghan platoon commander had to consult his Soviet adviser.

On his next visit the Afghan officer said that, with great difficulty, he had persuaded the adviser to allow the Mujahideen through, but only on condition that while the rocket attack was in progress the post could open fire, but in the wrong direction. When the firing party withdrew the garrison would open up on the area of the firing point. The Mujahideen Commander was quite satisfied with this arrangement, but, naturally, my team was far from happy. The decision was the Commander's, so the Pakistanis had to go along with it, although the major intended to position the mortars and machine guns to cover the post in case of treachery.

Starting from Chakri in the afternoon, moving fast, and on through the night the hide was reached two hours before dawn. The next day was spent crouched among the boulders under blankets, overlooking the Logar Valley. Immediately after last light they left for the 9-kilometre march to the firing position. The footbridge-crossing over the river and the move through the villages was disturbed only by a few barking dogs. Then, by 10.30 pm the force was approaching the gap between the Afghan posts. At a distance of 600 metres the major sited the mortars and machine guns on a low spur off the track from which the post could be covered. The team's sergeant was left with this group.

The main body moved, with the mules, in single file towards the post. This was the moment of truth, for no matter how careful they were it was impossible to avoid some slight noise as a mule kicked a loose stone, or a man's weapon knocked against a rocket or part of the MBRL. The column passed within 20 metres of the Afghans, with a sentry standing in his trench clearly visible. No challenge, no whispered exchange; the Mujahideen passed by like so many ghosts.

By midnight the covering party was deployed ahead of the firing point and the MBRL was ready. '*Allah o Akbar. Mordabad Shuravi*' (God is great. Death to the Soviets): with this shout the firing started. In less than half an hour all sixty rockets had gone and the Rishkoor complex was burning brightly. While the MBRL was in action the enemy opened up with a suitably impressive expenditure of ammunition, well away from the Mujahideen.

The move back was hurried, no attempt being made at silence as speed was more important in order to make the most of the remaining five hours of darkness. With much lighter loads now the firing was over, the column moved past the post at a brisk walk. The Afghans had stopped firing, but after the Mujahideen had disappeared into the gloom they opened up again, with streams of tracer rounds flashing down the track towards the firing point. They had kept their bargain to the letter. Later, back at Chakri, Kabul Radio confirmed that Rishkoor had been hit and that fires had taken several hours to bring under control. Like the other Pakistani teams, the major and his two NCOs were later congratulated and decorated by the President.

Kabul was well defended with a huge concentration of troops, guns and aircraft. By early 1985 no less than three rings of mutually supporting positions surrounded the city (see Map 13). We could not, until 1986, carry out stand-off attacks by day. Until the introduction of the Stinger in late

1986 and early 1987, the Soviets' complete control of the air prevented us applying the sustained pressure needed to isolate the city. Not only were our attacks confined to the night, but they were reduced to almost zero during the winter. These day and winter respites were enough to allow the enemy to recover, retaliate and retrieve lost ground. It was during the months from January to March that the Soviets extended their defences, pushed their perimeter outwards and captured Mujahideen bases and arms dumps in the hills surrounding Kabul.

The reason they were able to do this year after year was that most Mujahideen went home for the winter. I have indicated the main guerrilla operational bases within striking distance of Kabul on Map 13. In terms of time this meant they could reach firing positions in two night marches, anything more was too hazardous. Except for Koh-i-Safi each base had several Commanders from various Parties controlling anything from 100 to 1000 Mujahideen. The seemingly insuperable problem was that in winter, with heavy snow in the passes, supply columns could not get through. Much forethought, planning and logistic effort was required to pre-dump sufficient stocks at the bases to last until April. We made concerted efforts to do this, but the unforeseen problems in the pipeline, over which we had no control, often thwarted us. This, however, was not the only difficulty.

As I have previously explained, the Mujahideen were not expected to remain in the field indefinitely without respite. A few months' stint in the Jehad, then back home to see their families or to earn money was the norm. Couple this with the harsh conditions in caves or tents with little firewood, scarce rations, and no proper clothing, and the unpopularity of winter warfare is understandable. Most Afghans hibernate in winter, whether soldiers or civilians. It is stressful to venture out from the house, even for a few hours. The Mujahideen were human, and it was asking too much to expect them to tramp through the snow in open sandals, or sleep rough, wrapped in one threadbare blanket. To keep warm in a blanket you need to wrap it around your body with your arms inside, hardly conducive to firing a rifle, loading a mortar, or the freedom of movement needed to fight. We needed to give them proper winter clothing and equipment. By this I mean thick jackets, snow boots and ski tents. The fact that we failed to supply these items from 1979 through to 1985 was a shameful failure on our part.

During 1984 I held numerous discussions with my staff and Commanders as to how to maintain attacks on Kabul during the 1984/85 winter. In the end it boiled down to money. Did we have sufficient for the extra transport costs to pre-position stocks or for winter clothes? Regrettably the answer was no. It was decided to try nominating different Commanders for different sectors for two-month periods. Their task was to keep up regular rocket strikes on a nightly basis throughout the winter. We felt this could be done if the Commanders kept a minimum of 100 to 200 men in the field. Some

Map 13

KABUL UNDER PRESSURE

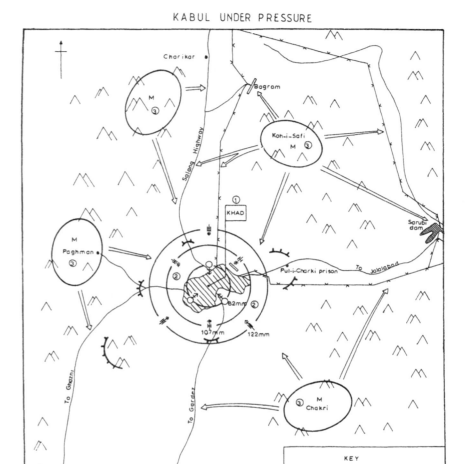

Charikar •

Bagram

Koh-i-Safi
M ③

Salang Highway

Sarubi dam

① KHAD

M Paghman • ③

Pul-i-Charki prison   To Jalalabad

② 82mm ②

107mm   122mm

To Ghazni

To Gardez

M Chakri ③

KEY
① KHAD HQ in city center
② Mortar & rocket attacks at max range
③ Mujahideen bases and attacks
} Kabul's outer defenses
Electricity power line

0   3   6   9   12 K

155

thirty Commanders were involved and we offered them extra MBRLs as an incentive.

For the first few weeks all went well, but with the heavy snowfalls in January movement towards Kabul became more and more difficult and expensive. Some commanders started to withdraw due to lack of shelter, food, clothing and equipment with which to counter the freezing conditions. This created a vacuum around Kabul of which the Soviets were quick to take advantage. They mounted offensives against Chakri and Paghman where resistance was light. The result was that we lost ground gained in the summer, the enemy built another series of posts to consolidate their gains and protected them with wire and mines. We had been pushed back, the range to our targets in the city had been lengthened, and our grip weakened. In 1985 we lost Chakri completely. In 1986 Paghman was taken, with only Koh-i-Safi remaining unscathed. It was not until the introduction of Stingers in early 1987 that we were able to regain some lost ground in the Paghman area. Until then the inevitable pattern was repeated annually: a successful campaign of attacks up to December, a winter withdrawal, with the Soviets pushing their defences outwards, leading to our needing longer-range weapons. Thus was our ability to strangle Kabul eroded.

I believe that if we had diverted enough money for appropriate clothing from the start we could have kept fighting throughout the year. I tried hard during 1985 not to repeat the errors of previous years, putting forward urgent requests for 5,000 sets of winter clothing to General Akhtar. He did not have the money. The best he could hope for was 1,000 sets, which, in order to save funds, were to be purchased from Pakistani manufacturers. Despite ISI's best efforts they did not honour their commitments.

Some Commanders did make an effort to keep a token force of 30-40 men operative throughout the winter, with personnel changing over after about two months, but it was seldom effective. To live in a tent placed on top of the ruined walls of a house, with the temperature of minus 15-20 degrees, completely isolated, living on a meagre ration of nan bread, as for most of the time there were no civilians within 15 kilometres, was asking a lot. These men had to remain alert, do sentry duties, and go out to launch rocket attacks or collect firewood. If they were lucky they obtained a little flour or tea, but not sugar. Tea was often drunk while eating a sweet to make it slightly more palatable. Without warm clothing or boots, the battle against the cold was unremitting and unsuccessful. Mujahideen in these conditions all lost 20-25 pounds in weight, came back haggard, their faces drawn, aged and blackened by fire smoke. Winter was an infinitely tougher opponent than the Soviets.

During 1985 operations elsewhere were, I believe, showing that the Mujahideen could get the upper hand. If only we had had Stingers I am certain the war would have been winnable much earlier. As it was, we were struggling to maintain the fight, and around Kabul, our primary target, we were losing momentum. The CIA had provided me with a series of excellent satellite photographs of dozens of enemy posts within a 20-kilometre radius of Kabul. With the aid of these I set about renewed planning.

It was at this time that General Akhtar came up with the idea of a concerted attack to capture a part of Kabul and hold it for up to 36 hours. If it could be achieved, it would have a tremendously favourable effect on Mujahideen morale. I asked for time to study the proposal, but the General had mentioned it to Hekmatyar and Sayaf, both of whom were enthusiastic, provided they got more heavy weapons, so I was ordered to discuss plans in detail immediately.

The results of my talks were that such an operation would need to be a joint one, with at least two Parties cooperating. In the absence of an effective anti-aircraft weapon, the attack could not succeed by day. We would need to mount simultaneous diversionary attacks on Kabul, Bagram and Jalalabad airfields. Finally, secrecy would be of paramount importance – hard to ensure if we were to group 5,000 Mujahideen around Kabul. This was the number that the Leaders insisted was the minimum necessary.

Our view was that, instead of holding Kabul for 36 hours, which meant fighting throughout at least one day, we should confine the operation to the launching of numerous small attacks from multiple directions. These should be during one night only, with exfiltration complete by dawn. Neither of the Leaders was prepared to accept a joint operation, and our alternative plan did not meet with their approval either, as it did not, in their view, involve a sufficiently generous allocation of heavy weapons.

I was never able to coordinate truly joint attacks on Kabul, although I believe I created this impression to the enemy by a system of briefing numerous Commanders to carry out operations against targets from multiple directions during the same period.

Kabul was the key to Afghanistan; of this I have no doubt. It should have fallen within weeks of the Soviet withdrawal in 1989, but the story of why it did not belongs to a different chapter.

CHAPTER TEN

The Bear Attacks

'This animal is very bad; when attacked it defends itself.'

THE Soviet high command was acutely sensitive to the activities of the Mujahideen in the eastern border provinces of Kunar, Nangarhar and Paktia. Just across the frontier in Pakistan were the Mujahideen's forward supply bases, training facilities and scores of refugee camps. From this area the great bulk of arms and ammunition poured into Afghanistan in an endless stream of caravans, or pack trains of animals, moving along the tracks and trails through the mountains. The strategic importance to both sides of this border zone, from Barikot in the north, to Urgun in the south, is illustrated on Map 1.

A main road ran from Kabul to Peshawar, via Jalalabad, over the Khyber Pass. For the Soviets Jalalabad was a key city. All roads, tracks and valleys from the frontier converged on Jalalabad. Here were the headquarters of the Afghan 11th Division, the Soviet 66th MRR, a Spetsnaz battalion, plus the 1st Afghan Border Brigade. Half-way up the Kunar Valley to the NE was another Afghan division, the 9th, at Asadabad, with a second Spetsnaz battalion further up still at Asmar (Map 11). At the Afghanistan end of the Khyber Pass was Torkham, overlooked by a high, dominating feature occupied by the Afghans, called Shamshadsar. In early 1984 I was awakened one night with the news that Shamshadsar had fallen to the Mujahideen and that the Soviet/Afghan counter-attack had failed to dislodge them. Apparently the Afghans had given an ultimatum to the local Pakistan border post that unless the Mujahideen withdrew they would shell the nearby Pakistani civilian population. This had caused considerable panic. The Mujahideen had refused to budge unless so instructed by General Akhtar, who was in Karachi. The governor of the NWFP was furious and had complained to President Zia. The upshot was I had to go, reluctantly, to get the Mujahideen to pull back. Eventually I succeeded, but thereafter there was a presidential ban on any Mujahideen offensives within 10 kilometres of Torkham, or of Chaman on the Khojak Pass in Baluchistan.

The Soviets were equally touchy about the Parrot's Beak peninsula which outflanked both Jalalabad to its north and Khost to its south. The Mujahideen dumps concentrated in this area were closer to Kabul than either of these two Afghan towns. We despatched nearly 40 per cent of our supplies for the entire guerrilla war effort from this area around Parachinar. The cork intended to stem the flow was the Afghan garrison at Ali Khel, 12 kilometres from the border.

Of similar significance to Jalalabad, but south of Parrot's Beak, was the town of Khost. Its garrison, from the Afghan 25th Division and 2nd Border Brigade, was responsible for maintaining the small border posts facing Miram Shah in Pakistan. Through Miram Shah ran another branch of our supply pipeline, carrying a good 20 per cent of the Mujahideen's arms requirements.

Soviet border strategy was based on maintaining a multitude of posts, large and small, close to Pakistan. They were intended to seal the border and interdict our supply routes. It was rather like a person trying to shut off a large tap by putting his hand over it. Throughout the war the majority of these garrisons have been under at least partial siege, and many times small posts have fallen to attack. These eastern provinces have seen some of the fiercest fighting of the campaign, with battles resembling conventional war being fought in several instances. In fact, with hindsight, these towns and posts probably diverted our efforts too much from Kabul and other more suitable guerrilla targets. It was tempting to try to take isolated garrisons adjacent to the border. They were close to our main base with all the advantages that gave; small successes were not difficult to achieve and Commanders could be certain of recognition for their victories. Plunder and publicity were the rewards of some comparatively easy, low-risk triumphs.

In strictly military terms an isolated fort is only beneficial if it ties down more enemy in besieging it than its own garrison, or it threatens a supply line which necessitates a strong enemy masking force to prevent forays. Judged by these criteria perhaps the continuous and costly efforts of the Soviets and Afghans to maintain these posts was worthwhile. There is little doubt they tied down large numbers of Mujahideen. Two examples of this were the garrisons at Ali Khel and Khost, both of which were under continuous siege from early in the war. At both these locations operations alternated, with the Mujahideen concentrating up to 5,000 active fighters, cutting off supplies to the garrisons, seizing outlying posts and threatening to capture the town, followed by a major Soviet/Afghan thrust to break the investment. These were usually successful, with the Mujahideen melting back into the mountains along the border, only to return again when the enemy columns withdrew. In 1983 it looked for a while as if Khost would fall. At the end of August, with the situation critical, the Kabul régime flew in Colonel Shahnawaz Tani's 37th

Commando Brigade by helicopter. This forced us back after bitter fighting. By October the commandos were back in Kabul and we were closing in again.

By 1985 the Mujahideen Leaders and senior Commanders were determined that Khost should fall, and a major offensive was mooted to this end. To take a strongly-held town such as Khost was not really a task for a guerrilla force. It would require the cooperation of at least two parties and their Commanders to mobilize sufficient men. Even then, the militarily desirable ratio of 3:1 in favour of the attacker could not be achieved. Couple this with the Mujahideen's exposure to air attack and the likely massive Soviet/Afghan response that would be provoked, and the doubtful wisdom of such an assault is apparent.

I called a conference in Peshawar to discuss the problems. It was to be a combined effort between Khalis' and Gailani's Parties, with Jalaluddin Haqqani, a renowned Khalis Commander, playing a leading role from his forward base at Zhawar only 6 kilometres over the border opposite Miram Shah, and some 20 kilometres south of Khost. I found that Gailani was not ready, while Khalis pressed me hard to give the go-ahead, and issue the necessary heavy weapons and ammunition. Although I had misgivings I had previously decided I would give this operation my full support provided the Commanders would mount a joint attack in accordance with a sound tactical plan. I had resolved to go into Afghanistan myself to coordinate the assault, and to send in several Pakistani teams of advisers with various Commanders. On Map 14 I have shown the tactical situation.

Khost was surrounded by mountains in which sat the Mujahideen. All around were a series of defensive posts and minefields, with a substantial garrison at Tani. The Mujahideen were particularly strong to the south and SE of the town, with their outposts overlooking the plain along the line shown on the map. The only feature that they did not occupy, as it was held by the enemy, was Torgarh. This mountain ridge was about 9 kilometres from Khost, with its northern end curling round to within 4 kilometres of the totally exposed airfield. In fact this strip was seldom used by the Afghans as we could bring it under fire so easily that they often resorted to parachute dropping of supplies. Torgarh was what the military term vital ground for any force wishing to defend or attack Khost.

I explained to the assembled Commanders that phase one of any assault on Khost must be the taking of Torgarh by night. To my dismay they all wanted a daytime attack. For hours I tried to convince them that this would be folly, with the Mujahideen exposed to heavy fire from the air and artillery long before they could reach Torgarh itself. The principal Commander, Haqqani, would not budge. My attempts to enlist the support of ex-Colonel Wardak, the military representative from Gailani's Party, failed, as he was reluctant to oppose Haqqani for political reasons. Haqqani argued that by

Map 14

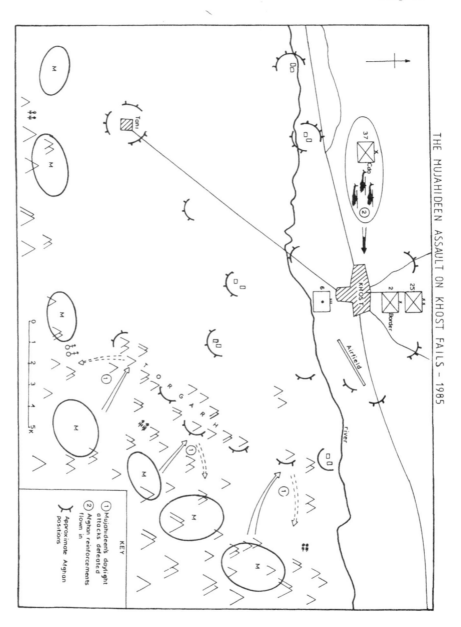

THE MUJAHIDEEN ASSAULT ON KHOST FAILS – 1985

KEY

① Mujahideen's daylight attacks defeated

② Afghan reinforcements flown in

⌣ Approximate Afghan positions

day everybody would do their best, nobody would hold back in front of his comrades, while in a night attack nobody would cooperate and everybody would blame each other for failure. He believed that only by day could Commanders exercise control. He assured me of success, and accepted full, personal responsibility for the operation.

At the end of a day of fruitless discussions I said to Haqqani, 'I am not prepared to be a party to a plan which I know for certain will not only fail, but result in heavy casualties.' I withdrew Pakistani adviser support, but later relented and allowed two teams to go in.

The Torgarh attack was timed to start at 10.00 am (H-hour), but the inevitable delays meant that it was midday before the Mujahideen started moving forward. Regrettably, as I had forecast, the attack was broken up by concentrated fire. The Mujahideen suffered numerous unnecessary casualties. After dark some progress was made up the slopes of Torgarh, but, with the exception of taking a few bunkers, little could be achieved. By midnight they had had enough and fell back, carrying their dead and wounded with them.

After two weeks Haqqani came to me to apologize for rejecting my advice. He admitted his error, and in the same breath urged me to allocate him more weapons and ammunition. He wanted to try again — by night. But by then the Afghan hold on Torgarh had been consolidated. I declined a second attempt. Reinforcing failure has never been a sensible military tactic.

My prediction that such a large-scale attack would provoke a correspondingly strong retaliation was also proved correct. On 20 August the enemy launched their second eastern offensive of 1985, involving some 20,000 men. A series of pincer movements (shown on Map 15) were aimed at flushing out the Mujahideen from their strongholds west of the Parrot's Beak around Azra, Ali Khel and Khost. From the latter their intention was also to move south, up to the border, and demolish the Zhawar base area. Considerable use was made of heliborne encirclement, particularly around Azra. No less than nine landing zones were used to position the cordon troops of Soviet air assault units around guerrilla bases or villages. It was a similar story around Ali Khel, with the attackers able to secure several small arms caches and inflict losses on the Mujahideen.

The thrust from Khost, through Tani, towards Zhawar was also worrying. In fact any strong offensive from Ali Khel, or towards Zhawar and Pakistan, always produced squeals of alarm from both politicians and the military in Islamabad. If ever the Soviets contemplated ground incursions into Pakistan these were two obvious routes. Just inside Pakistan the huge Peiwar Kotal mountain feature dominated, not only the approaches to Afghanistan but, more importantly, the whole of the Kurram Valley back through Parachinar and beyond. To lose these heights would mean our border defences had been pierced. I can vouch for the fact that during these months of intense activity

Map 15

THE SOVIET'S SECOND EASTERN OFFENSIVE OF 1985

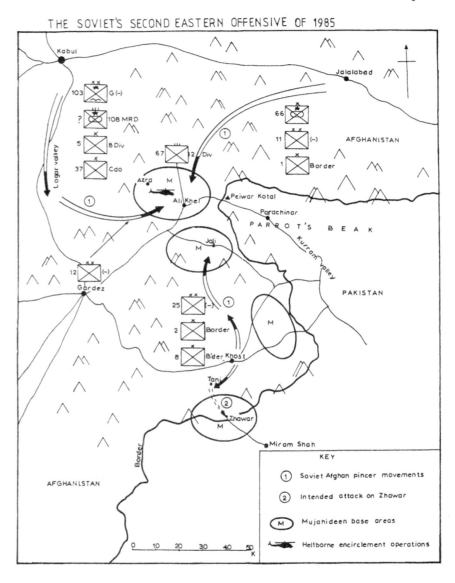

and probing of the border the Pakistan Army in the NWFP was on full alert, and indeed had deployed units forward to prepared positions – just in case.

Although our siege of Khost was broken by the enemy counter-attack, Zhawar did not fall. In fact the Afghans did not make headway south beyond Tani due to some skilful and courageous fighting by Mujahideen forces operating from the Zhawar area. We were somewhat handicapped by the absence of many Commanders, including Haqqani, who had left for the Haj (pilgrimage to Mecca). His second-in-command was Shaheed in these battles, and it was quite a close-run thing. The Soviet/Afghan forces had shown that their tactics and techniques were improving, they had been able to penetrate into areas long held to be inaccessible, and had they been able to close right up to the border and destroy our bases there, the entire campaign might have been put in jeopardy. I decided to ensure that any future attempt should also be defeated.

Throughout mid-1985 I did much soul-searching as to whether my overall strategy was working. Our efforts to keep the enemy away from the border areas seemed to have failed, we had suffered casualties, our attempt to seize Khost had been badly flawed, and the Soviet high command had apparently gained the initiative. I spent many hours in front of the map of Afghanistan as I pondered and debated in my mind how best to prosecute the war. My conclusions were that the Soviets had not inflicted any serious defeat on the battlefield; in fact the border engagements although intense, had been indecisive. I believe the enemy had launched its offensives in order to relieve pressure elsewhere in Afghanistan, particularly around Kabul; that they were designed to disrupt and destroy our base areas south and east of Ali Khel and Zhawar with this as their primary aim. I felt that there was nothing wrong with our basic strategy; in fact with our increasing efforts against Kabul, and in the north across the Amu, I was certain we could expect the Soviet/Afghan forces to lash out again at our border strongholds. It would be a sign that we were succeeding elsewhere. In this connection I made a controversial decision. I decided that should any future offensive attempt to take either the Ali Khel or Zhawar base areas they would be defended, we would not withdraw into Pakistan, but attempt to hold our own and fight a conventional defensive battle. This was against the normal principles of guerrilla war. Some in my staff felt I was making an error of judgement, that to hold ground against superior forces who had complete air cover was tactically unsound and would lead to defeat with heavy losses. I understood the wisdom of what they said, but I was convinced that other factors overrode their arguments. War is an art, not a science.

First and foremost I felt that with up to 60 per cent of our supplies passing through these two forward base areas we just could not afford to lose them.

They were essential jump-off points for the entire campaign. If they were occupied for any length of time by the enemy, with their forces close up to the frontier, they would have effectively blocked our major logistics artery feeding the war. These areas were vital ground to us and merited determined defence.

The establishment of strongpoints along the border in these areas would act as a trip-wire should the war escalate. In the event of the Soviets moving on Pakistan these two routes would certainly be used by ground troops. Mujahideen defensive positions would delay the advance, cause casualties and gain time for the Pakistan Army to complete its forward deployment and rush up reinforcements.

It took us three months finally to decide to adopt these measures, at the end of which time General Akhtar and President Zia were both in favour. It was with the President's approval that, in September/October, 1985, I visited the Ali Khel and Zhawar areas to put in motion the necessary defensive preparations to try to convert the bases into defensive localities.

My first trip took me to Ali Khel, accompanied by the members of the Military Committee of Hekmatyar's and Sayaf's Parties, who had undertaken responsibility for the work in that area. I wanted a close look at Ali Khel and the surrounding enemy posts, so I took forward a reconnaissance party to a ridge within 2 kilometres of the village. Later, we pulled back to an observation post (OP) some 4 kilometres away to watch a Mujahideen fire-power demonstration scheduled to start at 4.00 pm. This would give insufficient time for gunships to scramble from Kabul or Jalalabad and get overhead before last light. I was suitably impressed. Over 1,000 rounds from 107mm rocket launchers, 82mm mortars, and recoilless rifles were rained down on Ali Khel and associated defences during a two-hour period. The response was unimpressive, as the enemy artillery counter-battery fire was wide of all our firing points, with the closest shell to my position, from which we were adjusting the fire, falling 500 metres away.

That night, back in a bunker at Sayaf's base, I was touched by two brief but revealing examples of Mujahideen hospitality in the field. Several local Commanders dismissed my escort of three Pakistani soldiers and themselves took turn at sentry duty outside my bunker. Rather thoughtlessly, I had asked one of my soldiers to get me a bucket of hot water in the morning. There was no bucket in the entire base. They only had a plastic jerrycan, which they filled laboriously by continuously heating water in a kettle over an open fire. I felt most ashamed in the morning when I realized that I was the only person among several hundred to wash in hot water.

We spent a second day on reconnaissance from a forward OP. Again we arranged for an MBRL bombardment of the Ali Khel positions. It was followed by a pause of about 30 minutes to deceive the enemy into thinking we had finished. As soon as movement was spotted we opened up again, continuing until nightfall. Back at the base I met Professor Sayaf and some of his Commanders from Kabul. He was keen that his Party alone should be responsible for the defence, and I had great difficulty persuading him otherwise.

The next day was spent in touring the base area and discussing with the Commanders how best to prepare to withstand an assault. Areas for minefields were defined; AA guns, machine guns, recoilless rifles and mortars were sited to cover likely approaches; possible helicopter landing zones (LZs) were identified for mining and heavy weapons designated to cover them by fire.

I stressed the urgent need for communication trenches and for all weapon pits or bunkers to have overhead protection. There was a great deal to do and I could only hope that the Commanders would galvanize their men into action. I gave them two months to complete the tasks, with the promise of extra heavy weapons as an incentive.

I suppose I had expected too much. My officers spent considerable time giving guidance and checking progress, but at the end of two months the Parties asked for more time. Again I went into Afghanistan to see for myself. It was disappointing. Even taking into account the Mujahideen's antipathy towards digging and reluctance to defend static positions, I was inwardly exasperated by what I saw. Trenches had not been dug, gun positions were exposed without proper camouflage, tents were conspicuously pitched close to forward positions and overhead protection was lacking everywhere. In contrast with the forward positions, great efforts had been made to construct a series of tunnels to house the headquarters and administrative facilities. I was forced to release some heavy weapons, but on the understanding that considerable improvement must be made to all defences before the balance was allocated.

The situation at Zhawar was identical. The Mujahideen worked enthusiastically at tunnel-building, using bulldozers and explosives to produce seven tunnels dug into the side of a wide, dried-up nullah. They included shelter for a mosque, garage, armourers' shop, small medical aid post, radio station, kitchen, guest house and stores. A generator provided power for the aid post, mosque and guests' tunnel. It was even possible to watch video films at the base. This work always had priority over the tactical defences facing the enemy. The Parties and Commanders were eager to have an impressive 'showpiece' for visiting journalists. The fact that the previous attempt to reach Zhawar in September had petered out gave them a false sense of security.

Map 16 shows the approximate defensive deployment for the battle of Zhawar, which took place in April, 1986. Zhawar was a substantial administrative base. From there operations against Khost were planned and conducted; it was a Mujahideen centre for training recruits on both small arms and heavy weapons; it was the focal point of what was regarded as a liberated area, where a sort of mini-government had been set up, courts were held and delegations and journalists were received. The principal Commander was the tall, blackbearded, 50-year-old Haqqani from Khalis' Party, although Hekmatyar, Nabi and Gailani also had Commanders in the vicinity. Haqqani had some forty to fifty subordinates under his direction, with probably 10,000 Mujahideen spread over the border district between Ali Khel and Zhawar. I have shown the line of the forward defences at Zhawar as following the foothills of the mountains up to 10 kilometres from the frontier, although smaller outlying groups were located on the Khost plain.

The AA defences were dependent on three Oerlikon guns, the 12.7mm and 14.5mm machine guns, and shoulder-fired SA-7s, which were often sited up to 7 kilometres forward of Zhawar itself. Likely ground approaches for armour or infantry were protected by anti-tank minefields, mortars, recoilless rifles and RPGs. Some positions were connected by field telephone or walkie-talkie radios. While, in theory, the tactical handling of the defence was Haqqani's responsibility, in practice individual Commanders would fight their own battles, with Haqqani devoting his efforts to coordinating logistic support. The weapon positions shown on the map are not completely accurate but are indicative of the layout and type used.

In Zhawar base itself, in and around the tunnels, about 400 men were deployed for its close protection, or to work on administrative support. Here also was Haqqani's headquarters. These Mujahideen lived in or near the tunnels, while those in the forward positions lived, ate and slept at their posts. Food was often prepared centrally, operations permitting, or even cooked in Pakistan and carried forward to the Commanders. Once fighting started everybody survived on what he carried.

Although the Soviets masterminded the attack on Zhawar, they only deployed one Soviet air assault regiment from the 103rd GAAD at Darulaman, the remainder of the 12,000 men assembled for the advance being Afghans. Tactical control was to be exercised by the staff of Major-General Shahnawaz Tani, who four years later, as Defence Minister, was to launch a coup attempt against the Kabul régime, and then flee to join the Mujahideen. The Afghan Army commander on the spot was Tani's deputy, a talented officer of Baluchi origins, Brigadier Abdol Gafur.

The Soviet/Afghan objective was to smash the guerrilla base infrastructure around Zhawar, occupy the area and seal off this important Mujahideen supply route (see Map 17). It was an ambitious undertaking. The operation was certain to involve tough fighting, with the Mujahideen able to call in reinforcements quickly from Pakistan. There was no way that the Khost garrison of the 25th Division and 2nd Border Brigade could undertake a

Map 16

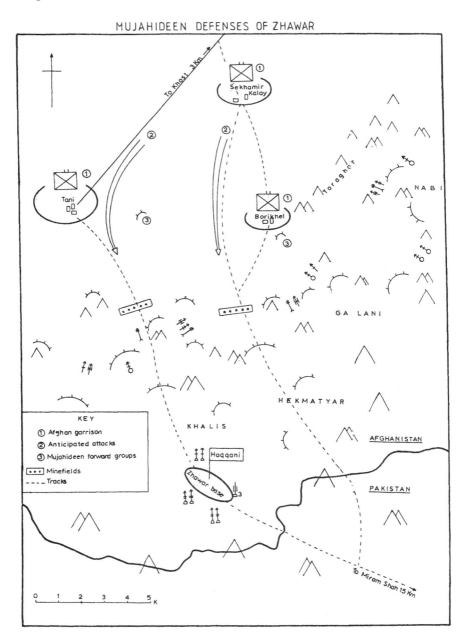

MUJAHIDEEN DEFENSES OF ZHAWAR

KEY

① Afghan garrison
② Anticipated attacks
③ Mujahideen forward groups
[•••] Minefields
- - - - Tracks

168

mission of this size. Khost would provide a convenient jump-off point, but the bulk of the troops would have come from elsewhere. Showing a remarkable display of staff work, Gafur used the month of March to assemble his task force. Units from the 7th and 8th Divisions in Kabul, the 12th at Gardez and 14th at Ghazni were concentrated at Khost. Three battalions (1,500 men) of the 37th Commando Brigade and the Soviet AAR (2,200 men) were flown in to spearhead the offensive into the mountains. The entire operation would have the usual air umbrella, artillery and rocket support, together with scores of transport and gunship helicopters. That the Afghan Army was able to put together such an operation was striking evidence of how it had regained much of its military competence. Such an undertaking would have been unthinkable three years earlier.

As the winter weather abated in the first week of April the advance began, under cover of air-strikes and gunfire, led by Soviet and Afghan commandos in helicopters. Immediately, the ground columns came under fire from pockets of Mujahideen south of Khost and around Tani, which slowed progress to a crawl. South of Tani the operation bogged down for several days as the leading elements of the enemy came up against stiffer resistance from the mountains north of Zhawar, and groups of Mujahideen fired hundreds of 107mm rockets into Khost airfield to disrupt helicopter sorties. The second phase from Tani to Zhawar was going to require rethinking and reorganizing, so Gafur paused until 11 April.

His final plan envisaged the bold use of heliborne commandos to seize dominating ground in a coup-de-main operation close to Zhawar base, the extensive use of airpower to smash the Mujahideen positions, and the use of ground forces to link up with the commandos, and mop up what was left.

For ten days Gafur struggled to get from Tani to Zhawar, ten days of heavy fighting in which the Mujahideen resistance took a severe pounding, but during which they proved they could hold their ground even in adverse circumstances. Their outstanding triumph of this battle was the complete destruction of a battalion from 37 Commando Brigade, which was a part of Gafur's plan to land troops behind the Mujahideen positions. In this instance they miscalculated badly in selecting as a landing zone (LZ) a flat, open plateau close to the base, but within range of higher ground held by some of Haqqani's and Hekmatyar's men. In broad daylight ten or more helicopters came in in waves to set down the 400 commandos. As they flew overhead they were met by a barrage of fire from SA-7s and heavy machine guns. Three helicopters crashed, while the others disgorged their troops under intense cross-fire from both Mujahideen positions. In the open ground the commandos were badly cut up and demoralized. By nightfall there was nothing left of this battalion: all were either killed or captured. Had we had the Stinger missile I doubt if any helicopter could have escaped.

From 11 to 22 April Zhawar was isolated from the rest of the area by

Map 17

THE BATTLE FOR ZHAWAR

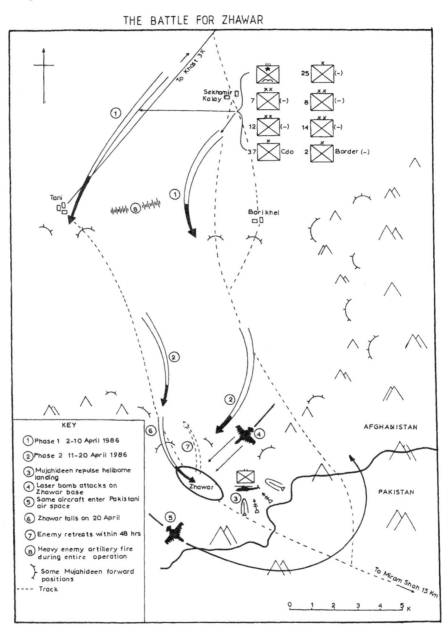

KEY

1. Phase 1 2-10 April 1986
2. Phase 2 11-20 April 1986
3. Mujahideen repulse heliborne landing
4. Laser bomb attacks on Zhawar base
5. Some aircraft enter Pakistani air space
6. Zhawar falls on 20 April
7. Enemy retreats within 48 hrs
8. Heavy enemy artillery fire during entire operation
} Some Mujahideen forward positions
---- Track

artillery and air strikes. Pakistani air space was violated countless times as enemy aircraft wheeled overhead before diving down on their targets. Some used laser-guided bombs for pinpoint accuracy in taking out the Zhawar tunnels. A direct hit on one tunnel caused it to collapse, crushing many of its occupants, including Haqqani who was injured, but survived. Back at Rawalpindi I received frantic calls from the Parties to do something to alleviate the rain of rockets and bombs from the air. In desperation I briefed General Akhtar that I proposed asking for Pakistani volunteers from my staff to take in some more Blowpipe missiles. My logistics colonel, who had been in the anti-aircraft artillery, offered his services. He was to be accompanied by several others, including a young captain. General Akhtar agreed, so the team was rushed to the frontier. Within 24 hours they were in Zhawar.

Early in the morning the Blowpipe party climbed up a prominent peak nearby to set themselves up for the day's shooting. It was to turn out to be a duck shoot in which the ducks won. From their hide on the hill they had a magnificent view of the enemy aircraft as they banked, turned, dived and pulled up again, in their efforts to strafe our defences. The first Blowpipe missile roared majestically upwards but wide of its mark. From then on the firing point had been identified. Within a few minutes the colonel had been slightly wounded and several Mujahideen hit, but the captain kept the Blowpipe firing. In all thirteen missiles were fired before a direct hit severely wounded the captain and his JCO assistant, and killed several men nearby. Not a single missile had hit an aircraft. For me it was the final proof that this weapon system was useless on the battlefield. We had said so from the outset, and now it had failed us at a critical juncture of a desperate battle. A British artillery officer who saw the Blowpipe in action in the Falklands excused its poor performance by saying that at least it frightened pilots into veering off and leaving the firer alone. This was not our experience, and anyway we needed to knock them down, not frighten them.

Our team was evacuated under the directions of my colonel, back to a military hospital in Pakistan. Weeks after the incident I asked the captain why he had not tried changing his firing point once it had been located by the enemy. It was the obvious thing to do as both he and I knew. His reply was interesting. He had felt that to move would have damaged his reputation for courage in the eyes of the Mujahideen around him. They showed no inclination to move, they intended to stand their ground under fire, and the young officer felt that the honour of the Pakistan Army was at stake, so he stayed until hit. He was later decorated by the President.

With Haqqani out of the fight, there was even less coordination of the defences, and I was alarmed at the series of conflicting and worrying reports that came in daily. I urged General Akhtar to let me go forward, but he refused. Meanwhile, I arranged for all the military representatives of the Parties to go personally to Zhawar to organize operations aimed at the enemy's rear areas and Khost airfield. The ferocity of the fighting may be judged by the fact that the barrels of many of our AA guns had been worn out, and there were instances of hand-to-hand combat.

Again I pleaded with General Akhtar to let me at least go up to the border, as I felt my presence close to the fighting would be a steadying influence, and that from there I could coordinate things. After all, the enemy were now within 3 kilometres of Pakistan, and for all we knew might come across the frontier. On my assurance that I would not venture into Afghanistan, he let me go. The day I reached Miram Shah Zhawar fell. Soviet and Afghan commandos secured the tunnels and set about completing the destruction of the base. The Mujahideen had eventually been forced back in some of the toughest fighting of the war in which they had used every weapon in their armoury, including several captured tanks.

At Miram Shah I met Hekmatyar and Khalis who had gone to the border for the same purpose as myself. The news was bad, but large numbers of Mujahideen were still in the area, and not all the bases had been lost. Hekmatyar agreed to lead in reinforcements that night to secure his base. To try to find out the exact situation I went to a suitable vantage point from which I could observe enemy movement around Zhawar. I gazed long and hard through my binoculars, but saw nothing. There was no enemy in Zhawar. I hurried back and spoke to Haqqani, who was recovering well, telling him that Zhawar appeared unoccupied. He ordered a Commander to take in a patrol that night.

During the night I watched an impressive 107mm rocket barrage by Hekmatyar's men on to suspected enemy rear areas. Others joined in, confirming that the Mujahideen were far from defeated. The next day it was confirmed that the enemy had withdrawn. Within 48 hours Zhawar was back in our hands.

The Kabul régime celebrated a major victory. According to radio broadcasts hundreds of Mujahideen bunkers and fortifications had been destroyed; thousands of weapons and mines captured, and millions of rounds of ammunition secured. According to their account we lost 2,000 dead and 4,000 wounded. To say that this propaganda stretched the truth would be a serious understatement. Mujahideen losses at Zhawar did not exceed 300 killed, together with a few truck-loads of arms and ammunition. Although Zhawar base fell, other nearby strongpoints did not, and within a few hours the enemy pulled back to Khost, making no attempt to hold the ground they had won. We had shot down thirteen helicopters and aircraft, captured over 100 Afghan soldiers and killed or wounded about 1,500.

Our decision to fight a conventional defensive battle at Zhawar came under great criticism. We were accused of violating the principles of guerrilla war. As I have explained earlier, we had valid reasons for developing Zhawar and Ali Khel into strong points, and holding them if attacked. Our conduct of the war was dependent on these operational and logistic jump-off points. After the Zhawar battle we rebuilt the base and continued to use it throughout the rest of the campaign. It was Zhawar that so impressed Mr Wilson when I took him there about a year later. As far as I know it continues to function as an essential part of the Mujahideen's military strategy.

By all this I do not mean that we had not been dealt a severe tactical blow. We had, but it was not as serious as was made out at the time. I have no doubt that the Mujahideen would have repulsed all the assaults, with fewer losses, had two matters been resolved beforehand. First, if the Commanders had properly constructed their defences, ensured overhead cover and dug in with enthusiasm in the preceding weeks, the Mujahideen would not have received such a bloody nose. Second, and more importantly, if the US and Pakistan had not procrastinated for so many years over supplying us with an effective anti-aircraft weapon, we would assuredly have beaten off the attack with comparative ease. The Mujahideen, properly dug in at Zhawar with the Stinger, would have been unbeatable. Of that I have no doubt.

CHAPTER 11

Wonder Weapons — Gunships versus Stingers

'Aeroplanes are most effective against morale. They frighten; they exhaust; they break nerves. They do not, usually, in fact, kill many men.'

Captain Tom Wintringham, British guerrilla warfare instructor, 1939.

ON 25 September, 1986, some thirty-five Mujahideen crouched excitedly in the scrub on a small hill only a kilometre and a half NE of Jalalabad airfield runway. It was mid-afternoon and they had been hidden in this position for over three hours. They had done remarkably well to get so close to the strip undetected as they were now well inside the Afghan defences. The Commander, Engineer Ghaffar, could clearly see the soldiers in the perimeter posts around the runway, just inside the boundary fence. At either end of the strip were several tanks and APCs. Ghaffar had exceeded his instructions in getting so close, but he knew the area intimately, and his reconnaissance had confirmed a good covered approach that was useable even by day.

I had personally selected Ghaffar for this operation, together with another Commander called Darwesh, who had been assigned a similar task near Kabul. For us it was a moment we had been anticipating for four years, a chance to confront our most hated opponent of the war on equal terms. These two Commanders had been entrusted to attack the helicopter gunship, or indeed any aircraft, with the US Stinger anti-aircraft missile. On this first occasion it had developed into an outright competition between these two Commanders. Back at Rawalpindi, where they and their teams had been trained, they had challenged each other as to who would get the first kill. To encourage their enthusiasm I had gone along with their game, to the extent of allowing Darwesh a two-day start on his rival as he had the longer journey to Kabul. It was one of the crucial moments of the war. After years of being unable to strike back effectively at the enemy in the air, the Mujahideen had at last received a weapon worthy of their spirit.

The long wait for a suitable target was rewarded at 3.00 pm. All eyes gazed up into the sky to pick out a magnificent sight − no less than eight

174

helicopters, all their bitter enemy the Mi-24 Hind gunship, were approaching for a landing. With Ghaffar's group were three Stingers, whose firers now lifted their already loaded launchers on to their shoulders and stood up. Another Mujahid, armed with a video camera, was shaking with nervous excitement as he tried to focus on the rapidly descending aircraft. The firing parties were within shouting distance of each other, deployed in a triangular pattern in the bushes, as it had not been certain from which direction the target might approach. We had organized each team to have three men — the firer, and two others holding missile tubes for quick reloading.

Although the Stinger has an effective ceiling in excess of 15,000 feet, Ghaffar waited for the leading helicopters to begin their final approach. The Hinds were about to be ambushed by the West's most sophisticated shoulder-fired, man-portable air defence system. It was the Stinger's first use against a real enemy anywhere in the world. The Stinger had become operational in Germany in 1981, and with the 82nd Airborne Division in the US the following year. Stingers had been taken into Grenada in October, 1983, during the US invasion of that island, but were never fired. It fired an infra-red, heat-seeking missile, capable of engaging low altitude, high-speed jets, even if flying directly at the firer. The missile carried a high explosive warhead with significant countermeasure immunity. Once a missile has locked on to a target no other heat source, such as flares, can deflect it. The only possible way to avoid the lock-on is to keep so high as to be out of range, or to dispense flares at such a rate that there is virtually no interval between them. This entailed knowing when to start firing flares and having an inexhaustible supply. On this occasion not a single flare was fired as the eight helicopters came in. The attack would have the added advantage of total surprise.

The three firers waited for Ghaffar's shout. They would then fire almost simultaneously, selecting their own targets. Aiming and firing had been made simple. The firer held the launcher, or grip-stock as the military called it, on his shoulder. On top was the tube containing the missile, which jutted out beyond the end of the grip-stock. The tube was left behind when the missile was fired and would normally be discarded, but I had insisted that these tubes must be collected and returned for security reasons. Also it was proof that the Commander had actually fired his weapon, and so was not hoarding or selling missiles. Without an empty tube I would not issue more ammunition. Each Mujahideen selected a helicopter through the open sight on the launcher, the IFF (Identification Friend or Foe) system signalled a hostile target with a pinging noise, and the Stinger was then locked on to the heat of the aircraft. If the target was out of range no lock-on could be achieved, or pinging heard. The trigger was pressed, the missile fired, and the firer could immediately reload, take cover or move away. It is a 'fire and forget' weapon, with no need to remain exposed to guide the missile to its target. Nothing, short of a miracle, could stop the missile, travelling at over 1200 miles per hour, from homing on its target.

When the leading Hinds were only about 600 feet from the ground Ghaffar yelled 'Fire' and the Mujahideen's shouts of 'Allah o Akbar' rose up with the missiles. Of the three, one malfunctioned and fell, without exploding, a few metres from the firer. The other two slammed into their targets. Both helicopters fell like stones to the airstrip, bursting into flames on impact. There was a mad scramble among the firing parties to reload and change over firers as everybody in the teams wanted their chance to shoot. Two more missiles were fired, with another success and a near miss with a helicopter that had landed. I believe one or two others were damaged due to heavy landings as the frantic pilots sought to touch down in precipitate haste. Five missiles, three kills — the Mujahideen were jubilant.

Their cameraman was so overcome with elation that he tried to film while running around, so his record of the event consisted largely of blurred images of sky, bushes and stony ground. He only steadied himself sufficiently to film the black smoke pouring from the wrecks. Later, this video was shown to President Reagan, while the tube from the first missile was handed over to the CIA for them to make into a suitable presentation piece.

It was a memorable day. Ghaffar had won his bet and became an instant celebrity. In the coming months he went on to shoot down ten helicopters or aircraft with Stingers. I subsequently had him called to Islamabad to meet General Akhtar, who rewarded him with a special presentation for his achievements.

His rival, Darwesh, did not fare so well at Kabul. He had been tasked, not to get close to the airport, but rather to position his men on the usual approach flight path, some distance from the runway. From there he was to launch rocket attacks on Kabul to try to tempt aircraft to take off on retaliatory strikes. I also suggested he could attempt to get in closer to the airfield at night to take on Soviet transport aircraft. After several days of fruitless waiting for a suitable target, his frustration got the better of him and he let fly at a fast-moving jet at extreme range that was moving away from the firer. It missed, as did two further missiles. He had broken the rules for engagement we had given him during training, so he was recalled for a thorough debriefing and more tuition. This was always considered to be a personal insult, but Darwesh came with comparative good grace for his refresher training. Within two weeks of returning to Afghanistan he redeemed himself with two confirmed hits.

After firing, Ghaffar's men quickly gathered up the discarded tubes and destroyed the unexploded missile by smashing it with stones; they had no demolition kit and could not leave it to fall into enemy hands. Their dash back to base was uneventful, although about an hour into their journey they heard jet aircraft in the distance, together with the crump of exploding bombs.

At Jalalabad there was no immediate reaction that afternoon, just stunned disbelieve. In the event the airfield was closed for a month. When flights resumed, flying techniques had changed dramatically. No longer did helicopters come cruising in on a straight, gradually descending flight path, but rather in a tight, twisting spiral from a great height and firing flares every few seconds.

Both these two Commanders belonged to Hekmatyar's Party, so the second Stinger training course was allotted to two of Khalis' Commanders, Mahmood from Jalalabad, and Arsala from Kabul. They were both veterans, much respected for their operational performance, and highly reported on by my officers who had previously accompanied them inside Afghanistan. Our confidence in them was subsequently confirmed when they both successfully fired their Stingers.

Mahmood's achievements were, however, seriously marred by his irresponsibility afterwards. His indiscretion was the equivalent of making a broadcast to the world that Stingers were now in use against the Soviets. After his first 'kill' near the Sarubi dam he gave an extensive and revealing briefing to a journalist. He gave out highly confidential information, including the general location of the training school and details of my policy of rewarding each confirmed kill by issuing two more missiles to the Commander. Mahmood even went so far as to have a Mujahid carrying a Stinger photographed.

It was an infuriating breach of security, but it could not detract from our delight that at last we had a weapon which could be a war-winning acquisition. When the news broke, and spread throughout the Mujahideen, there was a wave of jubilation. Morale soared, and I was almost overwhelmed by the clamour of every Party to receive their share. To have a Stinger was the ultimate status symbol. It was also, I believe, the turning-point of the campaign as far as the four-year period of my stint with ISI was concerned. Unfortunately, its arrival had been needlessly delayed – not by soldiers, but by American and Pakistani politicians.

We felt it was appropriate that the first Stinger victims should be the Hind D helicopter gunship (MIL Mi-24). It was particularly loathed for its destruction over the years; not so much for the casualties it had caused to the Mujahideen, which were comparatively light, but for the countless hundreds of civilians and women and children it had gunned down.

It was a formidable helicopter, designed by the Soviets for a battlefield assault role — not only could it deliver massive firepower but also up to eight fully equipped combat troops. It was, like the American equivalent, the Black Hawk, the workhorse of the war as far as the Soviets and Afghans were concerned. Under its auxiliary wings were four pods for rockets or bombs. With a full load 128 rockets could be carried, plus four napalm or HE bombs, while its cannon could fire at the rate of 1,000 rounds a minute. Within a year of the Soviet invasion the Hind D model, with its heavily armoured belly and cockpit for the pilot and copilot, appeared in large numbers. Its armour made it almost immune to our medium or heavy machine guns. By staying high, over 5,000 feet, it could strafe the ground with impunity as our SA-7 could not reach it at this height. Even when within range of this outdated SAM a few flares could usually be relied on to deflect our missiles off course. The technical details of these state of the art aircraft were top secret. At one stage a US magazine offered a million dollar reward for the first intact Mi-24 to be captured. I have already described in chapter five how two were handed over by us to the US authorities after their pilots defected. As far as I know nobody got the reward – we certainly didn't.

We did, however, manage to hit some of these helicopters in the years preceding the arrival of the Stinger. Our successes were always the result of superior tactics, of achieving surprise, and thus getting in a shot at close range before the pilot was aware of danger. Sometimes we positioned firers high up the slopes of a valley, hoping to fire down on to a helicopter if it came up the valley floor. For a while this worked; we even killed several with our anti-tank launcher, the RPG-7, in this way, but pilots are quick to learn when their lives are at stake, so they mostly kept high.

One of our most startling achievements against aircraft prior to the use of Stingers was in 1985, when we downed a MiG-21 piloted by a Soviet Air Force major-general. He was flying from Kandahar to Shindand when his plane was hit by an SA-7 missile. The general ejected safely but was captured by the Mujahideen, although at the time they did not realize his importance. The disappearance of the general triggered perhaps the most massive air search of the war. Scores of planes were scrambled to find the missing MiG. Fearing the scale of retaliation the captors shot their prisoner, not knowing for several days that he was a general. Later the Mujahideen brought his parachute back to Pakistan, where it is still kept as a souvenir of success.

The Mi-24 has a crew of three. The pilot and copilot, who is also the gunner, sit in tandem one above the other in the front cockpit, while the flight engineer/mechanic sits in the main cabin with the troops. The Soviets had hundreds of helicopters, including reconnaissance and transport types, in Afghanistan. The main bases for the Hind D were Bagram, Shindand, Jalalabad and Kunduz. The Afghan Air Force had large numbers at Kabul airport, including a squadron of Hinds, with another at Jalalabad. With these Afghan-operated helicopters it was normal for a Soviet or a KHAD agent to be a crew member. This was considered necessary to ensure missions were carried out as ordered. As the war progressed, and particularly after we started using Stingers, all helicopter pilots began to show a marked disinclination to press home attacks. The Soviets would tend to send Afghan units on difficult missions, while Afghan pilots would sometimes fire off their ammunition at any soft target, and report a successful strike, when they had not flown near their intended objective. A lot of distrust built up, confirmed via the interception of radio conversations.

Both the Soviets and Afghans flew their missions in pairs whenever possible. From early in the war road convoys were given air cover, with the gunships either flying overhead as the column crawled along the road or, for the less important convoys, on immediate call. The Hind was conspicuous in all retaliation strikes or in protecting and supporting a ground advance. Sometimes it operated as airborne artillery, sometimes it combined strafing with dropping commandos in cut off positions, but it was as the primary instrument in search and destroy operations that the gunship earned its infamous reputation.

The attack on the village of Rugyan in 1982 was typical of Soviet methods. Rugyan had a population of about 800 people and lay 8 kilometres NW of Ali Khel. It was an agricultural village set in the narrow valley of the Rugyan River and was, at that time, a thriving community which supported the Mujahideen. The mud-brick houses were clustered together on the lower slopes of the mountains on both sides of the valley, and up a smaller side valley, whose stream joined the Rugyan from the east. In the centre of the village were numerous wells and more houses. Every possible use had been made of terraces to give maximum soil and space for crops of wheat or maize.

On the day in question the villagers were going about their normal chores when at around 9.00 am six helicopters were spotted high above the valley. The leading pair came lower, straight at the village. At about 2,000 feet the first rockets were fired, then another salvo, then another, the high explosive ripping apart the flimsy dwellings and killing or maiming the occupants. For at least two hours the endless bombardment continued with short intervals as one pair flew off to make way for the next. As a gunship ran out of rockets it circled round hosing the houses and fields with machine-gun fire. On the ground a few younger men fled up into the hills, while the remainder, the elderly and the women and children cowered in the rubble or behind boulders. Many died outright, many more were to die later from shock and loss of blood. If there seemed to be a lull in the firing uninjured people would come out to attend the wounded. It was futile; any movement below was the signal for the next pair of gunships to attack. There was no defence. The number of Mujahideen in the village at the time was negligible. There were no anti-aircraft weapons and no caves in which to shelter.

The next phase was heralded by the approach of ground troops from the direction of Ali Khel. Two hundred infantrymen, with several tanks, APCs and mortars, halted a few hundred metres from the village. They spread out before opening fire. For another half an hour gunfire, mortar bombs and heavy machine-gun bullets pummelled the rubble and every possible place of concealment. At last, by about midday, the Soviet commander stopped the firing. None of his men had been scratched. It was a search and destroy operation in which the destruction preceded the searching An Afghan officer yelled through a bullhorn for anybody still living to come out. The shocked, petrified, wailing women and children were segregated from the handful of men still able to walk. The searching of the ruins began, with the soldiers setting fire to any building left intact. No attention was given to the wounded, they were ignored until the troops finally departed, taking a few men for interrogation.

It was the end of Rugyan village. All 200 or so survivors trekked to Pakistan, carrying their injured strapped to horses and mules, or carried on beds. It took them ten hours to reach Parachinar hospital. On that occasion the surviving women had been fortunate to escape with a few blows and curses. There was no rape or cold-bloodied butchery as it was not just a Soviet operation. When Afghan troops were present the Soviets usually refrained from their more gruesome atrocities. After a similar mission elsewhere three young girls had been taken up by the Soviets in a gunship, raped, then thrown out while still alive. Multiply Rugyan by hundreds and you get some idea of what the Soviets' scorched earth strategy meant. Not for them any attempt to win hearts and minds, but rather wholesale destruction, the killing of civilians, or the driving of them into exile. This was their way of rooting out opposition, of depriving the Mujahideen of support, and of putting pressure on Pakistan through the refugees. I must confess that it was partially successful. Had we had the Stinger in 1982 or 1983 I believe countless civilian lives would have been spared.

For almost six years it was politics that prevented us from receiving Stingers. Not long after I had taken up my duties with ISI, and before I became aware of the political issues, I had advocated their use by the Mujahideen. In early 1984 a delegation of US officials, who were advising Congress on the war, visited me at Rawalpindi. A member of the delegation asked me which weapon system I would recommend to counter the growing Soviet air threat. Without hesitation I replied, 'The Stinger'. Back at their embassy my visitors had asked the CIA station chief why the Mujahideen were not getting this weapon, as it had been strongly advocated by Brigadier Yousaf. The CIA's answer was that it was the Pakistani government that would not allow its introduction. This was only half the truth, as neither would the US administration, but I had inadvertently touched on a very sensitive spot.

The CIA chief had immediately contacted me to protest that the delegation seemed to be convinced that it was they, the CIA, who were preventing the issue of the Stinger, whereas I knew full well it was my own government. At the time I knew no such thing, but I had obviously caused problems with my ignorance. That evening I had to explain what I had done to General Akhtar. I stressed that I was unaware of any political motives for not accepting this weapon, and that my recommendation had been entirely a professional, military judgement. The General called a meeting with the delegation to clarify our position. I was conspicuous by my absence.

While it was not denied that the Stinger was the ideal weapon with which an infantryman can knock an aircraft out of the sky, as far as Pakistan was concerned it was too good. It was the best of its kind in the world at that time, and had recently been issued to US forces, so its technology was still top secret. President Zia took the view, changed in 1986, that for the Mujahideen to be given this sophisticated American weapon would contradict the policy of keeping all arms supplied to the Mujahideen of communist origin. Its introduction could not be kept secret for long; missiles, or even the weapon, might be captured or seen by enemy agents. In this event how could Pakistan maintain the pretence that it was not allowing the US to support the Jehad directly? Also, but never openly admitted, the President was worried that a Stinger might get into the hands of a terrorist organization and be used against his own aircraft. He had many enemies, and already they had tried to shoot down his plane. Ironically, President Zia was right in so far as he later met his death by terrorist sabotage of his aircraft, but not by the use of a Stinger missile.

What the CIA did not explain to my visitors was that the Pakistan government's view coincided with their own. The US Administration were equally terrified that their new wonder weapon might fall into the wrong hands. If it was supplied to the Mujahideen then, inevitably, sooner or later, they could lose one to the enemy either in action or to a KHAD agent, or even by sale by an unscrupulous Mujahid. Selling one Stinger would enrich a man for life. Rightly, the Americans were scared of the technology being obtained by the Soviets. They were also worried that the weapon might end up with a terrorist group for use against a civil airliner. In this connection they had a dread of it getting into the hands of Iran, which in the circumstances of the war in Afghanistan was quite probable. In the event they were proved justified, in that both the Soviets and Iranians obtained Stingers in 1987, although their fears about it being used against them were groundless.

By late 1985 I considered the Stinger issue to be the single most important unresolved matter in defeating the Soviets on the battlefield. I became more and more vocal in my demands to obtain an effective anti-aircraft weapon. As I have narrated before, I was fobbed off with, first, Oerlikon guns, and then Blowpipes. Always the civil authorities of both Pakistan and America responded by saying, 'Supposing it falls into the hands of the Soviets;

supposing a terrorist uses it against the president; can you guarantee these things will never happen?' Of course I could offer no such guarantee, but as a Stinger had apparently already been stolen from a US base in West Germany, the strength of these arguments was questionable. All I knew was that without it Mujahideen morale would not hold out indefinitely.

By a strange twist of fate it was the temporary loss of Zhawar, and the Soviet/Afghan successes around Ali Khel, that finally swung opinions to my point of view. Although I was severely criticized for developing these strongholds, and defending them in a conventional battle, it turned out that this error, if error it was, got me the Stingers. They were to tip the balance on the battlefield in our favour. It was the heavy fighting along the border with Pakistan in April, 1986, that frightened everybody into forgetting the risks and giving us what we wanted. I made the most of the opportunity to press my demands, both to General Akhtar and to the CIA. I reinforced my appeal with the opinions of US analysts, who were then saying that the Mujahideen could not continue to fight on with this rate of attrition; that manpower shortages were growing; that the men in the field were tiring; that the younger generation were hesitating to join the Jehad. I did not altogether go along with these theories, but they provided additional ammunition for me. By the middle of that year the President had been prevailed upon to agree. Suddenly, we were to get the Stingers.

The first problem was training. Even with this weapon, we still insisted that the Mujahideen be trained by Pakistanis, not Americans. This meant our instructors had to be trained in the US. They flew there in June. Meanwhile the Stinger training school was set up in my backyard, at Ojhiri Camp in Rawalpindi, complete with simulator. In practice all training was carried out on this simulator, with no live firing ever taking place before the teams fired Stingers for real in Afghanistan.

Our main constraint was that we could not train more than twenty men at a time, due to the limitations of the training equipment. The agreement with the Americans was for an annual allocation of 250 grip-stocks, together with 1000-1200 missiles, so it would be some time before we could field sufficient teams to absorb all the Stingers. There was no question of us suddenly being able to swamp Afghanistan with the weapons. The build-up would be more a gradual affair.

I personally interviewed and selected the majority of the Commanders for training. I looked for men with a proven record on the battlefield, particularly those who had performed well with the old SA-7. In the event, half of the Stinger trainees were already competent SA-7 operators with one or more kills to their credit.

US officials insisted on a four-week course for Mujahideen. Our ten Pakistani instructors, who had completed an eight-week course in America, felt three would be sufficient. Our first courses were as long as was felt necessary to produce competent operators. In the event three weeks was normally enough, with some only lasting 15 days. The US sent over an officer to watch our first course, and from him I learned that the average hit rate by American troops trained on the Stinger was 60-65 per cent in a non-hostile situation. They regarded this as satisfactory. From statistics we compiled later during actual operations the Mujahideen's success rate was 70-75 per cent, while our Pakistani instructors reached 95 per cent.

I put these excellent results down to the high standard of training imparted, the determination of the trainees to succeed, the natural affinity of the Mujahideen for weapons and the aggressive anti-aircraft tactics we employed with Stingers. By contrast, the Pakistan Army's efforts with this weapon were dismal. A number of Stingers were provided to units in the border areas to respond to the countless 'hot pursuit' incursions into Pakistani airspace. To my knowledge the Pakistan Army fired twenty-eight Stingers at enemy aircraft without a single kill. In early 1987 the Pakistan Army claimed to have hit an aircraft with a Stinger. There was great excitement. The corps commander at Peshawar, General Aslam Beg (now head of the Pakistan Army, and the only general not to board the President's aircraft at Bahawalpur in August, 1988) wanted to interrupt a meeting to inform the Prime Minister personally. I happened to be in Peshawar at the time, and asked Hekmatyar, in whose area the plane was supposed to have crashed, to check it out for me. He was in radio contact with his base, so within minutes he informed me that no aircraft had been shot down.

That evening back in Islamabad I received a telephone call from General Akhtar who wanted me to arrange to have the wreckage retrieved. He was dumbfounded when I explained that there was no plane and insisted I send an officer to check personally. I did, and he confirmed our version of the story, much to the embarrassment of the Pakistan Army. They had even sought to authenticate their claim by sending an officer to the Mujahideen to collect together some debris from another crashed aircraft, as evidence of their achievement. Fortunately better sense prevailed.

The US flew out a special team to find out why our Army could not get results with the Stinger. Senior Army officers refused to accept the numbers of Mujahideen kills as anything other than propaganda. When the President and General Akhtar insisted, they claimed they had been given a worthless, outdated version of the Stinger. I believe part of the reason was that the Pakistan Army did not use the weapon offensively; they did not set out to ambush aircraft, tempt them into vulnerable positions, before catching them by surprise. They were content to sit in a static defensive position and wait for a target to come their way, although to be fair that was really their only option in the circumstances on the frontier.

Early in 1987 I was informed that a PAF F16 had been shot down near Miram Shah, with the wreckage falling inside Afghanistan. The report alleged that it was the victim of a Stinger fired by the Mujahideen. There was a monumental rumpus. Everybody turned on the ISI with cries of, 'I told you so. The Mujahideen should never have been given this weapon. They haven't been trained properly. They can't differentiate between Soviet and Pakistani aircraft.' I was sceptical from the start, as no Stinger team had either been deployed in that area or was moving through it. I informed General Akhtar accordingly, but rumours abounded, including one that the missile had been fired from inside Pakistan. The panic prevailed for 24 hours, until proper investigation revealed that the plane had been downed by another Pakistani fighter. There was acute embarrassment when it became known that it was the PAF, rather than the Mujahideen, who needed to brush up their aircraft recognition training.

How best to deploy our wonder weapon was the subject of much animated discussion. As we could not suddenly flood Afghanistan with hundreds of Stingers, the strategic choice lay between concentrating first around enemy airfields, or deploying them close to the Afghanistan-Pakistan border, thus retaining a tighter control over the teams, and perhaps lessening the likelihood of one being captured. I argued strongly for the first option. I felt that the teams should be used boldly to strike offensively at important airfields. This was where our targets were concentrated. If we could achieve surprise, and hit hard at the outset, we would gain a tremendous moral advantage. To position them to protect our border bases would hand the initiative back to the enemy. All our American friends agreed, except for their Ambassador. He was fond of passing judgement on military matters about which he was imperfectly qualified to speak; this was such an occasion. He wanted the initial deployment around Barikot and Khost.

Military good sense prevailed (see Map 18). As previously narrated, the first Stingers achieved spectacular success at Jalalabad airfield. We also included Kabul — Bagram in phase one of their deployment. This was followed by sending them over the Hindu Kush to the airfields at Mazar-i-Sharif, Faisabad, Kunduz, Maimana and close to the Amu River. The third phase envisaged a more defensive role in the provinces bordering Pakistan, with the final deployment being around Kandahar and Lashkargah airfields. This area had a low priority because the terrain was so flat and arid that it favoured the enemy who, with the advantage of airpower, were able to spot Mujahideen movement with comparative ease.

The use of Stingers tipped the tactical balance in our favour. As success followed success, so the Mujahideen morale rose and that of the enemy fell. We now had the Soviet and Afghan pilots running scared; they were on the defensive. They became reluctant to fly low to push home attacks, while every transport aircraft at Kabul airport and elsewhere had its landing and take off protected by flare-dispersing helicopters. Even civil airliners, which we did not attack, adopted a tight, corkscrew descent to the runway, causing

Map 18

STINGER DEPLOYMENT PHASES 1986-87

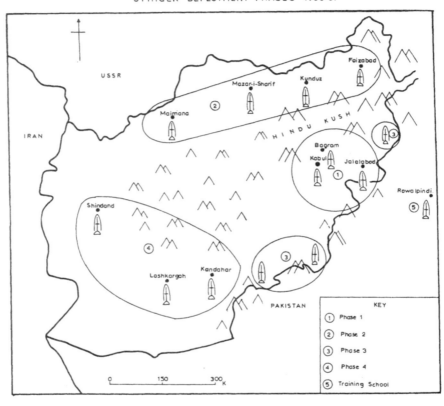

KEY

① Phase 1
② Phase 2
③ Phase 3
④ Phase 4
⑤ Training School

much nervousness and vomiting by the passengers. We had instructed Commanders to hunt not only aircraft, but the crews as well. We wanted dead pilots more than dead planes, as the former were far harder to replace than the latter. We set out to kill or capture more pilots by training special 'hit' groups for this task, who accompanied each Stinger team whenever possible. We even went to the extent of targeting pilots' messes at Kabul and Bagram for stand-off rocket attacks.

Although it was never our policy deliberately to kill captured aircrew, Soviet propaganda had instilled in many that to be taken prisoner was a fate infinitely worse than death. This had been the position long before we introduced Stingers. Back in 1984 the courageous British photographer John Gunston had captured this terrible fear in a photograph of a dead Soviet MiG-21 pilot, published in the French news weekly *L'Expres*. It showed the pilot lying amongst the shrouds of his collapsed parachute, still in his ejection seat with his hand cocked to his head. He had ejected, but had his leg ripped apart as his seat cleared the cockpit. On landing, in dreadful agony, he had shot himself through the brain to avoid capture. Later, the Mujahideen had removed the pistol from his hand. In his book *Soldiers of God* Robert Kaplan quotes Gunston as saying, 'The pilot had been there for several weeks, and had turned black in the sun, though the snow had kept his body from decaying. Maggots were eating a hole in his face. I found his radio sigs and MiG-21 instruction book. But damn, the muj wouldn't let me keep it.'

In 1987, in the Logar Valley, a Stinger missile downed a helicopter which burned like a furnace on impact with the ground. The Mujahideen raked through the debris, and filmed one guerrilla lifting up the tiny, shrivelled, blackened body of the pilot with the end of his stick. It looked like a grotesque charcoal doll.

In the ten-month period from the first firing up to when I left the ISI in August, 1987, 187 Stingers were used in Afghanistan. Of these 75 per cent hit aircraft. By this time every province, except for three, had them. Always we taught Commanders to plan and act offensively. They would put pressure on a post hoping that it would radio for assistance. If helicopters arrived they were ambushed. Similarly rocket attacks were used in broad daylight to tempt the Hinds into the sky. Sometimes they came, stayed high, fired a few rockets and disappeared. With high-flying helicopters the Mujahideen would often deliberately expose one or two vehicles, drive them so as to make a lot of dust, thereby hoping to entice the victim down. If he came he was usually killed. More often he stayed high.

There is no doubt that the introduction of Stingers caused considerable alarm among the enemy air crews. On one occasion two gunships were strafing a village when one was hit by a Stinger missile, whereupon the pilot of the second helicopter bailed out in panic. The winter of 1986/87 was the first time that Commanders and Leaders were prepared to continue operating in strength throughout the severe weather, provided they had a good supply of Stingers. We exploited their enthusiasm to the maximum. It was the first winter in which we did not lose ground around Kabul; in fact some outposts were recaptured by the Mujahideen as the enemy gunships' pilots were often too frightened to intervene effectively as before.

Despite our continuous emphasis on security, on the need to prevent any Stingers or missiles reaching the enemy, the inevitable eventually happened. Twice, in early 1987, we lost Stingers, firstly to the Soviets, and then to the Iranians.

We had trained a team destined to operate in the Kandahar area under the infamous Mulla Malang ('the Butcher'). On his way back to his base of operations with three Stingers he was successfully ambushed by a Spetsnaz unit. Despite my personal briefing on how to move tactically and remain alert, he managed to break all the rules of security. He put two grip-stocks and four missiles in his advance party, while he, with the remaining Stinger, followed some way behind with his main body. The advance party had halted and were caught napping by the Spetsnaz, who suddenly descended on the Mujahideen in helicopters. Far from being shot down, the gunships landed and disgorged the commandos who proceeded to kill or capture the entire group, with the exception of one man who escaped. The Soviets must have been well rewarded when they returned with such valuable booty.

For months I hesitated to deploy Stingers in the provinces bordering Iran. There was a real risk of its being sold or given to the Iranians. However, after we knew the Soviets had captured some I decided to take the chance. I introduced the weapon to sensitive areas near Herat, Shindand and other suitable areas near the Iranian border. Tooran Ismail of Herat was the first Commander of this region to get Stingers through his deputy, former Colonel Alauddin, who came to Pakistan for training, and later escorted the missiles himself. Thereafter we selected a less important Commander from Khalis' Party. After training, he was given two new vehicles and escorted up to the border, where he was briefed at length on the route he should take through Helmand Province. On no account was he to go into Iran. Inexcusably this Commander returned to Quetta after a short journey into Afghanistan, on the pretext of collecting more weapons, leaving his party to continue without him. They had difficulty crossing the Helmand River and deviated from their intended route. Whether by accident or design they ended up being arrested in Iranian territory by the Passadars (Iranian Border Scouts). They had with them four Stinger launchers and sixteen missiles. Repeated efforts by Khalis and Rabbani, who had excellent contacts in Iran, failed to get them returned. The Iranian authorities never actually refused to give them back, they just kept delaying their release with one excuse or another. To this day we have never seen these missiles again. I do not know if it is generally known that Iran has had access to these weapons since 1987. I can only pray they never end up with a terrorist organization. Needless to say, it was the last time Khalis got any Stingers while I remained in office.

CHAPTER TWELVE

Bear Baiting

'Alexander next marched to the Oxus [Amu] opposite Kilif, where the river was about three-quarters of a mile wide. It was crossed by means of skins stuffed with chaff .... it took in all five days.'
Major-General J.F.C. Fuller, *The Generalship of Alexander the Great*, 1958.

SOME 2,300 years after Alexander had crossed the Amu a high-ranking American official was examining this river on my map. His interest was focused on that part of it that formed the border between the Soviet Union and Afghanistan, particularly where it meandered for some 500 kilometres across the plain from Badakshan in the east to just beyond Kilif in the west. Then, using Winston Churchill's famous phrase, coined during World War 2 about Italy, he declared, 'This is the soft underbelly of the Soviet Union'. William Casey was thus the first person seriously to advocate operations against the Soviets inside their own territory. In his view the ethnic, tribal and religious ties of the people who lived on both sides of this river should be exploited. He was convinced that stirring up trouble in this region would be certain to give the Russian bear a bellyache. He suggested to General Akhtar that perhaps a start could be made by smuggling written propaganda material across, to be followed by arms to encourage local uprisings. Akhtar agreed to consider the written materials, but deliberately did not respond on the explosive issue of weapons.

Thus it was the US that put in train a major escalation of the war which, over the next three years, culminated in numerous cross-border raids and sabotage missions north of the Amu. During this period we were specifically to train and despatch hundreds of Mujahideen up to 25 kilometres deep inside the Soviet Union. They were probably the most secret and sensitive operations of the war. They only occurred during my time with ISI as, in 1987, an audacious, and successful attack on an industrial site well north of the river caused the water temperature to come perilously close to boiling, which compelled Prime Minister Junejo to halt them. There was, for a short while, real fear among the politicians that the Soviet Union and Pakistan might go to war. It was a dangerous game. Casey had been correct — we were touching an extremely tender spot.

As I write this the world has witnessed the communist empire crumbling round its edges, including its southern edges. The Kremlin has always been concerned to keep the lid on its ethnic minorities, particularly those who were faithful to Islam. The Afghan border touches three Soviet Republics — Turkmenistan, Uzbekistan and Tajikistan; it divides two countries but it does not divide the people (see Map 19). The Turkomens, Uzbeks and Tajiks of Afghanistan share the same culture, history, languages, apprearance and religion with their neighbours a few hundred metres away over the frontier. Moscow's specific worry was the spread of fundamentalism and its influence on Soviet Central Asian Muslims. This was one of the reasons for the invasion in the first place, to prevent the possibility of a Khomeini-style régime sweeping aside the fledgling communist government in Kabul. It had removed a threat to the Soviet Union's southern border. This fear of fundamentalism was one that they shared with the US, and which, I believe, was ultimately to prevent an outright military victory for the Mujahideen in 1989.

When Casey studied the map, what did he see? He was looking at a region that had political and economic, as well as military, importance. The Kremlin had no wish to see political instability in the area, no wish to see a religious revival which could not only disrupt the war effort, but might merge with a nationalistic movement aimed at greater autonomy, or even independence. The Soviet military presence in these republics, and in Afghanistan, was also protecting an investment. These southern regions were a rich source of natural gas, oil and minerals for Moscow. Considerable effort had been made to develop these natural resources, to build up an industrial infrastructure, and expand road, rail and air communications.

Over the past three decades the Soviets had used the mask of international aid to explore, identify and map the natural resources of Afghanistan. Their invasion was substantially motivated by the need to seize them. Indeed, within a few months they had stolen millions of dollars worth of precious stones, including 2.2 kilos of uncut emeralds, from government stores. Eighty per cent of all natural gas flowed from the fields around Shibarghan, north over the Amu. Even the metering of the amount was carried out in the Soviet Union, and Soviet officials decided the price they would pay, or rather be credited against Afghanistan's 'debt' to Moscow. As far as I am aware this milking of the Afghan economy continues today.

Southern Central Asia had only belonged to the Soviets for about a hundred years. It was a part of their empire acquired by force, and it still required force to retain it. Modern Termez, the centre of their base of supply for the war, had begun its life as a Russian fort in 1897, but for over 2,000 years before that few Russians had ever ventured that far south. This area,

Map 19

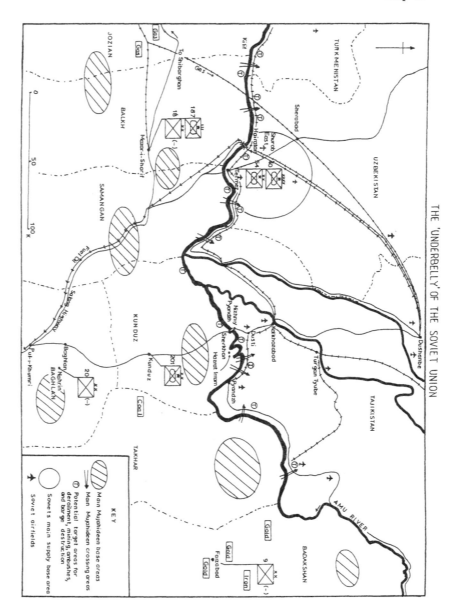

which boasted one of the hottest temperatures recorded in the Soviet Union, 50 degrees centigrade, had seen Alexander's army when it recrossed the Amu nearby on its return from Samarkand on the march to India. The ancient town of Termez flourished in the first century BC, welcomed Islam from the Arabs, was sacked by Ghengis Khan's Golden Horde, became a part of Tamerlane's empire, and was again destroyed at the end of the 17th century.

Into this melting pot of peoples, languages, cultures and Islam the Soviets had recently poured communism and quickly slammed the lid. The Army made sure it stayed shut. Casey had been right. It was an area of great potential for seriously damaging our enemy.

One of the men involved in our campaign of incursions over the Amu from the outset, indeed he later became the Commander of the raid that resulted in our being ordered to halt these operations, was Wali Beg. This is not his real name, as for obvious reasons it is essential for me to conceal his true identity. Wali Beg is an Uzbek, 53 years old but looks older, with a beard nearer to white than grey. He used to be a farmer and had a wife, two sons and a daughter. Now he has lost all his close family, and lives the life of a crippled carpet maker in a refugee camp in Pakistan. His original home was one of the tiny, long-since-destroyed villages on the south bank of the river in Kunduz Province. His house was only minutes walk from the water. It was also not far from the old Afghan river port of Sherkhan, which the Soviets had recently developed into a fuel storage area. A bridge now straddles the river at Sherkhan. This is a new structure, as trade and people had crossed the Amu for centuries in boats and barges at ferry crossing places. Wali remembers going over as a boy with his father to meet relatives and friends on the far side. Sometimes these people would visit his family. They would cross on flat-bottomed boats, towed by two swimming horses attached to outriggers. The horses were guided by the ferryman, and were partially supported in the water by the outriggers. By such means large loads of men and goods could be moved slowly across.

Wali's background is typical of millions of Afghans. Islam had dominated his village life, with the mosque as the centre of all social organization. Only boys received any education, and that was in the mosque school, where Wali had learned to read a little, and learned a lot of verses and prayers from the Holy Koran. At the age of ten he became a herdsman and fed the animals. In rural Afghanistan every family, except the very poorest, has a few animals: a donkey, or preferably a horse, for transport, a cow for milking and calves, an ox to make up a yoke with neighbours, and a few goats or sheep. At fifteen he learned to plough.

Wali told me that his wife had been selected for him when she was still an infant. When she was fourteen they were married without his ever having seen her face, although relatives had told him she was pretty. Marriage was for the production of children. Most young women in those days expected to have a child every two years, although many died in infancy. Instances of one woman having sixteen children, of whom only five or six reached adulthood, are not unknown. Allah blessed Wali with four children, of whom two sons and a daughter lived.

Wali grew up beside the Amu, so over the years he acquired an extensive knowledge of his area. He knew the river, the tracks leading to it, the reed swamps that clogged its banks, and its twists and turns and tributary streams. He knew the strength of the current, he knew the river in flood, and in the winter when the water was at its lowest. He knew the little sandy islands that sometimes split the sluggish flow.

With the Soviet invasion Wali's life was devastated. His sons had joined the Mujahideen, but the youngest, a boy of seventeen, was soon Shaheed in fighting along the Kunduz-Baghlan road. The eldest simply disappeared. To Wali this indicated arrest, infinitely worse than an honourable death in the Jehad. When I talked with Wali he was convinced his boy was dead, but it was the probable manner of his dying that consumed him. The tortures his son would have had to bear before death had released him made Wali's hatred of the Soviets totally merciless. The bombing of his village while he was in Kunduz had killed his daughter, so he and his wife had fled to Pakistan via Chitral. Within a few months she had succumbed to malaria. For our purpose Wali's knowledge of the border region, coupled with his oath of vengeance taken against the Soviets, made him an ideal Mujahid to carry the war over the Amu.

I had several options in attacking the Soviets in their own country. I could start with tentative incursions to distribute propaganda and to sound out how receptive the people would be to assisting with sabotage or other missions. Then I could confine our activities to firing into Soviet territory from inside Afghanistan, or sink barges and steamers on the river. Finally, I could send teams over the river to carry out rocket attacks, mine-laying, derailment of trains or ambushes. It was decided to start with the renewal of contacts, together with the distribution propaganda to test the water before anything more adventurous.

Casey had suggested sending books, and I had discussions on this with a CIA psychological warfare expert who recommended several books describing Soviet atrocities against Uzbeks. He was himself an Uzbek who had been working with the CIA since 1948. Although we agreed to use these books, our inclination was to send in copies of the Holy Koran that had been translated into Soviet Uzbek. We persuaded the CIA to obtain 10,000 copies.

While these were being printed we called in a number of Commanders and other suitable persons, including Wali, from the northern provinces. They were carefully screened, briefed to make contacts over the Amu and report back on whether the Holy Koran would be welcome, and whether some of the people would be willing to assist any future operations by giving information on Soviet troops movements, industrial installations, or act as guides. Later Wali explained to me how he had made his first trip in the late spring of 1984.

He decided to make for a village that he had last visited about ten years previously, as there was a good chance one or two of the families he knew would still be there. It was not safe to cross near Sherkhan, with its busy Soviet port of Nizhniy Pyandzh on the opposite bank, so he chose a quieter area where the river made several loops, and there were large expanses of jungle and reeds before reaching the bank. It would need to be a night crossing as he knew there were border security posts, and possibly patrols by day. Because of the distance he could not manhandle a boat, so it would mean swimming at least 600 metres, possibly more, as the Amu was full of icy water from melting snows. Wali had killed a goat, dried its skin and inflated it. He intended to cross as Alexander's soldiers had done.

He had set off after dark carrying his goatskin. Within two hours he hit the reeds and swamp on the south bank, which slowed progress and were noisy. When he finally reached the river he could dimly see the land opposite only about 300 metres away. He was in luck — only a short swim. In fact he only had to swim for about half the distance, with the goatskin easily taking the weight of his body. The ground on the far side was flat and sandy, but after walking for some time he came to the river again. For a moment Wali had been perplexed, surely he had not walked in a circle. The channel in front of him was barely 100 metres across. Then it struck him; he had been on an island. Although he did not know it, the boundary between Afghanistan and the Soviet Union ran through the island, so he was now in hostile territory. Another short swim, followed by a two-hour walk brought him to the houses of the village he sought. The first grey streaks of dawn were on the horizon when Wali quietly dropped on his knees, bent forward to touch the sand with his forehead, offering his thanks to Allah for his mercy so far.

Wali spent two days in the village, much of the time out in the fields as a shepherd with his friends and their sheep. His report was entirely favourable. His contacts would welcome copies of the Holy Koran, and, yes, they would pass them on. Two men had asked for rifles, but Wali had not been able to agree to this at this stage. Perhaps later, if things developed well, weapons would follow; for the moment information on which to plan, and a willingness to provide guides or shelter was all that was needed.

Wali's two days in the field were most revealing. There was a busy 25-kilometre road running NE between Nizhniy Pyandzh and the town of Dusti. Close to Dusti was an airfield. An overhead electric pylon line followed the road, upon which there was considerable traffic, including many military vehicles. Dusti had a Soviet garrison, and Wali's friends were certain military planes used the airfield. They told him of a railway line that linked Dusti with the riverside town of Pyandzh some 40 kilometres upriver from where Wali had crossed. This railway had a road paralleling it all the way, and was protected by border posts at regular intervals as it came close to the river for much of its length.

Wali was one of the dozens of Mujahideen who ventured across the river over a period of several months in 1984. Most of them brought back similarly encouraging news. We duly received the Holy Korans and the other books and began to take them over in batches of 100-300 at a time in small rubber boats, or Zodiacs (eight-man wooden recce boats) with small outboard engines. The latter were not popular as they were too noisy. The CIA had provided the boats but could not oblige with the specially silenced outboards that we had requested. About 5,000 Holy Korans were distributed, but the atrocity novels did not have much appeal. I was impressed by the number of reports of people wanting to assist. Some wanted weapons, some wanted to join the Mujahideen in Afghanistan, and others to participate in operations inside the Soviet Union.

We were now in a position to start raising the water temperature.

By 1985 it became obvious that the US had got cold feet. I had asked for more Holy Korans and large-scale maps of the Soviet Union up to 30 kilometres north of the border, on which to plan our incursions, but, while the Holy Korans were no problem, I was told no maps could be provided. It was not that their satellites were not taking the pictures, they were, but somebody at the top in the American administration was getting frightened. From then on we got no information on what was happening north of the Amu from the CIA. They produced detailed maps of anywhere we asked in Afghanistan, but when the sheet covered a part of the Soviet Union, that part was always blank (see Map 20). The CIA, and others, gave us every encouragement unofficially to take the war into the Soviet Union, but they were careful not to provide anything that might be traceable to the US. They quoted some article, which I do not remember, for their sudden inability to help in this respect.

The Afghanistan border with the Soviet Union is over 2,000 kilometres long. For more than half this distance it is the Amu River, but in the west the frontier is merely an erratic line across the desert and barren rocks of southern Turkmenistan to Iran. From my point of view, in selecting suitable Soviet targets, the border divided itself neatly into three. In the east, from Takhar Province to the eastern tip of the Wakhan peninsula where Afghanistan and China briefly touch each other, the border snakes its way through deep mountain gorges. The Wakhan was part of the roof of the world with towering, lofty, icy peaks over 20,000 feet high. Population was

Map 20

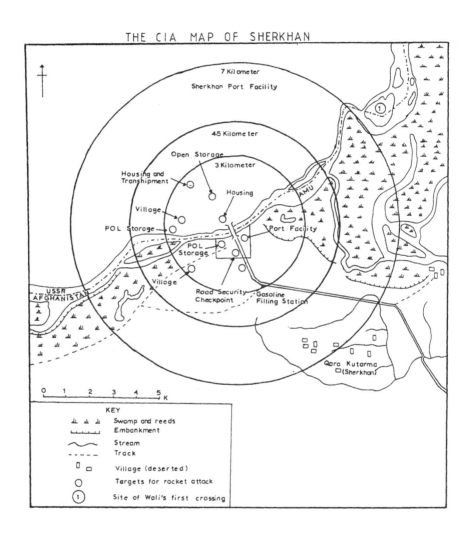

THE CIA MAP OF SHERKHAN

7 Kilometer

Sherkhan Port Facility

45 Kilometer

Open Storage

3 Kilometer

Housing and Transhipment

Housing

AMU

Village

POL Storage

Port Facility

POL Storage

Village

Road Security Checkpoint

Gasoline Filling Station

USSR
AFGHANISTAN

Qara Kutarma
(Sherkhan)

0 1 2 3 4 5
K

KEY

⊥ ⊥ ⊥   Swamp and reeds
⊥⊥⊥⊥⊥   Embankment

~~~~~~   Stream

- - - - -   Track

▯ ▫   Village (deserted)

◯   Targets for rocket attack

①   Site of Wali's first crossing

sparse, all the valleys cut off for months on end in the winter, and even in the less inhospitable Badakshan further west there were few worthwhile targets near the border.

Similarly, the western half of the frontier crossed arid land. Only around Kushka (see Map 9), which was the base of supply for the Soviet forces in the extreme west of Afghanistan, were there installations worth attacking.

It was the central 500 kilometres, from Kilif in the west to north of Faizabad in the east, that was the 'underbelly' that Casey had described. Throughout 1984 I had expended much time and effort in boosting the Mujahideen activities in the northern provinces. I had persuaded General Akhtar of their importance and managed to increase the allocation of heavier weapons to the more effective Commanders in this area. The problems were largely ones of distance and time. Winter closed our main supply route from Chitral, so much forward planning was necessary to get large convoys to the Mujahideen operational bases facing the Amu. A minor operation would take up to six months to plan and execute, while a major one would need nine. For this reason it was not until 1986 that our campaign started to be effective.

As the optimistic reports came in of contacts anxious to help I had many discussions with my staff as to how we should start bear-baiting in earnest. We decided on a cautious and gradual campaign of incursions, but spread out over a wide area. Depending on our success rate, we could increase the frequency and depth of the penetrations, although I had to assess the Soviet reaction with great care, as I had no wish to provoke a direct confrontation.

First, there was the river itself. There had always been a brisk trade both along and across the river. Now, with the Amu acting as the forward edge of the Soviet supply base, the traffic across had increased fivefold. All the Soviet freight in trucks and trains headed for the river. The choke points were the crossing places, mainly the bridges at Sherkhan and Hairatan (Termez). This latter was a newly built, 1000-metre long iron bridge over the Amu, about 12 kilometres west of Termez. Opened in June, 1982, it had been named the 'Friendship Bridge', and was the first road and rail link between the two countries. Built at a cost of 34 million roubles, this bridge was expected greatly to speed up the movement of goods and had greatly strengthened the Soviets' strategic position. It had enabled the Soviets to establish, for the first time, a railhead on the south side of the Amu. Hairatan was expanded as a port to handle the bulk of the river trade. The bridge marked the start of the Salang Highway on its long journey to Kabul. In addition to the road and rail it also carried the oil pipeline, and as such was second only to the Salang Tunnel as a critical congestion point on the Soviets' main line of communication.

I started the long process of planning, with the aim of blowing this bridge, in early 1985. I asked the CIA to provide technical advice. They cooperated to the extent of recommending the type and amount of charges needed, where they should be placed, also details of the current, flow and best time of year to destroy it. The expert favoured a summer attack, with a minimum of two spans, preferably three, collapsing. The actual operation would need to be an underwater demolition mission by night. The CIA did not, however, give us good photographs of the bridge; for these we had to rely on the amateur efforts of local Commanders. It was they who also reported on the security arrangements. These consisted of sentries and a company post on the Afghan side, plus an APC on permanent duty. We could identify the guard posts at the Soviet end. I went ahead with ordering all the equipment from the CIA. I called for a Commander to bring a team for special underwater demolition training at a suitable dam inside Afghanistan, but, in late 1985, the operation was called off. General Akhtar had explained what was to happen to the President who had vetoed it immediately. He was worried that its success might trigger a series of sabotage attacks on key bridges inside Pakistan. Personally, I did not consider this likely, but I could not argue. Once again I was thwarted in my efforts to hit the two main Salang Highway bottlenecks — the tunnel and the bridge.

Barges and boats were easier, although the high level of activity and security near crossing places meant that these attacks needed to be covert, and therefore during darkness. We required limpet mines that a small recce boat or a swimmer could carry, which could be clamped to the side of the boat just below the water line. For these we turned to the British, via MI-6. They obliged, and it was the UK's small, but effective, contribution to destroying a number of loaded barges on the Soviet side of the Amu throughout 1986. Others were sunk by recoiless rifle fire from positions in the reeds and swamps near the south bank.

Because the Americans declined to provide maps or photographs of Soviet territory I was hampered in selecting targets both for rocket attacks from inside Afghanistan and for the Mujahideen raiding parties crossing the river. I had to rely on information brought back from operations, such as Wali Beg had provided after his first mission. During 1986 some fifteen Commanders were specially trained in Pakistan for these operations. In particular we concentrated on derailment. A massive amount of freight came down the rail link from Samarkand to Termez, but there was also a link line that hugged the northern bank of the Amu, which was within striking distance. We did succeed with several such attacks, but two large-scale operations failed when the Soviets reacted quickly to cut off the invaders. I am certain they had been forewarned.

Commanders were issued with 107mm Chinese single-barreled rocket launchers (SBRLs) and 122mm Egyptian rocket launchers, with ranges of nine and eleven kilometres respectively, which meant they could set up their firing positions well south of the river, and still bring down effective fire inside the Soviet Union. Teams went across to hit border posts, lay anti-tank and anti-personnel mines on the tracks between posts, and to knock down power lines. Despite the CIA's advice to the contrary, as they were worried they might fall into Soviet hands, we positioned several Stingers in the north, close to the Amu. On one occasion, in December, 1986, some thirty Mujahideen crossed in rubber boats near the base of the Wakhan panhandle to attack two hydro-electric power stations in Tajikistan. This raid involved an assault on two small Soviet guard posts, during which some eighteen Muslim soldiers surrendered and joined the Jehad. It was later reported that a number were subsequently Shaheed in Afghanistan.

There were many operations launched from the Hazrat Imam district in Kunduz Province, the area from which Wali Beg came. An attractive target that came under rocket attack was the small Soviet town of Pyandzh, set among the cotton fields within a hundred metres of the north bank of the Amu. The attraction was the airfield on the northern edge of the town, which was in frequent use by military planes and helicopters launching retaliatory strikes at villages around Kunduz.

Just to the west of where Wali first crossed the Amu on his goatskin is Sherkhan river port, with its Soviet twin of Nizhniy Pyandzh on the far side (see Map 21). The main road from Kunduz comes north until it almost hits the river at Sherkhan village before swinging west for the 5-kilometre run to the port facilities. It used to be a busy ferry crossing point, but the Soviets built a pontoon bridge to take a road that has two branches leaving Nizhniy Pyandzh. One goes NE to Dusti, while the other goes NW, before turning back to become the river road that follows the north bank of the Amu all the way to Termez and beyond. The importance of this facility to the Soviets was that the road fed the 201st MRD at Kunduz, and then joined the Salang Highway at their main fuel and vehicle depot Pul-i-Khumri.

I was keen that the Sherkhan/Nizhniy Pyandzh fuel storage complex came under attack. The fuel was stored in tanks and open storage areas on both sides of the river, and there was barrack accommodation for the Soviet border security unit near the northern end of the pontoon bridge. The layout of the area on Map 20 shows it exactly as I was given it by the CIA, with all the territory north of the river blank. I had to pinpoint potential targets and other features from Mujahideen sources, and then try to locate them on the map. The concentric circles were drawn to assist the Commander in estimating the range to his chosen target. Using this map, and the Commanders' local knowledge, it was not difficult to select a series of alternative firing positions for his rocket launchers. The river, streams, tracks, houses, swamp and road were known to him, and he could point out likely positions and approaches to them on my map. We could then give him the various bearings and ranges from each position to each target. This was important, as few Mujahideen could read a map, but provided we supplied the technical data for firing, they were able to get good results.

In this instance we highlighted the facilities in Nizhniy Pyandzh (the blank area just north of the bridge), emphasizing that so long as the rocket launcher was located within the 7-kilometre circle he would be certain to be in range of the targets in the Soviet Union. The Commander was given complete discretion as to which target he engaged, from which firing position, and when he carried out his attacks. For example, we might ask that he did so once a week for two months, but nothing more specific. Within six weeks of our briefing the Commander at Peshawar, rockets started to rain down on Nizhniy Pyandzh.

These cross-border strikes were at their peak during 1986. Scores of attacks were made across the Amu from Jozjan to Badakshan Provinces. Sometimes Soviet citizens joined in these operations, or came back into Afghanistan to join the Mujahideen. As I have mentioned above, in at least one instance some Soviet soldiers deserted to us. That we were hitting a sore spot was confirmed by the ferocity of the Soviets' reaction. Virtually every incursion provoked massive aerial bombing and gunship attacks on all villages south of the river in the vicinity of our strike. These were punitive missions, with no other purpose than razing houses, killing people and forcing the survivors to flee, thus creating a belt of 'scorched earth' along the Amu, from which it would hopefully prove impossible for the Mujahideen to operate. Their aim was sufficiently to demoralize the population to halt our incursions.

In so far as destroying villages, killing women and children and driving survivors into Pakistani refugee camps were concerned, the Soviets succeeded. But if stopping our attacks or weakening the Mujahideen resolve were their objectives, they failed. We continued to bait the bear until April, 1987, when Soviet diplomatic reaction rather than military, sufficiently frightened Pakistani politicians into ordering us to stop. Perhaps our April attacks were just that much over-ambitious and represented too deep a cut in the Soviet anatomy.

During late 1986 we made tentative plans to continue operations inside the Soviet Union the following spring. With this in mind Commanders were trained, briefed and supplied with the necessary weapons and ammunition before winter set in. In April we hoped to start the offensive with three slightly more ambitious attacks. The first involved a heavy rocket attack on an airfield called Shurob East, some 25 kilometres NW of Termez, near the Soviet village of Gilyambor. It was not a major airfield, but it was in use, and lay only 3 kilometres north of the river, so the firing positions could be in Afghanistan. In early April this bombardment was successfully completed, with the airstrip being engaged several times over a period of ten days.

The second attack involved a party of twenty men armed with RPGs and anti-tank mines, tasked with ambushing the frontier road east of Termez, between that town and the Tajikistan border. They were to lay the mines

Map 21

WALI BEG'S INCURSION INTO THE SOVIET UNION

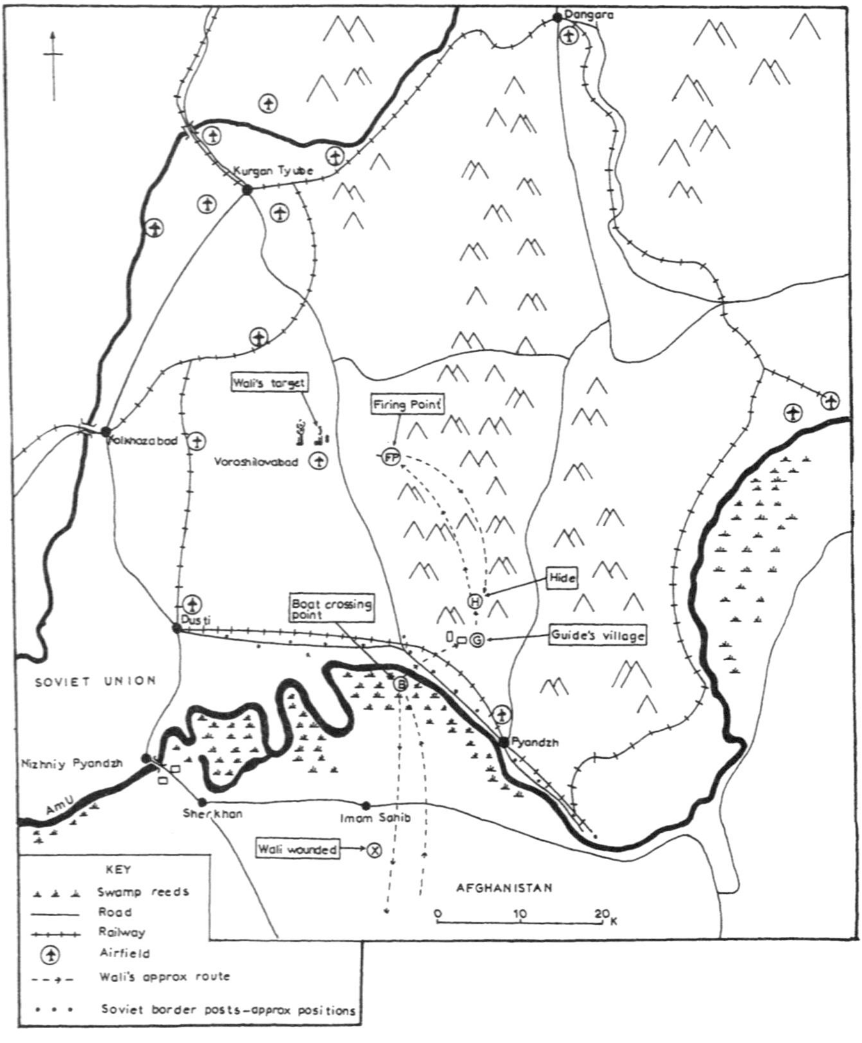

between two security posts, wait for some vehicles to hit the mines, then open fire and withdraw. In the event three soft-skinned Soviet vehicles drove along the road at night, one hit a mine and the two others were destroyed by RPG rounds. Several Soviet soldiers were reported killed or injured, the nearby post opened up with mortar and machine-gun fire, and the Mujahideen pulled back over the Amu. This was followed by the third, and most ambitious, mission which penetrated some 20 kilometres north of the Amu, and struck an industrial target close to the airfield at Voroshilovabad (see Map 21). This was Wali Beg's operation.

By 1986 Wali was a commander in his own right, with operational control over about 300 men. He had been inside the Soviet Union five times since his first reconnaissance mission in 1984. The area I had chosen for him was the large region between the Amu, north of Sherkhan, and the Soviet town of Kurgan Tyube. It was a well developed area with no less than nine airfields, industrial facilities, railway depots, and power stations (see Map 21). It was full of potential targets and I was hoping that Wali would be able to get much deeper inside than we had managed previously. Not that I was able to be specific as to what to expect, or exactly where he would find a worthwhile objective. The only guidelines I could give him were to go in on a long reconnaissance, make contact with his friends, then find a suitable target, firing positions and routes in and out. The detailed planning I left to Wali, who I had come to respect as a shrewd tactician.

He took two Mujahideen with him in early April. All three crossed the Amu in a small recce boat, not far from his first crossing place nearly three years earlier. After a night at his friend's house they were taken up into the hills behind the village to graze sheep. Leaving one man to tend the animals, Wali and his comrade set off north with the guide. He had a compass and binoculars, and wanted to reach a good position from which to observe the plain below him to the west. It was a clear spring morning. They would see the road from Pyandzh to Kurgan Tyube about 5 kilometres from the hills on which they stood. Even at this early hour there was some military traffic. They walked fast for several hours, keeping to the goat and sheep trails, until they had covered some 12 kilometres, and were overlooking the centre of the plain east of Kolkhozabad. They had only met a few shepherds, to whom their guide shouted a greeting as they passed.

Wali and his companions had no map, neither did they know the names of the Soviet industrial areas, factories or airfields that were scattered over the cotton-growing plain below them. Wali needed to find a target, one that he would be able to get within 9 kilometres of by night, and then withdraw from hurriedly while it was still dark. He slowly scanned the area through his binoculars. He could see vehicles on the road about 7 kilometers from his position, and near that what had to be a small airstrip upon which a light aircraft had just landed. Beyond, but close to the airfield, were a cluster of high chimneys belching black smoke. In front of the airfield, by the road, and on the far side of it, were several long, greyish buildings with a number of shorter chimneys, with more smoke – a factory of some sort. Wali took a bearing. From the spur on which he stood, the factory, airfield and high chimneys were more or less lined up on 283 degrees. The range to the factory? Hard to be sure, but not more than 9 and not less than 7 kilometres. However, it was spread over a largish area, with what seemed to be a lot of industrial-type buildings in the vicinity of the factory. If he missed the factory there was still a good chance of hitting something worthwhile. It would suffice. The firing position was easy, it could be anywhere on the spur on which he stood. Wali and his companions hurried home, rechecking the route as they went, noting the landmarks and timing themselves over the distance. They were back well before dusk – a round trip of eight hours.

Like most military commanders, Wali's problems were largely centred on getting to and from the target. The actual firing was the easy part. It was a question of time and space. He would need to go lightly armed, with only personal weapons and two Chinese-made 107mm SBRLs. These were ideal. With a range of 9 kilometres, they could each be manpacked by two men, one carrying the bipod, the other the barrel. Wali considered taking only one, but the thought of it failing at the crucial moment convinced him to play it safe. He wanted to fire up to thirty rockets, which, at one per man, meant a total force of at least thirty-four men.

With four recce boats, he would need one night to get his men and weapons across the Amu and safely into a scrub-covered gully in the hills beyond his contact's village. They would shelter in the gully that day and set off immediately it got dark at around 7.00 pm. That would give him 11 hours to do the job and return, walking at night carrying the SBRLs, rockets and rifles. By day it had taken eight, so it was cutting it a bit fine, but if they stopped an hour before dawn to find a suitable hide it should be enough. He was certain they would have to wait another day in the hills before re-crossing the river on the third night.

The operation went ahead in mid-April. After pre-positioning the recce boats in the reeds near the river bank the night before, Wali and his men crossed over and were met by their guide. He safely led them between the Soviet border posts up into their hide in the hills. A sweltering day was spent under blankets and rocks in a small gully, trying to sleep, occasionally nibbling at nan bread, or drinking a little water from chugals (water bottles).

It took five hours hard marching to reach the firing position. The night sky was lit by myriad stars, while the plain below sparkled with hundreds of electric lights. Both SBRLs were set up with fifteen rockets apiece. Wali took his bearing, then went to each launcher to check the setting. He adjusted the elevation to give a range of 8 kilometres on one launcher and 7.5 on the other, to give himself a better chance of hitting the factory with at least some of the rockets.

'Allah o Akbar — Fire'. With their distinctive whoosh and roar two rockets soared up in their graceful arcs. All eyes followed the trails until they both plunged out of sight into the blackness, the white flash of the final explosions just visible for a split second. Wali had included ten smoke rockets, for their incendiary properties, with the HE, as he hoped to set some buildings on fire. Now both launchers fired indepedently until all the rockets had gone, while Wali peered through his binoculars at the impact area. Something was burning over there, but Wali did not wait to watch for more than a few minutes, just long enough to know the strike was successful.

The journey back to the hide was uneventful. As Wali had anticipated, they did not have sufficient darkness left to cross the river, so spent a second day crouched among the boulders and scrub. From there they saw the start of the Soviet reaction. Within an hour of daybreak gunships and fighter bombers swarmed south over the Amu to pound the area around Imam Sahib and the high ground beyond. All day the planes flew back and forth, blasting every village, every valley that might conceal Mujahideen — not that the already ruined buildings housed more than a handful of people. By 1987 they had long gone to Pakistan, Kunduz or Kabul. The planes kept coming for a week. Wali's cut into the 'soft underbelly' had been deep and the bear's roar of rage was loud and long.

It was the next night, after recrossing the river, when the party was making its way round Imam Sahib that disaster struck. Unbeknown to the Mujahideen, the Soviet helicopters had been dropping hundreds of anti-personnel mines, mostly of the 'butterfly' type. They took their name from the little wings they had, which enabled them to flutter gently down without tumbling. Coloured brown or green, these vicious mines blended with the soil or rocks and could easily remove the foot of the unwary. This is what happened to Wali. A flash, a bang, and Wali collapsed with his left foot hanging by a piece of tendon and skin. A quick tourniquet with a piece of cord, a quick cut with a sharp knife to remove the foot before the numbing effect of the injury wore off was the best his companions could do; then a blanket tied to rifles as a stretcher, followed by the long, agonizing trek into the hills. They were hounded from the air for six days, during which four more men were wounded. Wali would have preferred to die. He would have been a Shaheed; he would have joined his family; Allah the Merciful would surely have welcomed him. Now, he was a cripple with nothing to live for. He could not even continue to kill Soviets.

Somehow, even though the will to live had gone, even though it was several weeks before he could be brought on horseback to Pakistan for proper attention, Wali survived. It was several weeks after I had left the Army that

I heard the full story of his raid into the Soviet Union from Wali himself, as he sat learning to make carpets in a camp not far from Peshawar. Had he been a regular soldier Wali would have received a high decoration for his leadership that day. As it was, he was content to know that his attack had been too successful, too damaging and too daring.

By one of those strange twists of fate 25 April, 1987, the date that brought the Soviet Ambassador in Islamabad to our Foreign Minister's office, was the same day that the Army Promotion Board declined to promote me to major-general.

Wali's attack had caused considerable damage and inflicted a number of Soviet casualties, although I was never able to establish exactly how many. The smoke rockets had started a fire which had consumed several buildings, but it was the suddenness, the ferocity and the distance (about 20 kilometres) inside the Soviet Union that was so galling to the enemy. It was the third successful attack within three weeks, and the Soviet Ambassador had been instructed by Moscow to use whatever language necessary to get future attacks halted immediately.

Our Foreign Minister, Sahibzada Yaqoob, was left in no doubt that if any further operation was conducted in the Soviet Union the consequences for the security and integrity of Pakistan would be dire. It was a threat of outright attack by the Soviet military. That they used this threat was itself confirmation that our raids were hurting. They were concerned, not so much with the actual damage caused, but by the effect they were having on the local Muslim population. If the attacks were to continue unchecked it might not be long before they had a general uprising on their hands. There was panic in our Foreign Office. The Prime Minister was informed that Pakistan might be on the brink of war, so he at once ordered General Gul, who had recently replaced General Akhtar at ISI, to cease all such operations at once.

Gul contacted me late at night in Peshawar, where I had gone to plan some operations with the Military Committee, telling me to halt these incursions immediately. I responded that it was impossible. I was not in communication with all the Commanders involved, and to pass on this order would take time. This infuriated Gul, whose head would roll if the Prime Minister's instructions were not obeyed, so he insisted that I confirm to him that these activities had been halted by the morning. I could only repeat that it was impossible, but I added that if any did take place no Commander or Party would claim the credit. I told him I would endeavour to pass the message by the quickest means. I myself felt that calling them all off indefinitely was too hasty, as we would lose the momentum. When I returned to Islamabad I tried to convince General Gul of the tremendous advantages of such operations. I did not want to abandon our contacts and stop everything, just when we were obviously hurting the Soviets. Of course, I spoke as a soldier, not a politician, and I knew there was no way the Pakistan Army could meet an all-out Soviet ground attack, but I believed they were bluffing.

Even the CIA was shaken. The local chief told me, 'Please don't start a third world war by conducting these operations inside Soviet territory'. There were no more. Looking back I believe I was right; the Soviets would never have launched an invasion of Pakistan. Within a few months they had agreed to withdraw from Afghanistan, so I do not see how Gorbachev would ever have escalated the conflict and brought the world to the brink of a world war. It was surely the last thing he wanted. I must acknowledge my limited wisdom in this matter, but I feel that had General Akhtar still been in the chair at ISI he would have allowed such operations to continue, but at a lower key.

Be that as it may, these attacks remain for me the high point of my career with ISI. My bureau was the only military headquarters in over 40 years to have planned and coordinated military operations inside the communist superpower. The great majority were successful; they wounded the bear and they proved the effectiveness of well-led guerrilla attacks to be out of all proportion to their size. That the small-scale raids by such Commanders as Wali Beg could influence the councils in the Kremlin was of itself a singular reward.

CHAPTER THIRTEEN

The Bear Backs Off

'To those who flee comes neither power nor glory.'
Homer, *The Iliad*, XV

IN late March, 1987, General Akhtar was promoted to four-star rank. This meant he had to relinquish his post as Director-General of the ISI and take up duties as Chairman, Joint Chiefs of Staff Committee. His promotion was not welcomed by the Parties, the Mujahideen, myself, or indeed by the General. For eight years General Akhtar had been the architect of the strategy for the Jehad. Under his overall direction the war had been brought to the point where ultimate military victory for the Mujahideen was in sight. It had been his recommendations to the President at the outset that had put Pakistan behind the guerrilla campaign. He had battled successfully on the political front to keep some semblance of unity among the Party Leaders, but only as a prerequisite for an outright military victory. He well understood the Afghan psyche and the imperative need to achieve military objectives before introducing the distractions of political wrangling. The Mujahideen Leaders and Commanders could only cope with one at a time. No one perceived better than he the debilitating effect of the premature debut of political power grabbing on the Jehad.

During 1986 he had seen the Soviet resolve beginning to crumble. That was the year when President Gorbachev told the 27th Communist Party Conference that 'counter-revolution and imperialism have transformed Afghanistan into a bleeding wound'. In May of that year, at the UN-sponsored Geneva peace talks, the Soviets had offered a four-year withdrawal timetable. In July they actually withdrew a token force of 6,000 men, which, significantly, included two MRRs and a tank regiment, as well as three, obviously superfluous, anti-aircraft artillery regiments. 1986 was also the year of the Stinger.

General Akhtar was going to a job that carried little authority or influence. From the most powerful position within the military in Pakistan, from a job that for all those long years had involved the struggle with the Soviet superpower on the battlefield, he was being 'kicked upstairs' to a sinecure.

For two weeks Akhtar did not hand over his Afghan responsibilities to his successor, Major-General Hamid Gul. There was talk of his retaining these duties in his new position. This is what he hoped for, as, for personal and professional reasons, he very much wanted to see the Jehad through to final victory. But it was not to be. President Zia did not relent, so, reluctantly, he handed over to Gul. It was the first of a series of major setbacks to the war that occurred both before and after the Soviets' withdrawal, and would eventually lead to the Mujahideen snatching defeat from the jaws of victory. General Akhtar was, I believe, the victim of American pressure. It was pressure that had been evident for years, but in April it finally coincided with our President's wishes. Although the US Ambassador protested to him that General Akhtar should retain his Afghan obligations, he did not speak with conviction. The Americans had never been happy with Akhtar as head of ISI.

For a number of years the US had made no headway with General Akhtar over a number of issues. At the start of the war the objective had seemed clear cut — to drive the Soviets from Afghanistan and make them pay for the US humiliation in Vietnam. It was primarily a military matter, involving massive support for a guerrilla campaign. But, as the tide of battle began to turn slowly in the favour of the Mujahideen, as the Soviets began to show they were less than totally dedicated to remaining in Afghanistan, that in fact a military pull-out was possible, so the Americans began to look at an Afghanistan without the Red Army. What they saw alarmed them. They did not believe the Afghan communist régime would survive a Soviet withdrawal any more than the South Vietnamese had survived the US retreat from Vietnam. They saw an Islamic fundamentalist government in Kabul. They saw leaders like Khalis, Sayaf, Rabbani and particularly Hekmatyar, establishing an Iranian type of religious dictatorship, which would probably make Kabul as anti-American as Tehran. For this reason the US sought, with increasing vigour, to break the hegemony of the Leaders. They wanted to exploit the differences between the Parties and their Commanders. General Akhtar understood their aims and methods and opposed their every move.

The CIA had always argued that ISI should issue arms direct to Commanders, by-passing the Parties. This, they claimed, made sense militarily. The CIA would have dearly loved to decide who got the weapons and who did not. Although we explained that our method was based entirely on operational factors, they would not accept this and grew increasingly frustrated with ISI's refusal to change the system. Had we distributed arms direct to Commanders it would have resulted in corruption, chaos and confusion inside Afghanistan. Interestingly, this is the situation today. In 1990 the Americans got their way. Weapons are now largely given to Commanders, with the ensuing infighting and lack of control. Commanders attacking Mujahideen convoys to steal arms they feel should have been given to them is now commonplace. This suits the US and the Soviets, who are equally fearful of a fundamentalist régime in Kabul aggravating their own problems within their adjoining Muslim republics.

General Akhtar was also strongly opposed to the Americans' bright idea of bringing back the long-exiled Zahir Shah to head a government of reconciliation in Kabul. This was suggested in late 1986 and was just another ploy to cause more dissension between the moderates and fundamentalists. The latter regarded the former king as being, at best, a vacillating incompetent who had got through five prime ministers in ten years, or, at worst, an American puppet. Gailani, the Leader of a moderate Party, had at one time been an unofficial adviser to the King, so putting Zahir Shah forward was guaranteed to keep resentment and rivalries simmering.

Then there was the General's resistance to the American and Pakistani foreign office demands that the Leaders call a Shoora (Council) to discuss arrangements for the future government of Afghanistan, on the basis of equal representation of each Party irrespective of its size. This would mean that some numerically large Parties, whose efforts and efficiency in the Jehad were poor, would have a greater say in politics and policy than some smaller ones who were more combat-orientated. Both General Akhtar and I were vocal against the injustice of this proposal. Similarly, we both opposed the formation of an interim government by the Parties until such time as the war had been decisively won, which to us meant when the Soviets had left Afghanistan and the Mujahideen had taken Kabul.

General Akhtar recognized that these US/Pakistani foreign office proposals were designed to increase the polarization between the Parties and to encourage dissension between Leaders and Commanders to the detriment of their efforts on the battlefield. He and I never wavered from our belief that the Mujahideen must secure a military victory before a political future for Afghanistan could be agreed. Once Commanders in the field became more interested in the politics in Peshawar than with fighting the war, they would soon, quite literally, abandon their operations to congregate in Pakistan. After all, why should they continue to prosecute the war with enthusiasm, at great personal risk, when potentially powerful political positions were up for grabs in Peshawar? Nobody was going to secure anything worthwhile unless they were there in person, to lobby and intrigue – as much a part of the Afghan character as fighting.

General Akhtar was conscious that if political activities were initiated before the capture of Kabul it would so weaken the Jehad that a military victory might prove unattainable. How right he was. Regrettably, General Akhtar had few friends. Within the military all the senior generals regarded him with a mixture of suspicion and envy. He was at loggerheads with the Prime Minister, while the Americans regarded him as the champion of the hated fundamentalists. The final decision to remove him from ISI was made by one man – President Zia. If the President had wanted him to stay, then nothing could have moved him, but by early 1987 Zia also wanted a change at the top in ISI.

General Akhtar had achieved a miracle – almost. The possibility of the Mujahideen defeating the communist superpower was beginning to look like a probability. The Soviets were talking about troop withdrawals and the Stinger was now deployed against them. With a military triumph, Akhtar would be the hero; he had first advocated fighting, and he had devised and overseen the strategy of the war. It would be his victory. I believe that President Zia promoted General Akhtar so that the credit would be his, Zia's. It would strengthen his personal authority and prestige enormously. He would be seen as the victor in the greatest Jehad for centuries, and it would surely have made his position as President unassailable. When these thoughts coincided with the other, American and Pakistani, pressures to move General Akhtar, the decision was irreversible. Akhtar was not the first senior officer to be dropped when it was felt he posed the slightest threat, direct or indirect, to the President's personal interests.

My reaction to General Akhtar's leaving ISI was one of dismay. As a soldier, I sought a victory on the battlefield as the first priority. My views on this coincided with the General's. First win the war, then hand back authority to the politicians. I appreciate that this was perhaps too simplistic, naive even. Nevertheless, events were to prove that premature political squabbling was instrumental in bringing about the military chaos that reigns in Afghanistan today.

My efforts were devoted to operations, but the intrusion of politics on to the battlefield was a part of my everyday life. Always it seemed that politics hampered rather than helped the Mujahideen. The Pakistani Foreign Minister, Sahibzada Yaquoob, was deeply committed to the UN-sponsored Geneva talks between Pakistan and the Soviet Union. He would brief the Leaders on progress at these discussions, but I found it frustrating to see the way he would only reveal what was already public knowledge, what had been reported in the press. He never took them into his confidence or disclosed his intentions. Nor was he prepared to accept their views. Our Foreign Office was determined to do a deal and under no circumstances would the Mujahideen's leaders be given the right to veto any agreement. By the end of 1986 confidence and respect between the Leaders and the Foreign Office was at its lowest ebb. On one occasion the Foreign Minister asked the Leaders' views on the Soviets' withdrawal time-frame. Hekmatyar replied: 'It is very simple. The Soviets should be given as much time for withdrawal as they took when moving into Afghanistan, i.e. not more than three days.'

The Leaders were of the view that the Soviets should be asked to negotiate with them directly. Whether the Soviets would have accepted this in 1986 I do not know, but the Foreign Office was certainly not prepared to lose its importance or control over our side of the talks. The Leaders also insisted that they would never share any interim government with Najibullah or Soviet stooges, even for a single day. They were emphatic. Their struggle had been in the name of Allah and for the establishment of an Islamic government in Kabul. They spoke of such a sharing as a betrayal of the sacrifices made by millions of Afghans. Even President Zia tried to persuade them to show a little more political wisdom by sharing power in an interim government for a token period, but they could not budge. It was the Afghan at his most inflexible. In the end I gave up attending Sahibzada's briefings; they were too depressing.

Major-General Hamid Gul replaced General Akhtar at ISI in April, 1987. He was to last two years. His previous post was that of Director of Military Intelligence at GHQ and I had heard much of his professional competence and strength of character. Looking back now, I can sympathize with him. He was destined to preside over a series of disasters which, despite the Soviet retreat from Afghanistan, culminated in the chaos of today. During his stint at ISI military victory was snatched from his grasp and instead stalemate was substituted.

Being a new broom, General Gul wanted to start sweeping immediately. He also needed time to settle in, to meet the Leaders, to start to understand the Afghan way, and so be able to sort out what was possible and what was not. At the beginning Gul sometimes found this difficult. As a soldier with a cavalry (armoured) background he was a forthright advocate of an army having a mobile, hard-hitting task-force as a reserve — a formation that could move at speed to a crisis point, influence the battle at the right moment, and with which to exploit success. A fine idea, essential for success in a conventional war, desirable perhaps in a guerrilla war, but an impossibility for the Mujahideen in Afghanistan. At the outset General Gul had little inkling of the infighting between Parties and Commanders, no idea of how this affected what was practical operationally, and had yet to realize that most Commanders would not tolerate Mujahideen from other Parties moving through their area, let alone allowing a large force to come and take over operations in their territory.

I pointed out these problems, but he rebuked me for being a defeatist and opposed to new ideas. Out of loyalty to my superior, I made strenuous efforts to collect Mujahideen from all Parties for training for this 'strike' force. For four weeks we struggled to sort out the difficulties of finance, logistics, command and control, but could make little headway. By this time General Gul was starting to grasp some of the quirks of the Afghan character and agreed with me to drop the idea for the time being.

By this time I knew I was retiring from the Army. I was told in late April, 1987, that the selection board had passed me over for promotion to major-general. I was disappointed, but not surprised. Virtually none of the generals on the board knew me; I had not served under them in a senior appointment; all they knew was that I had been working in ISI for four years. They promoted the men they knew in preference to an unknown brigadier who had spent such a long time outside proper soldiering and in an organization they viewed with misgiving. I believe the President spoke out in my favour, but he was not prepared to overrule so many. For him it was not a crucial issue at that moment. I could have continued in ISI as brigadier, but this I refused to do. I had long before decided to retire if not promoted, so this is what I set out to do. The snag was that I could not retire with a pension unless given permission by the Army. As a brigadier I could have been required to continue to serve. This is what Generals Akhtar and Gul tried to convince me to do; even the President sent word that I should not be allowed to retire as I was still needed.

I was prepared to stay for a few months to settle in my successor, but no more. Having directed the war (I thought reasonably successfully) for so long my professional pride was hurt. But, much more importantly, I could detect the general atmosphere of change towards a policy that, in my view, would weaken the Jehad just at the time when military pressure had to be maintained. I was starting to lack confidence that an outright victory in the field was the aim of the game. The smell of political expediency and compromise was in the air. Even President Zia was talking to the leaders of sharing power within an interim government with Najibullah. To me this was anathema. With victory on the cards, I could see that the Americans were beginning to assume the war was won and to concentrate their thinking on how to prevent the fundamentalist Parties taking over in Kabul.

I cannot resist quoting from a letter written by a well known Commander, Abdul Haq, to the *New York Times* on 1 June, 1989. Although it was written almost two years after I retired, the sentiments it expressed were exactly those of the rank and file Mujahideen throughout the war. Referring to the US government he wrote:

Your Government always claimed to support the resistance against the puppet régime of the Soviets. That puppet régime is still in Kabul. President Najibullah was not the minister of health or education, he was the minister of torture and killing [as head of KHAD]. Since he became President, we have had thousands more victims .... More than one and a half million people have been killed, 70 per cent of all the country has been destroyed, and five to six million people have become refugees.

It is said we should make a broad-based government with President Najibullah and his cronies. Yet American won't give a visa to Kurt Waldheim because he was alleged to have a role in war crimes more than 45 years ago. But you want us to compromise with the Hitler of our country.

For some time it was touch and go whether I would be allowed to leave. General Akhtar and I had a heated exchange in his office. He insisted I remain, offering me several other posts by way of persuasion, but I was adamant. At the end of the interview, when I had told him nothing would induce me to change my mind, General Akhtar lost his temper, telling me that under no circumstances would I be retired. I told General Gul that I was prepared to forego my pension and resign my commission if need be, but go I would. Thereafter, Gul did his utmost to convince the authorities to release me and eventually he succeeded. For this I owe him a debt of gratitude.

Before leaving the ISI and the Army, which I did on 8 August, 1987, I had promised the Military Committee that I would return as a civilian to offer my services to the Jehad as a private individual. After settling myself, and my family, back into civil life in Karachi, I booked a flight to Rawalpindi for 4 April, 1988. I was going back to the war. At the last moment I telephoned my successor in ISI to tell him of my intentions, but he advised me to postpone my journey as there was insufficient arms or ammunition forward with the Parties for any worthwhile operation. This was a bad sign, as the system called for a steady flow from the rear to the front. I decided to wait a bit. Within a week I received the dreadful news that all the ammunition stocks at my old headquarters at Ojhri camp had been destroyed in one devastating explosion.

January, 1989, was one of the coldest months in Afghanistan for a long time. By the middle of the month the bulk of Soviet troops had gone; many were back home in the Soviet Union leaving only the rearguards to ensure the withdrawal was complete by 15 February. Radio operator Vasily Savenok looked forward eagerly to leaving and to future reunions with his comrades in Moscow. He had spent a year in a small, fortified outpost overlooking the Kharga reservoir and the Ghazni road NW of Kabul. It was marked on the Soviet military maps as Hill 31. It had been built around an old, circular concrete water tank, with tunnels leading from it to underground command and communication bunkers. In the central dormitory bunker a wood fire burned, with the bodies of several soldiers wrapped around it, trying to thaw out before the next two-hour sentry duty outside, without gloves. On one wall a poster proclaimed, 'Paratroopers, accomplish your duty in Afghanistan with honour'. Outside, the world was black and white and freezing. Dug into the hillside, and protected by sandbags, were two 122mm howitzers and a T-62 tank, each with piles of empty shell cases half-buried in the snow. The post was part of the inner ring of Kabul defenses, whose purpose was to prevent the city falling to the Mujahideen as the Soviets left. The garrison waited impatiently to be relieved by the 'Greens', as the Soviets called the Afghan Army.

To the NE of Kabul, at the airbase, Colonel Alexander Golovanov had a heavy responsibility. His task was to keep the airfield open round the clock until the last Soviet unit had left. Although the great majority of the troops drove out up the Salang Highway, Kabul airport had never been busier, with Ilyushin military transport aircraft arriving every few minutes from Tashkent. Backfire bombers flew missions from the Soviet Union, dropping 12,000 lb bombs to secure the withdrawal route, while Colonel Golovanov organized continuous gunships patrols around the perimeter of the airfield to divert missile attacks from the transports. His comment to the *Sunday Times* correspondent was, 'They [the Mujahideen] are well prepared and well trained for combat in mountainous terrain ... they are still bandits. You never see them in the field face to face. They always shoot [from] behind the corner.' A nice compliment to the guerrilla fighters.

In Kabul there was great elation among the resistance supporters. The Soviets were going. With them out of the way the Afghan communists could not last long. This seemed to be the view of the diplomatic community as well. Led by the Americans, most embassies were closing down. The diplomats and their families gave a good impression of scuttling for safety, from a ship they were convinced was about to sink. Perhaps they would all return as soon as a new government emerged in Kabul, but for the moment the city looked like being under seige for some weeks. I found it a bit odd, seeing the Americans pulling out at this moment. It seemed as though it was the Soviets that had been protecting them all these years, and now they feared for their safety, just as the Mujahideen appeared about to win the war. We were supposed to be their allies. The eleven staff, including four marines, watched sombrely in a biting wind as the national flag was hauled slowly down before hurrying to the airport. There they were disappointed. Heavy snow had delayed their flight for 24 hours. Next, the British abandoned their elegant colonial building. The following week it would be the French and Austrians − all promising to return when things had settled down.

The Soviets kept to their withdrawal timetable exactly. The last Soviet soldier to cross the bridge at Hairatan to Termez did so on 15 February, 1989. During the previous weeks thousands of troops had driven up the Salang Highway in tanks, trucks and APCs, running the last gauntlet before gaining the sanctuary of their motherland. They had left Kabul a battalion at a time, usually at night, overloaded with Panasonic TV sets and other Western electrical goods unobtainable at home. They wore their medals and some took their pet dogs. It was a more or less dignified departure. Their diplomats did not have to climb desperately on to the last helicopter from the roof of their embassy, as the Americans had done in Saigon 14 years earlier. The next day in the Chicken Street bazaar, a trader commented: 'The Red Soldiers had no money and no manners. I had no time for them at all – they seemed like peasants to me. I think there will be a lot more fighting before we see the hippies back again.'

The very last man to cross into the Soviet Union was the 45-year-old widower, Lieutenant-General Boris Gromov. He walked over without a backward glance to embrace his teenage son, Maxim, who had been brought to welcome him. Gromov was a veteran of three tours in Afghanistan. His had been the difficult job of extracting the Soviet Army without a bloodbath on the way to the border. Although the Mujahideen did their utmost to hamper the withdrawal, the weather and the elaborate security precautions prevented any major Soviet disaster. According to Gromov, only one soldier died on 15 February. He had been shot by a sniper some 20 kilometres north of Kabul. Moscow was impressed with Gromov's performance; he was to be promoted to command the Kiev Military District, an extremely prestigious appointment, and made a Hero of the Soviet Union.

On the same date, thousands of miles away, at the CIA headquarters at Langley, Virginia, William Webster, the man who had replaced Casey as director, gave a champagne party. The toasts were to victory; the Vietnam débâcle had been reversed; now it was the Soviets in retreat and counting the cost in men and money of a nine-year war. The Soviets were out of Afghanistan. Revenge, for the rough handling the US forces had received in Vietnam, due in part to the Soviet Union's supplying America's enemies with the means to fight, was complete. I believe that, with the fulfilment of the Geneva Accord, which had been signed in mid-April, 1988, the US lost interest in finishing the war. From that moment on my doubts were confirmed and it became clear to me that their aims had now diverged away from a military victory towards a compromise peace, towards a stalemate. As I will explain in later pages, the objective of the US became to ensure that no Islamic fundamentalist government was established in Kabul. For the Americans, if that happened, it would merely be replacing one adversary with another. Ironically, in this they had the support of the Soviets, who were equally fearful of Islam stirring up religious or nationalistic feelings in their republics north of the Amu River. From the moment the Soviets agreed to quit Afghanistan it was in the interest of both superpowers to prevent an outright military victory for the Mujahideen.

The Soviets set about achieving this by pouring in vast quantities of military hardware for the Afghan Army. In fact, as I know full well, General Gromov was certainly not the last Soviet soldier in Afghanistan. Several hundred remained in the guise of advisers, and to service and fire the Scud medium range, surface-to-surface missiles that were to feature prominently in the battle for Jalalabad in mid-1989. Their Afghan venture had cost the

Soviets over 13,000 dead, 35,000 wounded and 311 missing. Reportedly, it had required one million roubles a day to keep the war going. In terms of cash, the price rose steeply as soon as they withdrew. Only the most massive logistic effort could keep Najibullah's men fighting, and the Soviets supplied it. American officials estimated that Afghanistan received military supplies worth up to $300 million a month after February, 1989 In the six months following their withdrawal at least 3,800 aircraft flew in, carrying food, fuel, weapons and ammunition. Compare this with the US aid for 1988, valued at $600 million, and the imbalance is crystal clear.

There are those who say the Soviets did not suffer a military defeat in Afghanistan. As a soldier who fought them for four years I disagree. Without the efforts of the Mujahideen on the battlefield no amount of political expediency would have got the Soviets out. At no time during the war were the communists able to do other than hold the towns and bases, try to secure their lines of communication and carry out a series of search and destroy operations of varying sizes. By and large the Soviet soldier fought poorly, as he lacked motivation. He was frightened of night operations, he seldom pressed home attacks, he was casualty shy and kept behind his armour plate on the roads instead of deploying into the hills. With the introduction of the Stinger, which boosted aircraft losses to an average of one a day, the Soviet high command tacitly acknowledged they could not win the shooting war. If you cannot eradicate a guerrilla army you have lost. The Soviets acknowledged that when they left Afghanistan. To win in the field would have meant a vast escalation of men, money and equipment. There was no way that Gorbachev was even going to contemplate such a price.

Gorbachev, who had nothing to do with invading Afghanistan in the first place, must have been hugely delighted with the kudos he gained from withdrawing. The invasion had cost the Kremlin dearly in terms of international goodwill. It had antagonized the Muslim world, damaged Soviet influence among the non-aligned nations and set back Sino-Soviet reconciliation. When, as I am sure they did, the Soviet supreme command told Gorbachev the costs of a military victory, he quickly decided to make the best of a dignified pull-out. The blaze of international publicity was just what he wanted. The Western nations were eager to see Gorbachev as the great reformer, and the Afghanistan invasion would be quickly forgiven and soon forgotten. At the time of writing (September, 1990) this is the precise position, with the Soviet Foreign Minister at the UN castigating Iraq for its invasion of Kuwait, as though his country could never contemplate such aggression, let alone carry it out. Politicians' memories are conveniently short.

With the signing of the Geneva Accord, the whole fabric of the strategy to win the war started to come unravelled. Incredible though it may seem,

216

when the Soviets left Afghanistan and military victory by the Mujahideen was anticipated by everyone, including both the Soviets and Afghans, there was a deliberate change of policy by the US to prevent it. Both superpowers wanted a stalemate on the battlefield. The Soviets sought to achieve this by their massive beefing up of the Afghan Army and Air Force, by the importing of Scud missiles, by the continued use of advisers and by getting the Afghans to concentrate their forces in a few strategic cities and bases, particularly Kabul, with orders to hold them at all costs. Above all else they had to keep Kabul. To do this they had merely to stay dug in, stay on the defensive, make the maximum use of airpower and missiles and keep open an air and land bridge to the Soviet Union. The Soviet planners had grave doubts as to whether or not the Afghan army could survive after they withdrew. If Najibullah could hang on to what he had got, then the chances of a compromise political solution were good. On the battlefield winner takes all. Neither the Soviets nor the Americans wanted to see the Mujahideen in that position.

The US now had the same goal as the Soviets. They set about achieving it by both military and political means.

First the military. Although there was no agreement with the Soviets in the Accord that the superpowers were to cut back on arms supplies to their respective allies, this is precisely what the US did. In order to hinder the Mujahideen, who were determined to harass the withdrawal, there was a substantial cut in arms shipments. I was told that this was to ensure the Soviets had no excuse for delaying their departure, but I believe this was a cover for a real change in their policy, as the cutbacks continued after the Soviets had gone.

Mujahideen supporters in Congress voiced their concerns. Two US senators requested a congressional inquiry into why arms shipments had been curtailed. As the *Washington Times* reported in early April, 1989, Senator Orrin Hatch, a member of the Senate Intelligence Committee, wrote to the chairman requesting an inquiry as to what the CIA was up to in Afghanistan. Mr Hatch was worried by the rate of the Soviet arms build-up, whereas, by contrast, US weapons shipments 'have slowed down to nothing'. Four months later the *Times* of London reported the chairman of the Intelligence Committee as confirming and supporting the cutback. Mr Anthony Beilenson stated, 'Supplying military aid to the Afghan rebels is no longer in our interest now that the Soviets have withdrawn'. There can surely be no clearer statement of the new American policy.

Even my friend Charles Wilson has, I understand, lost his former enthusiasm for a military victory. As I know from experience, most American officials were always resentful of the ISI, and how my bureau would brook no interference with arms allocations or operations. The Americans always wanted to control the war. With General Akhtar gone, and myself retired, the Americans were able to concentrate their efforts on the less experienced newcomers to ISI. House of Representatives member Bill McCollum from Florida put it neatly when he was reported by *Insight* magazine in April, 1990, as saying that all US military assistance to Pakistan, the third largest recipient of US foreign aid, should be re-evaluated, if not cut off, if ISI was not brought under control.

Next, the Americans' political tactics to secure a stalemate. In this they played on the well-known tendency of all Afghans for political infighting and the rivalries between Parties. With the Soviets out of Afghanistan the Mujahideen had achieved a notable victory, the Jehad had succeeded, the infidel had been driven from their homeland. This common enemy, this common mission, had gone a long way towards uniting normally irreconcilable and fractious Mujahideen groupings. Without the Soviets there was bound to be a tendency for Parties and Commanders to think more in terms of their future political positions and authority. Old jealousies and ambitions that had temporarily submerged in the anti-Soviet crusade would rise to the surface again. The US deliberately set out to encourage these dissensions. They now wanted to direct the attention of the Mujahideen from military to political matters. The more the Mujahideen squabbled, the more their Leaders and Commanders concerned themselves with what was happening in Peshawar rather than in Afghanistan, the less likely they were to win on the battlefield. The US promoted the idea of bringing back Zahir Shah, supported the calling of a Shoora with equal numbers of representatives from each Party, irrespective of its size, and encouraged the setting-up of an interim government of Afghanistan in Pakistan, knowing it would be recognized by nobody, including themselves. I have no doubt all these things were designed to foster the break-up of Mujahideen unity in prosecuting the war.

In this endeavour they were assisted, unknowingly, by the actions of General Gul. It was to be expected of him that he would wish to make his mark professionally, that he would institute changes to the existing system in order to prosecute the war more effectively. He seemed to want to give the Mujahideen forces a more conventional flavour and he obviously wanted to deal more directly with the military leadership of the Jehad, rather than through its political Leaders. It was in furtherance of this that he took over the chairmanship of the Military Committee. Gul felt, and in this he had the support of the President, that some Leaders were getting too powerful. To reduce their authority and, at the same time, he hoped, improve the combat effectiveness of the Mujahideen, General Gul re-started the system of allocating weapons direct to Commanders. This delighted the US and CIA who had advocated this method from the start.

During my time at ISI the Americans genuinely believed that giving arms direct to the people they wanted to use them would lead to a better battlefield performance by Commanders. While this might have been true in the short term, or for a special operation, we knew from past experience that in the end this method led to corruption and chaos. Certainly it cut out the Party Leaders from the supply system, and thus antagonized them, but it also promoted infighting between Commanders, as those who could not get the weapons they considered their entitlement from ISI resorted to looting from fellow Commanders. How could ISI deal directly with hundreds of Commanders? This was the system that had led to the 'Quetta incident' in 1983, which had been instrumental in my appointment to ISI.

Another facet of this new arms distribution system, and one which was to have a catastrophic effect on supplying the Mujahideen during the actual withdrawal, was that it necessitated the build-up of stocks at Ojhri Camp. This ISI arms and ammunition depot had to hold the bulk of the weapons destined for the Commanders. The individual 'packages' had to be sorted out at Ojhri, as it was no longer policy to keep stocks moving quickly to the Party warehouses. In early April, 1988, a few days prior to the Soviets signing the Accord, we lost the entire stock of arms and ammunition at Ojhri in a devastating explosion. Add to this the US cutback on supplies and the disastrous strategic error of the attack on Jalalabad a few weeks after the Soviets had left Afghanistan, and the real reasons why the Mujahideen snatched defeat from the jaws of victory become clearer.

CHAPTER FOURTEEN

Two Disasters

'You want to know why it's dumb to attack Jalalabad? Because it's dumb to lose ten thousand lives .... And if we do take it, what's going to happen? The Russians will bomb the shit out of us, that's what.'

Abdul Haq, Mujahideen Commander, May, 1988, to Robert D. Kaplan, *Soldiers of God*, 1990.

AT about 10.30 am on a bright, sunny morning in early April, 1988, the city of Rawalpindi was rocked by a colossal explosion. Many people thought that India had attacked Pakistan or that our nuclear plant or bomb had been detonated. A massive, mushroom cloud of black smoke soared thousands of feet into the air. It heralded the start of a rain of rockets and missiles that continued throughout that day. The crash and crump of secondary blasts could be heard for the next two days. People 12 kilometres away were hit by falling rockets, although fortunately they were not fused, so were not exploding on impact. The entire arms and ammunition stock held by ISI at the Ojhri Camp for the Afghan war had gone up – all 10,000 tons of it. Some 30,000 rockets, thousands of mortar bombs, millions of rounds of small-arms ammunition, countless anti-tank mines, recoilless rifle ammunition and Stinger missiles were sucked into the most devastating and spectacular firework display that Pakistan is ever likely to see.

There was absolute chaos. One moment the roads around the camp were thronged with people, bicycles, carts and cars, the next the ground was littered with dead and dying. Almost 100 people died, and over 1000 were injured. These included five ISI staff killed and 20-30 wounded.

From the point of view of the enemies of the Jehad the timing was perfect. Within a few days the Soviets signed the Geneva Accord and the following month began their withdrawal in the knowledge that the Mujahideen had been deprived of all their reserves of ammunition at a stroke. The explosion occurred when the depot was fully stocked, in fact it was overflowing with at least four months' supply. While I was at Ojhri we tried to keep stock levels as low as possible, using the camp as a transit facility with daily deliveries forward to Peshawar. General Gul's new system of building up special composite packages of various types of weapons and ammunition for numerous Commanders required all kinds of supplies to accumulate at Ojhri. Only when sufficient quantities of all types had built up could individual arms packages be made up. As the CIA's part of the pipeline was so erratic, with shipments often being deficient of particular items, there was inevitably delay at Rawalpindi. On this occasion hundreds of packages had to lie at the depot for weeks. It was made worse by the fact that, for the previous three months, those packages destined to go straight to Commanders at the border had been held up because of the winter weather. At the exact moment when the Mujahideen would be expecting their depleted reserves to be replenished at the start of the spring operations there was nothing. If it was deliberate sabotage, it was a masterstroke.   Before the last rocket had fallen the verbal accusations and recriminations were flying thick and fast. How could it happen? Why was so much ammunition stored in a densely populated area? Who was responsible? The civil authorities, led by the Prime Minister, blamed the Army and the ISI. The Army accused the ISI of gross incompetence, and both the Prime Minister and the Army turned on General Akhtar. It had been over a year since he had left ISI, but it was he who had authorized Ojhri as the main arms dump for the Jehad, so he must take the blame, or so his accusers thought. The fact that both the President and Prime Minister knew the camp's location, had visited it and had made no complaint as to its whereabouts were conveniently forgotten. This was the ideal opportunity to destroy General Akhtar and condemn the Army and ISI. President Zia, who was still Chief of Army Staff, was left with little option but to defend the military. His relations with the civil government and the Prime Minister were already strained, so there was no way he could meekly agree that it was all the Army's or ISI's fault. He supported his generals, Akhtar and Gul, in particular. The civil government used this tragedy to push their opposition to the military too far. Within a few weeks Zia had sacked the Prime Minister and dissolved the national and provincial assemblies when the Prime Minister tried to block the promotion of some generals, and insisted that the findings of any inquiry be made public.

An official military Court of Inquiry was immediately set up to investigate the disaster. It was headed by Lieutenant-General Imran Khan, the corps commander at Rawalpindi. He did not relish the job. There is no doubt in my mind that he did not know what to do, as he was being pushed by the Prime Minister in one direction and pulled by Zia in another. The former, I believe, wanted General Akhtar to be blamed, while the latter was insisting everything be hushed up, with no finger pointing at a culprit. The result was that Imran Khan dithered, which infuriated both his civil and military seniors. Eventually, perhaps not surprisingly, the court reached a finding that did not attribute blame to any individual. Whether or not the explosion was put down to an accident or sabotage I do not know for certain, as the court's conclusions were never made public. I do know that nobody was punished. Both Generals Akhtar and Gul continued in their careers. It was the Prime Minister who lost his job.

I was called as a witness to the inquiry, but was not greatly impressed with its methods or motives. Nevertheless, some basic facts emerged. A fire had started from one of the boxes containing Egyptian rockets, which had been sent to the ISI by the CIA for trials, before issue to the Mujahideen. Contrary to all safety regulations, these rockets had been armed with fuses by the Egyptians before shipment. A box fell down, either as a result of mishandling by the loading party, then in the warehouse, or due to a small explosive device. When it fell there was a minor explosion which started a fire. At that time several personnel in the warehouse were injured so there was a rush to treat and evacuate them by nearby staff. There was no attempt to extinguish the fire that had started as everybody was too busy moving the injured. After some eight to ten minutes the entire dump went up with one gigantic bang.

As to how it occurred there is no definitive answer that I know of. It could have been accidental, it could equally have been sabotage. If it was an accident then it could not have happened at a worse time as far as its effect on the prosecution of the war was concerned. The accident scenario has the fused Egyptian missiles falling due to mishandling; one went off causing a fire, perhaps in the wooden crate. The fire was not tackled as everybody was too concerned with the injured, so it took hold and set off the main explosion. This was not the first fire at Ojhri.

Almost exactly a year before fire had broken out in the same ammunition warehouse. On that occasion it had been due to some old World War 2 WP (white phosphorous) smoke grenades leaking and igniting. The NCO in charge had broken down the door and dragged out the offending box with complete disregard for his own safety. The fire was extinguished so there was no explosion. The inquiry recommended improved precautions. The staff at Ojhri were therefore conscious of the dangers and of the need to fight fires.

Those who feel it was sabotage base their argument on the fact that it could have been done and, perhaps equally importantly, on the perfection of the timing, on the amazing coincidence that at that moment the depot had never been so full, that the Soviets were about to start their withdrawal and they wanted to do so with the least possible harassment, and that the Mujahideen were depending on these supplies for their spring offensive. The sabotage theory has the rockets being tampered with in Egypt or in Pakistan, possibly at the request of the KGB. Once they were in the store then the device was detonated by a remote-control exploder from outside the camp. Alternatively, the device was planted by somebody who had access to the warehouse. It was guarded 24 hours a day, so no outsider could enter. In this case the initial explosion, which caused the box to fall, could have been triggered by a timing or remote-control device.

If it was sabotage the Soviets had the most obvious motive, but, far-fetched though it may appear, the Americans also had reasons to wish the Soviets an uninterrupted retreat. As I have stressed, their policy was changing, they now wanted a stalemate, they wanted to prevent fundamentalists winning the war, and so Mujahideen without ammunition at this critical juncture coincided nicely with their objectives. The suspicion that, just perhaps, the US was not entirely blameless is heightened by the fact that the explosion was followed by the cutback in their shipments of arms. Had they really wanted to, I feel sure that strenuous efforts would have been made to replenish Ojhri Camp. No such efforts materialized; in fact it was not until the following December that further supplies arrived. The CIA knew that delivering arms at that time of the year effectively meant that nothing would reach the Mujahideen for a further three months, by which time the Soviets had gone. It all fell into place rather too neatly. For me, the destruction of all the Mujahideen's war reserves of weapons and ammunition was one of the turning points of the war. At the very time that the Soviets were pouring munitions and equipment into Afghanistan at an unprecedented rate, the Mujahideen were deprived of the means of carrying out any prolonged or large-scale operations. ISI remained in a state of shock for some time. They did not recover sufficiently to formulate strategic plans to clinch a victory in the field either during or after the Soviet withdrawal. A crucial period was wasted. To achieve the victory that everybody expected it was vital that the period of the withdrawal be used to plan, train, coordinate and dump the logistic requirements of the Mujahideen in various parts of Afghanistan. These activities should have been carried out in accordance with a sound military strategy, and should have been completed prior to the onset of winter. Nothing of the sort happened. No sooner had ISI begun to show signs of recovery than President Zia's aircraft was sabotaged, killing both him and General Akhtar. Within the space of sixteen months General Akhtar had been removed from ISI, Ojhri Camp was destroyed, the President, along with Akhtar and other senior generals, murdered, and the US was making it obvious that its support for the Jehad was now half-hearted at best.

In these circumstances the capture of Jalalabad was supposed to be the answer.

By early 1987 General Akhtar and I were confident that it was only a matter of time before the Soviets quit Afghanistan. 1986 had witnessed Gorbachev's bleeding wound speech, their offer of a four-year withdrawal timetable, the actual withdrawal of six regiments and the introduction to the battlefield of the Stinger. We began to discuss an operational strategy to cover this event and to bring the war to a successful conclusion after they had gone. General Akhtar's relations with the Americans were somewhat cold and formal. He told me on several occasions that he did not trust the US to continue to support the Jehad wholeheartedly if the Soviets withdrew. I was inclined to agree, as I knew their antipathy towards fundamentalism and their desire for a moderate-nationalistic postwar government in Kabul.

One of the most difficult decisions that a guerrilla commander has to make once his forces begin to get the upper hand is the precise moment in the campaign when he should go on the offensive, when he should progress from guerrilla to conventional strategy and tactics. It is a matter of shrewd judgement. He has to assess the enemy's position with care. Is he sufficiently weakened numerically and materially? Is he demoralized, collapsing from within? Does he lack the means to keep his units adequately supplied? If the answer to these questions is yes, then perhaps the time is ripe to shift to the conventional phase of guerrilla war. But before doing so the commander must also examine his own forces. Are his men sufficiently trained to adopt coordinated conventional attacks, and if so on what scale? Are they well equipped with heavy support weapons? Can they cope with the enemy's likely control of the air? Can the scattered groups be supplied, concentrated, and then cooperate in joint offensives? Again if the answers are affirmative, then, probably, it is time to launch the offensive that will end the war.

There are numerous instances in military history when the guerrilla commander has moved into the conventional phase too soon, got a bloody nose, and as a result the campaign has been set back for months, even years. General Giap made this error in the early fifties against the French. The Communist Tet offensive in early 1968 in Vietnam failed, with losses of around 45,000 men, because their assaults were badly coordinated, communications were poor, the South Vietnamese Army fought well, and there was no demoralization within it ranks, or among the South Vietnamese population. Both the French and Americans lost eventually, but their opposing high commands had misjudged the timing of raising the stakes.

General Akhtar and I had considered this matter and decided that, even without the Soviet ground forces, it would be too risky to switch to a conventional strategy. Before General Akhtar was promoted away from ISI we had formulated an operational strategy to be applied during, and after, a Soviet withdrawal. Its objective was collapse in Kabul. If the people of Kabul, if the Afghan Army in Kabul, gave up, the war was won; but we did not feel this would be possible by direct assault. Kabul must be cut off, starved of food, fuel, men and munitions; the garrison must be demoralized and deprived of the means to fight. Then, and only then, were we confident they would surrender or turn on their Communist leaders. We did not consider the Mujahideen were ever likely to be ready for a conventional

Map 22

GENERAL AKHTAR'S STRATEGY TO FINISH THE WAR

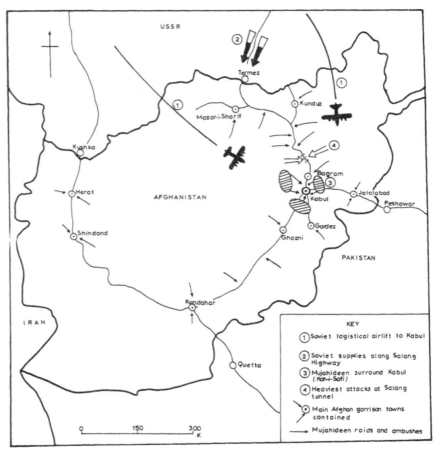

KEY

(1) Soviet logistical airlift to Kabul

(2) Soviet supplies along Salang Highway

(3) Mujahideen surround Kabul (Koh-i-Safi)

(4) Heaviest attacks at Salang tunnel

(⊙) Main Afghan garrison towns contained

→ Mujahideen raids and ambushes

attack, or that one was necessary. We agreed that the strategy of a thousand cuts should continue, but with the emphasis on Kabul and its supply lines.

Map 22 shows what we had in mind. Kabul was to be surrounded by Mujahideen bases from which attacks were to be continuous. The Koh-i-Safi area would provide the main base for our efforts against Kabul airfield, which had to be made unusable. A series of blocking positions were to be established along all the main lines of communication from the Soviet-Afghan border to Kabul and Kandahar to deny logistic support to the Afghan régime. The strongest blocking positions were to be around the Salang Tunnel, the choke point for Kabul. We hoped that threats there would draw out forces from Kabul to clear the route, thus providing us with good ambush opportunities. Finally, the Mujahideen would contain and fix, as distinct from assault and capture, all the remaining Afghan garrisons in Afghanistan.

We could not of course decide on the timings for implementation as these would be dependent on the Soviets' withdrawal time frame, the weather (winter), and on our being able to bring forward our logistic requirements to the right places. Before we could take this strategy further General Akhtar left ISI and I retired in August, 1987. April, 1988, saw the Ojhri camp disaster; the Soviet withdrawal started the following month; President Zia and General Akhtar died in the air crash in August; the US cutback on arms supplies started; the 1988-89 winter was particularly severe. The Soviets had gone by mid-February, 1989, and in March the Mujahideen took to conventional warfare with a full-scale assault, not on Kabul, but on Jalalabad.

Why was such an attack mounted? Why was there no strategic plan to finish the war after the Soviets had gone? These questions are difficult to answer. Part of the problem was the euphoria, the elation, that gripped everybody at the prospect of imminent, easy victory. Certainly the Mujahideen Leaders and Commanders made the fatal mistake of assuming that the Communist government would collapse by the middle of 1989, that without the Soviets' presence its defeat was inevitable. This attitude was enhanced by the fact that most Mujahideen were busy making postwar plans and political manoeuvring. The Afghan Interim Government (AIG) had been formed in December, 1988, and was sitting in Peshawar. Although unrecognized internationally, its members saw themselves as about to take over in Afghanistan within a matter of months. Peshawar politics became more important than military operations. There was a feeling that Peshawar was the place to be, securing a position in the AIG rather than risking life and limb in the field when the war was all but won.

The AIG, which was basically controlled by the seven Parties, backed by Pakistan, and seemingly with the support of ISI, selected Jalalabad as their target of their post-Soviet strategy. It was to be a conventional attack on a major city (but not the key city of Kabul). The time had come, so they thought, to abandon guerrilla warfare. Jalalabad was tempting because it was so close (50 kilometres) to the Pakistani border of the Parrot's Beak. This meant that Mujahideen reinforcements and supplies should have quick and easy access to the front line. A main road led over the Khyber Pass to Peshawar. A victory at Jalalabad would enable the AIG to move forward with ease to Jalalabad. There they could declare a part of Afghanistan liberated and a new government established. This political objective had some merit, but depended for its fulfilment on military success. Could the Mujahideen surround and storm the city, and if they did would the Afghan Army collapse, or would they just get bombed out of existence? Above all would the loss of Jalalabad also lead to the loss of Kabul?

I believe General Gul allowed himself to be persuaded that it was militarily a sound proposal, partly by some of his younger operational staff, partly by the Leaders, and also by pressure from the Pakistan government, who saw it as a way of shifting all the Peshawar politicians and their countless followers back into Afghanistan. The easy capture of smaller garrisons at Barikot, Azmar and Asadabad in the Kunar Valley added to the Mujahideen's over-confidence.

In contrast to the dubious military strategy of the Mujahideen, that of the Afghans was simple and sound. To survive they had to hang on to Kabul and, if possible, the major population centres and military bases. Map 22 shows their strategic situation. To succeed in this they must concentrate their resources of men and munitions, and not be concerned if minor posts fell. They had to retain the ability to reinforce key positions by air if necessary, and above all they must keep Kabul supplied with food and military supplies.

With logistic support the Soviets continued to be more than generous. Although only a few advisers remained, Afghanistan was still the Soviets' war, as Vietnam remained an American one even after they too had left their allies to fend for themselves. Vast infusions of money and materials arrived. The war was able to continue due to the massive in-place transfers of weapons and equipment as well as the huge re-supply effort. In 1988 over 1,000 armoured vehicles were handed over by the departing Soviets. It is estimated that the first six months of 1989 saw the transfer of $1.5 billion of military support to the Kabul régime, including 500 Scud surface-to-surface missiles. The Afghan Army still had tremendous superiority in what I call the three As — armour, artillery and aircraft. If they could bring these assets to the battle, if they could combine them effectively, then the Mujahideen would be defeated. The initiative was with the Mujahideen, but they had to use it both strategically and tactically.

By March, 1989, the Mujahideen had assembled 5,000-7,000 men in the hills around Jalalabad. However, their impending attack would not achieve surprise, as it had been heralded with too much publicity. The Jalalabad garrison knew what was coming and had made the necessary preparations.

The 11th Division had been brought up to strength and other reinforcement units deployed in a ring of defences. Bunkers, barbed wire and extensive minefields surrounded Jalalabad. The outer defences extended 20 kilometres from the city, particularly to the east. Highway 1, the link to Kabul, was protected by scores of posts throughout its length. Map 23 depicts the approximate layout of the Afghan defences and the main topographical features of tactical importance.

The Mujahideen assault began in early March with a direct, frontal attack from the east, up the Kabul river valley and on either side of Highway 1. Their first objective was the Samarkel position on the road 12 kilometres SE of Jalalabad. The ragtag warriors stormed ahead under cover of a heavy rocket, mortar and machine-gun barrage. Their initial impetus and enthusiasm carried them forward. The ridge east of Samarkel fell, and shortly afterwards the little village itself. Next the airfield, only 3 kilometres from the city, was taken by jubilant warriors yelling their war cries. This advance was led by several captured T-55 tanks crewed by the guerrillas. I believe this was the only tank versus tank engagement of the war. The Mujahideens' success was short-lived, as the coordinated use of the three As drove them back from the strip.

The battle gradually became a stalemate, with more and more Mujahideen being sucked into the siege, but unable to coordinate their efforts, and wasting lives in reinforcing failure rather than success. Although some eight senior Commanders and their groups were deployed, there was no overall leader who could command obedience or devise a sound tactical plan. Attacks were invariably by day, with the Mujahideen walking or cycling forward in the early morning for a day's shooting, and returning at dusk to sleep in the deserted villages in the surrounding rich farmland.

From the outset a steady stream of miserable refugees, old men, women and children, tramped towards Pakistan. By June 20,000 had gone. Meanwhile the siege of Jalalabad ground on with the Mujahideen unable to improve on their initial success. A decisive factor in the attackers' failure was a lack of cooperation between the Commanders. They attacked when the mood took them, and without thought to concentrating or coordinating their efforts. As one exasperated Commander was quoted as saying in the London *Sunday Times*, 'There is no coordination. If the Mujahideen attack on one side and keep the government busy, the Mujahideen on the other side are sleeping'. This lack of an overall plan led to many setbacks. The vital highway to Kabul, which, after the airport was closed, was virtually the only way of reinforcing or supplying Jalalabad, was seized by the guerrillas. But instead of closing the road permanently, the Mujahideen kept rotating the groups responsible which enabled the enemy to keep slipping convoys through.

All through April, May and June the position of the Mujahideen gradually

Map 23

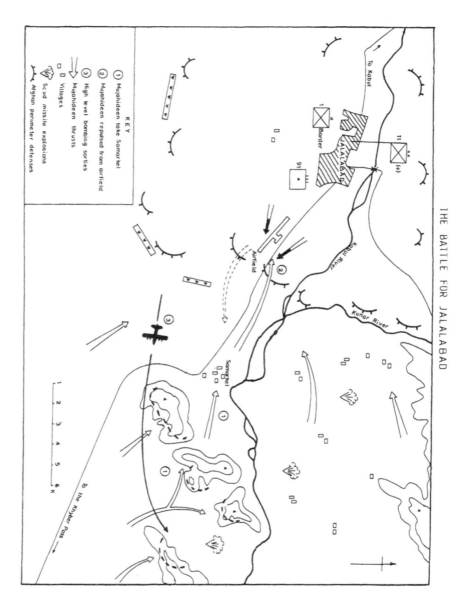

THE BATTLE FOR JALALABAD

KEY

① Mujahideen take Samarkel
② Mujahideen repulsed from airfield
③ High level bombing sorties
⟱ Mujahideen thrusts
□ Villages
⟰ Scud missile explosions
⌒ Afghan perimeter defenses

To Kabul

JALALABAD

Border

Kabul River

Kunar River

Samarkel

Airfield

To the Khyber Pass

1 2 3 4 5 6 k

229

worsened. Within a matter of a few weeks ammunition shortages became critical. The heavy, and at times wasteful, expenditure in the early days could not be made good. The US shipments were still substantially less than necessary, the reserve stocks had never been built up again after the Ojhri Camp disaster, and there had been little forward planning or dumping of available stocks prior to the battle. Not only was the strategic wisdom of attacking Jalalabad doubtful, but the tactics and logistics of carrying it out were quickly revealed as inadequate.

The Afghan resistance had also been underestimated. These soldiers had to fight to survive. Some early killings by the Mujahideen of prisoners confirmed in their minds that surrender was no answer. They were supported by enormous firepower; they had the advantage of being in strong defensive positions; numerically they equalled, if not outnumbered, their attackers, and their logistic needs were met. Aircraft, including Antonov-12 transports converted into bombers, flew up to twenty sorties a day. Heavy bombs, and cluster bombs that exploded above the ground scattering scores of bomblets over the target area, were used. These were extremely lethal against infantry. The effect on the ground is rather like the effect on a pond of throwing a fistful of gravel into the water, but over a far wider area. Although the Antonov is a slow-moving, propeller-driven aircraft, on these bombing missions it kept high, above the Stingers' ceiling.

Then there was the psychological as well as the physical effect of the Scud missiles. At least three firing batteries of these missiles had been deployed at Kabul, where they were maintained and operated by Soviet personnel. They were new weapons, introduced to help compensate for the Soviet troop withdrawal, and they were technically complicated, which explained the Soviet crews. A battery consisted of three launcher vehicles, three re-loading vehicles each with one missile, a mobile meteorological unit, a tanker vehicle towing a pump unit on a trailer, and several command and control trucks. Getting ready to fire took an hour. It involved a lengthy survey procedure at the firing position, using theodolites and optical devices, being completed before the missile could be raised upright for launching.

The Scuds fired in Afghanistan carried high-explosive warheads weighing over 2,000 pounds. Jalalabad was comfortably within range. The only warning the Mujahideen had was if they heard the sonic bang as the missile crashed through the sound barrier. They were area weapons, that is they could not achieve great accuracy. Their manuals indicate that when firing at a range such as from Kabul to Jalalabad, about half the missiles would fall in a circle with a radius of 900 metres. Over 400 Scud missiles thumped down among the hills around Jalalabad during the siege I believe at least four fell inside Pakistan.

In four months of fighting the Mujahideen failed to take Jalalabad. It came as no surprise to me, or anybody else who took the trouble to study the situation. Their losses in men exceeded 3,000 killed and wounded. They expended what little reserves of ammunition had been accumulated, and their inability to breach the minefields and fixed defences boosted the morale of their enemies. The battle for Jalalabad renewed the Afghan Army's confidence in its own ability, as well as telling the world that the Mujahideen were not yet able to march into Kabul. It was another major setback to the Jehad, from which the Mujahideen have not recovered to this day. Nor do I believe that their leadership has understood the lessons.

ISI and the Party Leaders made a strategic blunder in moving from guerrilla to full-scale conventional warfare too soon. They compounded it by selecting Jalalabad, whose capture would not necessarily bring down the Communist régime, instead of Kabul which would. They made no attempt to tie down Afghan reserves by keeping up the pressure at airfields such as Kabul or Bagram.

It was during the latter stages of the siege that Hekmatyar's men ambushed Massoud's forces in Takhar Province, sparking off the campaign of vengeance that resulted in the public executions described in chapter eight. That outright civil war should break out among the Mujahideen at such a critical juncture is indicative of the rapid erosion of what little unity was left for the Jehad.

Tactically, it was a textbook example of how not to fight a battle. There was no surprise; inferior forces attempted to assault prepared positions frontally in daylight. The attacks were poorly coordinated and the Mujahideen were subjected to a continuous barrage of shells and bombs from which there was no respite. Logistically it was grossly mismanaged. Due to the US cutback and the loss of all the strategic reserve stocks of arms at Ojhri, there was insufficient ammunition for a large-scale offensive lasting more than a week at most. The Mujahideen leadership knew all this, but still persisted with their plan.

General Gul was removed from his post at ISI in June, 1989, when it was clear to everybody that Jalalabad was a catastrophe. His two-year involvement with the Jehad must have been a bitter experience for him. He came at a time when military victory was in sight; he left when Mujahideen defeat was distinctly possible. The falling away of American support, the Ojhri explosion, the air crash which killed the President, the fractious political infighting of the Leaders, which increased markedly as the Soviets left, and finally Jalalabad, demanded a scapegoat – General Gul. Prime Minister Benazir Bhutto had him transferred back to the Army whence he came.

His replacement was General Shamsur Rahman Kallu. He was brought out of retirement for the job. Zia had got rid of him for having the temerity to suggest that the President should relinquish the post of Chief of Army Staff. He has closely followed the American line, bending to their pressures and thus effectively scuttling the chances of a Mujahideen victory. He has failed to retain unity among the AIG.

The Jehad has never recovered from Jalalabad. The Mujahideen had showed the world that they had the courage and skill to apply the pressures of guerrilla warfare to bring about the retreat of a superpower. Given the means to fight, given the cause of Jehad, and given a modicum of sensible military leadership, they could not be defeated. Take away these props and no army can win. Military history is a great teacher for both soldiers and politicians. Its lessons are few and oft repeated. The problem lies in the learning.

POSTSCRIPT

'Helplessness induces hopelessness, and history attests that loss of
hope and not loss of lives is what decides the issue of war.'
Captain Sir Basil Liddell Hart, *The Real War 1914-1918* (1930).

I have recently revisited Peshawar, spoken to the Leaders, renewed friendships with some of my former comrades-in-arms, and again gone inside Afghanistan. I wanted to see for myself what had happened to the Jehad which defeated the Soviets, but cannot defeat the Najibullah régime. It was a depressing visit. The ordinary Mujahid is bewildered, exhausted and angry with the endless political and military feuding that continues to sap the strength of their efforts against the Kabul government. They certainly seem helpless, and many have lost hope.

The more I look back, the more I re-think events of the past three years, the more convinced I am that it was the deliberate policy of the US government that we should never achieve a military victory in Afghanistan. Once the Soviets were out America had avenged Vietnam; she then concerned herself with bringing about a stalemate. Both superpowers will be content when Najibullah and his leftists shake hands with the moderates in some government of reconciliation. When this happens it will not bring peace or stability either to Afghanistan or the border areas of Pakistan.

The millions of refugees and the thousands of Mujahideen living in Pakistan will be required to return to Afghanistan, aid will be curtailed, but I do not believe the majority will go. They outnumber the local population, many are armed, and for a high proportion the prospect of returning to their devastated villages and fields, sown with millions of mines, is hardly an appealing proposition. There is the danger that the situation will be exploited by the KGB, by KHAD and RAW agents, to try to bring about another Lebanon, with serious fighting between the umpteen rival factions. In this scenario Peshawar would become a Beirut. India would certainly welcome such a state of affairs.

I believe the first move to undermine the Jehad was the removal of General Akhtar. This was done by Pakistan's President, but at the instigation of the

US. Once Akhtar had gone the whole process of political intrigue, and the weakening of the military effort, gathered momentum. It was Akhtar who had resisted all the American pressures; he was seen as the champion of an outright military victory and the establishment of an Islamic government in Kabul. He was inflexible, so he had to go. The US exerted pressure on Zia to remove him with perfect timing. It coincided with the President's belief that victory was assured, so he wanted to claim the credit. At the same time Zia would please the Prime Minister whose relations with Akhtar were poor.

Next came the explosion that destroyed all the war stocks of the Mujahideen at Ojhri. The camp was full because it was the Americans who had got their way with the newcomer, General Gul. In order to supply Commanders directly, ammunition had to be stockpiled in the warehouse at Ojhri in far greater quantities, and for far longer periods, than previously. The Americans had always insisted in the run-up to the Soviet withdrawal that they should be given a safe passage. The Mujahideen consistently refused to countenance this. The US, understandably, did not want anything to delay or halt the Soviet retreat, so they cut back their arms shipments to Pakistan. But there were 10,000 tons sitting at Ojhri. One big bang and it had gone. The following week the Accord was signed, the Mujahideen's ability to sustain prolonged operations had disappeared and the Soviet withdrawal proceeded reasonably smoothly. A convenient coincidence?

The CIA's arms supply continued to be an erratic trickle rather than a steady stream, while the Soviets flooded Kabul with weapons and equipment on a scale never experienced before. Another unfortunate fluke?

Then came the air crash which killed both President Zia and General Akhtar deliberately, and the US Ambassador and Military Attache accidentally. Immediately the Americans blocked any attempt to uncover the culprits. The likelihood was that the KGB or KHAD had been involved, with the collusion of some Pakistani military personnel. To expose them would upset American plans and probably lead to public demands for retaliation − after all two senior US officials had been murdered by an act of sabotage. The US shed a few crocodile tears over Zia's death, but the reality was they were not sorry to see him go. They believed, wrongly, that he was secretly pro-fundamentalist; they disliked his military rule and dissolution of the democratic assemblies; they were concerned at the progress of his nuclear programme; and they regarded him as a liability who could not be removed by political means.

At the end of 1988 Pakistan, pushed by the US, cobbled together the AIG. It was created before the Soviets were out of Afghanistan, and before the war had been won. Its only purpose has been to divert the Mujahideen from fighting the war to fighting politics. It was, and is, irrelevant. Without military victory no Islamic government could be set up in Kabul, but with a military deadlock all sorts of compromises are possible. It fitted in perfectly with American aims.

By mid-February, 1989, the Soviets had gone, with the exception of some advisers and their massive logistic support. The withdrawal had been successfully achieved, except for a period in November, 1988, when they threatened to halt it due to Mujahideen attacks. But after this the winter and a lack of ammunition secured a smooth departure. Then came the Jalalabad fiasco. The ISI, Pakistan, the Mujahideen leadership and their CIA backers moved from guerrilla to conventional warfare prematurely. Men and munitions were frittered away on an objective that could not have won the war. Both the strategy and tactics of Jalalabad were hopelessly flawed. Failure there was, I believe, the final blow to the original Jehad. It set the seal on a compromise political solution. Although I am reluctant to admit it, I feel the only winners in the war in Afghanistan are the Americans. They have their revenge for Vietnam, they have seen the Soviets beaten on the battlefield by a guerrilla force that they helped to finance, and they have prevented an Islamic government replacing a Communist one in Kabul. For the Soviet Union even their military retreat has been turned into a huge political success, with Gorbachev becoming a hero in the West, and still his hand-picked puppet, Najibullah, remains unseated, dependent on Soviet aid for his survival.

The losers are most certainly the people of Afghanistan. It is their homes that are heaps of rubble, their land and fields that have been burnt and sown with millions of mines, it is their husbands, fathers and sons who have died in a war that was almost, and should have been, won.

INDEX

Oerlikon AA guns, 87, 167, 181
Ojhiri Camp, 27, 100-101, 182; explosion at, 213, 219-223, 230-231, 234

Paghman, 119, 156
Pakistan, 2-3, 8, 12-13, 18, 22-26, 28-29, 32, 35, 39, 47, 50, 58, 65, 69, 74, 83, 85, 88, 90, 93, 95-98, 100, 108-109, 132, 162, 172-173, 180-181, 190, 204-205, 209, 218, 220, 226, 230, 234-235; assists Majahideen, 4, 40, 49, 64, 120; Staff College of, 20
Pakistan Air Force, 8-9, 15-16, 92, 98, 100, 118, 183-184
Pakistan Army, 2-3, 5, 9, 17, 20, 27, 86, 102, 107, 113, 117, 130-131, 164-165, 206; instructors of, 96; personnel of in Afghanistan (see also ISI), 113-115, 151-153, 162, 171; Promotion Board of, 205; use of Stinger by, 183-184
Pakistan International Airlines, 11
Pakistan Mobile Training Teams, 117
Pakistan Police, 107
Pakistan Ordnance Factory, 86
Paktia Province, 42, 128, 140, 158
Panjsher Valley, 6, 50, 69, 71-72, 141, 144; Soviet offensives in, 72-73, 121, 128
Parachinar (see also Parrot's Beak), 67, 107-108, 110, 144, 159, 162
Parcham Party, 143
Parks Mr D., 54
Paris, 11
Parrot's Beak (see also Parachinar), 68, 140, 158-159, 162, 227
Passadars, 187
Pawan Province, 119
Pech Valley, 134
Peiwar Kotal, 162
Persian Gulf, 48
Peshawar, 5, 28, 37, 40, 50, 62, 65, 97, 101, 105-106, 108-109, 117, 123, 135, 140, 144, 158, 160, 183, 200, 205, 209, 221, 226-227, 233
Peshghor, 73, 141
Pol-i-Charki, 113, 142-143, 145, 147
Prague, 143
Pul-i-Khumri, 65, 76, 199
Pushtun, 24-25, 31, 37, 114-115, 120
Pushtunwali, 34
Pyandzh, 195, 199

Quetta, 1, 20, 22, 25, 28, 37-38, 47, 49, 65,

97, 100, 102, 106, 108-110, 117, 130-131, 187

Rabbani, Professor, 41, 71, 105, 119, 187, 208
Raphel, Mr A., 10, 18
RAW, 12, 15, 233
Rawalpindi, 11, 27-28, 38, 91, 98, 100-102, 109, 136, 150, 171, 174, 180, 182, 213, 220-221
Reagan, President, 41, 79-80, 176
Red Arrow, 89
Refugee camps, corruption in, 138-140
Refugees, 23, 25, 28-29, 47, 49, 138, 180, 200
Revell, Mr O., 18
Revolutionary Guards, 112
Rishkoor, garrison, 147, 152-153
Rocket launchers, 87, 150, 165, 167, 172, 198
Rokha, 73
Rome, 144
Roosevelt, President, 78
RPGs, 36, 50, 83, 102, 116, 178, 200
Rugyan, attack on, 179-180

SA-7, 59, 118, 141, 169, 178
Saigon, 68, 215
Sajid, Flight-Lieutenant, 14
Salang Highway, 36, 47-50, 67-69, 71-73, 77, 102, 125-126, 144, 197-199
Salang Tunnel, 74, 197
SAMs, 59, 102, 118, 141
Samarkand, 46, 192, 198
Saradov, Major-General, 72
Sargodha, 9-10
Sar-i-Pul, 47
Sarubi Dam, 126, 177
Saudi Arabia, 20, 41, 80, 84, 98, 100; supports Mujahideen, 65, 77, 90, 96, 106, 120
Savenok, Vasily, 213
Sayad, Jamal, 129
Sayaf, Professor, 41-42, 119, 151, 157, 165-166, 208
SBRL, 109, 150, 203
Scud missiles, 215, 217, 230
Shaheed, 33, 126, 164, 193
Shakadara, 53
Shamshadsar, 158
Sherkhan, 93, 192, 194, 197, 199, 202
Shi'as, 31
Shibarghan, 47, 126
Shindand, 46-48, 59, 65, 67, 141, 178, 187
Shoora, 209, 218
Shultz, Mr G., 19

241